KINGS & QUEENS

AN ESSENTIAL A–Z GUIDE

This is a Starfire Book
First published in 2001

04 05 03

3 5 7 9 10 8 6 4 2

Starfire is part of
The Foundry Creative Media Company Limited
Crabtree Hall, Crabtree Lane, Fulham, London, SW6 6TY

Visit the Foundry website: www.foundry.co.uk

ISBN 1 84451 0 62 X

A copy of the CIP data for this book is available from the British Library

Printed in China

SPECIAL THANKS TO EVERYONE INVOLVED WITH THIS PROJECT:
Anna Amari, Frances Banfield, Lucy Bradbury, Roger Buckley, Helen Courtney, Claire Dashwood,
Giskin Day, Karen Fitzpatrick, Vicky Garrard, Phil Hempell, George Keyes, Lesley Malkin,
Geoffrey Meadon, Sonya Newland, Colin Rudderham, Mel Shaw, Andrea Simmonds,
Graham Stride, Helen Tovey, Helen Wall, Sharon Weiss, Nick Wells.

KINGS &
QUEENS

AN ESSENTIAL A–Z GUIDE

Paul Cheshire

GENERAL EDITOR – PROFESSOR DAVID LOADES

SELECT
EDITIONS

CONTENTS

THEMES

Each A–Z entry is tagged by themes which can be followed as threads throughout the book

Danes/Vikings   House of Lancaster   Saxons   Wales

England   Normans   Scotland   House of Wessex

Ireland   House of Plantagenet   House of Stuart   House of Windsor

House of Hanover   Saxe-Coburg-Gotha   House of Tudor   House of York

INTRODUCTION

TRADITIONALLY there have been two ways of looking at British History; from the top down, and from the bottom up. Roughly speaking, these are now expressed through political and ecclesiastical history on the one hand, and religious and social history on the other.

Even the earliest chronicles show a mixture of these two approaches; on the one hand the *gestes* or deeds of kings, princes and princesses; and on the other destructive storms, monstrous births and cattle plagues. We must also remember that the written chronicles which survive were only the tip of an enormous iceberg of interest. Before the sixteenth century, very few people could read or write, and these chronicles represent generations of folk myths, stories and traditions, filtered eventually onto parchment by a monk or some other clerical scribe. The reasons for the absorbed interest shown in the doings of royal families were rather different from those shown today. There was the same kind of voyeurism; but also an awareness that these people exercised real power. The wars of princes were defining episodes in the lives of their peoples, particularly if they happened to get caught up in them.

The balance between the 'real' and the voyeuristic has, of course, shifted dramatically in recent years. Firstly, the number of royal families (or families calling themselves royal) declined sharply between the ninth and the thirteenth centuries, from more than a dozen to three or four. By the seventeenth century it was down to one, both simplifying and elevating the process of study. Until the eighteenth century monarchs wielded real power; and then it became influence, and has so remained, more or less concealed. Since the beginning of the twentieth century, political, and even constitutional interest has declined, but recent events have shown that personal interest flourishes as never before. Once upon a time, when the king was believed to be the mediator of divine authority to his people, his behaviour was of critical interest to those who wanted the country to keep on the right side of God; now the behaviour of the royal family is treated as a kind of social thermometer. It may come as a shock to learn that the present practice of succession, whereby the oldest surviving child of the monarch inherits the Crown was not always followed. In the early days (and particularly in Wales and Ireland, where the rules were different), siblings often succeeded, even when there were direct heirs. It was normal for the most suitable member of the royal family to be promoted, irrespective of his exact relationship to the deceased king. As late as the end of the fifteenth century Richard III attempted such an approach, and got away with it for a while. Unlike France, none of the British monarchies operated a so-called 'Salic Law', barring women from the succession; but women were frequently pushed aside, even when they were the direct heirs – as happened to Matilda in the twelfth century.

So how do we know about all these things? For the recent monarchy there is a great wealth of literature, both scholarly and popular, based upon State papers, private correspondence, and the memoirs of those who were involved. For the early modern monarchy, from the late fifteenth century to the eighteenth, much the same applies, although the sources are less abundant. However, before that the nature of the material is different. There are very few letters before the sixteenth century, either official or personal, but contemporary chronicles or annals are important, and a good deal can be deduced from the legal and financial records, where these survive. Such records are good for England, less good for Scotland, and almost non-existent for Wales and Ireland, where (as we have seen) the monarchies came to an end at an earlier date. For the early period, we are heavily dependent upon such annals as have survived, usually either embroidered *gesta* of the kings themselves, or the lives of contemporary churchmen, particularly those with any claim to sanctity. Many of these annals are redactions of long-running oral traditions. For the Celtic kingdoms, there are also some early bardic writings, particularly hero stories and genealogies; while some of the early English kings issued charters which have survived. Archaeological evidence is mainly contextual. We can deduce that a large building was a royal hall or fortress, but not who built it, or exactly when. Only coins really contribute to the histories of kings, but early examples are rare.

This brief Biographical Dictionary should give the reader some idea of the richness of the history which the royal dynasties of these islands represent, and satisfy most curiosity about such matters.

PROFESSOR DAVID LOADES
Research Professor, University of Sheffield;
Director of the British Academy John Foxe Project

EARLY RULERS OF ENGLAND

When Roman Emperor Julius Caesar first reached England in the summer of 55 BC, he set foot in a land inhabited by tribes that spread across various English kingdoms. These kingdoms had evolved into more or less sophisticated and independent realms in the 2,000 years that had passed since the Celtic peoples had arrived and settled there, just as the Celts had done throughout western Europe.

The Celts had put down their roots in England during the Bronze Age, but it was in the Iron Age that the Greek historian, Herodotus, turned his attention to the British Isles, describing fifth-century Britain as the 'tin islands'.

Four centuries later Caesar arrived. He first landed in Kent in 55 BC, but it was not until the following year that he launched a full-scale attack. Having defeated the Catuvellauni king, Cassivellaunus, and other tribal leaders, Caesar returned to Rome. Then, in the first century AD, Cunobelin came to power as king of the Catuvellauni. The man on whom Shakespeare based his Cymbeline, Cunobelin became a dominant figure in South-East England in the years before the Roman conquest.

Ordered by Emperor Claudius, the invasion force of AD 43 was opposed by men such as Caratacus, the son of Cunobelin. However, the Roman legionaries won the war, Aulus Plautius and then Ostorius Scapula driving their soldiers relentlessly westwards and northwards. Eventually Caratacus was taken prisoner by the Romans, but a new resistance leader was ready to emerge: the formidable Boudicca (or Boadicea), queen of the Iceni tribe of Norfolk and Suffolk. In AD 61 Boudicca overran the Roman strongholds of Camulodunum (Colchester), Verulamium (St Albans) and London. Boudicca eventually suffered defeat, though, and committed suicide.

In AD 78 Gnaeus Julius Agricola began his six-year term as governor of Britain and with his arrival the conquest was consolidated so resolutely that the Romans were to remain the dominant force in England until the fifth century, almost 300 years after work had begun (in AD 122) on the construction of Hadrian's Wall between the Solway Firth and the River Tyne in the north of England.

In time, though, the Romans were forced to abandon Britain, the north-western outpost of their empire, the Emperor Honorius announcing his troops' withdrawal in AD 410. And so, after the cultured civilisation of the Roman era, the Dark Ages enveloped England. Yet as the Romans sailed away, new powers emerged to take their place. The mysterious Vortigern may have been one king to fill the vacuum, while the new kingdom of Kent may have been ruled over by Hengest during the second half of the fifth century.

Hengest was one of a number of Anglo-Saxon raiders who settled in Britain and who may have been opposed by the legendary sixth-century king, Arthur. Those settlers that did make their mark included the rulers of what became the royal houses of various English kingdoms. Writing his *Ecclesiastical History of the English People* in the early years of the eighth century, the Venerable Bede identified seven *bretwaldas*. These kings of kings were Elle

TOP LEFT: Roman bronze statue of Julius Caesar, Aosta, Italy
TOP RIGHT: Ethelbert is baptised by St Augustine
RIGHT: King Arthur

(Sussex), Ceawlin (Wessex), Ethelbert (Kent), Redwald (East Anglia) and Edwin, Oswald and Oswy (all of Northumbria).

Like Essex, the South-Saxon kingdom of Sussex was a minor power. Kent was the first such kingdom to be established and it was also the first to embrace Christianity, when Ethelbert was converted to Christianity by St Augustine in AD 597. In East Anglia, Redwald reigned supreme until his death sometime between AD 617 and 627. In the north was Northumbria, which consisted of the former kingdoms of Bernicia and Deira. There Edwin became a Christian before he was killed in battle in AD 633 and was succeeded first by his nephew, Oswald, (d. AD 642) and then, Oswald's brother or half-brother, Oswy, (d. AD 670).

Edwin and Oswald were both slain while fighting against Mercia. An emergent force, Mercia covered parts of the north and the Midlands and was led to glory by Penda, who was then killed by the Northumbrian Oswy in AD 655. Later Mercian kings were not quite as successful as Penda, but in Offa (r. AD 757–796) Mercia was blessed with a great leader. He was the king who ordered the construction of the Offa's Dyke earthwork that effectively separated Mercia from Wales. He was so omnipotent at his peak that he was recognised by the pope as 'king of the English'.

The most southerly kingdom, and in time the most powerful one, was Wessex. Possibly founded by Cerdic (d. *c.* AD 530), it was under Ceawlin (d. AD 593) that the West Saxons first flourished. In AD 577 Ceawlin claimed

a celebrated victory at Dyrham, Gloucestershire, where three British kings lost their lives in battle. Later, Cynegils (r. AD 611–643) became the first Christian king in Wessex, while the first truly great, all-conquering king was Egbert.

Egbert succeeded Beohtric in AD 802. He was to become the grandfather of Alfred the Great and the ruler who set Wessex on the way to becoming England's dominant kingdom. Egbert's success came at a time when the Vikings were beginning to raid England's coastal communities and he defeated the Mercian Beornwulf in AD 825. His control of Mercia was short-lived, but in the south-east and the south-west his victories were emphatic.

Acknowledged as the eighth *bretwalda*, King Egbert was succeeded by his son, Ethelwulf, in AD 839. Previously the ruler of Kent, Essex, Surrey and Sussex, he inherited his father's crown, but increasingly had to defend the realm against the first wave of attacks launched by the Viking 'Great Army'. Ethelwulf's son, Ethelbald succeeded his father while the older man was still alive. However, when Ethelbald died in AD 860 Wessex was ruled over briefly by Ethelwulf's younger sons, Ethelbert and Ethelred I. Dying in AD 871, the latter was succeeded by the man history came to know as 'Alfred the Great'.

EARLY RULERS OF IRELAND

Ireland was first settled about 9,000 years ago. Its earliest-known inhabitants were succeeded in the Neolithic era by the first Irish farmers. The County Meath sites of Newgrange are a product of this period. The status of Tara as a leading holy and royal site also began at this time and it remained a revered setting for centuries to come.

With the coming of the Bronze Age from around 2000 BC there arrived in Ireland a new group, known there and elsewhere as the Beaker people because of their distinctive pottery. It is believed that the next wave of peoples, the Celts, settled in Ireland during the Iron Age, from about the third century BC.

Despite their domination in mainland Britain, the influence of the Romans in Ireland was far less influential; their conquest of Britain reached its westernmost limit in Wales. As the Roman influence was negligible, Irish kings continued to hold sway. Among the early rulers of the Iron Age were legendary figures such as the third-century kings of Tara, Cormac mac Airt and Conn Cétchatha. Another heroic royal character was Lóegaire mac Néill, who was said to have been the country's ruler when St Patrick began his work as a Christian missionary in Ireland.

The exact life span of the man who became Ireland's patron saint is not known, but he was alive and preaching the gospel in the late fifth century. Many churches were built during his time in Ireland, and the period of Patrick's

teachings coincidied with the colourful life and times of Niall Noígallach. Like Conn Cétchatha, Niall was an ancestor of the Uí Néill dynasty, as well as a high king of Ireland.

The sixth century was the period in which the clan of Dál Riata of Ulaid became an established force in the west of Scotland. Sailing from Ulaid (which gives us the modern place-name of Ulster) settlers such as Aedán mac Gabráin were the ancestors of the Scots' kingdom of Dalriada.

Meanwhile, according to some annals, Diarmait mac Cerbaill of the southern Uí Néills was the Irish high king from AD 544, while yet another prominent figure alive at this time was Colm Cille. Also known as St Columba, he founded his famous missionary base at Iona in Scotland's Western Isles in AD 563, but was himself a native-born Irishman of the County Donegal clan that went by the name of Cenél Conaill. This was a branch of the Uí Néill dynasty, which was truly established as a power in the north during the seventh century. The southern Uí Néills were then the main force in the east, while in the west

LEFT: Beaker Burial
ABOVE: The Ardagh Chalice
RIGHT: St Columba

Connachta was ruled over by various local family groups. In the south-east, Leinster was home to to the Uí Failge, the Uí Dúnlainge and the Uí Chennselaig, whereas the sprawling province of Munster was the domain of the Eóganacht.

Consisting of different regional groups, this confederation became all-powerful Munster from the seventh century to the middle of the tenth century. The most successful king of the Eóganacht during this period was Cathal mac Finguine, who died in AD 742 following two decades of warmongering, which led some later writers to hail Cathal as Ireland's king of kings. Then, less than half a century after Cathal's passing, the Vikings arrived in Ireland. Their first recorded landing was made in AD 795 and for the

next four centuries the Norsemen were a force to be reckoned with. The arrival of the Vikings was announced by a series of lightning raids, but by the AD 830s the attacks had become more concerted, culminating with the fall of Dublin in AD 841.

At this time Fedelmid (also spelt Feidelmid) mac Crimthainn, king of Munster, was one of Ireland's mightiest men. Fedelmid challenged the supremacy of the Uí Néills, most notably his contemporary Máel Sechnaill I, the king of Tara, who became ruler of the southern Uí Néills in AD 846, the year before Fedelmid's death. Máel Sechnaill I notched impressive victories against Norse forces, while half a century later (in AD 919) Niall Glúndub was killed when he fought the Vikings of Dublin.

EARLY RULERS OF SCOTLAND

Inhabited during the Stone and Bronze Ages, for many centuries Scotland had been inhabited by Celtic tribes. Then the Romans arrived. Led by Agricola, the ninth Legion marched into southern Scotland in AD 80 or 81. Continuing to push northwards the legionaries eventually made Stirling their main base and fought and defeated Caledonian warriors at Mons Graupius. Yet this was as much as Agricola was allowed to achieve, for soon after this victory he was ordered to leave Scotland.

In AD 122 the Romans began the construction of Hadrian's Wall, between the Solway Firth and the mouth of the River Tyne. In AD 142 they started building the more northerly Antonine Wall. Like its southern counterpart, this stretched from west to east, running from the mouth of the River Clyde to the Firth of Forth.

On the offensive again from AD 207 or 208, Severus made little headway when he attempted to colonise eastern Scotland. Thereafter the Romans all but abandoned Scotland, then populated by Celtic tribes and Anglo-Saxons. The northernmost kingdom was ruled by the Picts (or 'painted people'), while their rivals in the west were the Irish Scots of Dalriada (or Dál Riata). In the south lay the Strathclyde realm of the Britons, whereas the south-eastern corner of Scotland was the territory of the Anglo-Saxons of Lothian.

Following the Roman invasion, the next major outside influence to be exerted on Scottish life was Christianity. Missionaries such as St Ninian were active early in the fifth century. Then as more Irish Scots arrived from the west, a second famous missionary followed in their wake. His name was Colm Cille. Better known today as Columba, he made Iona his home. A holy man and a politician, Columba died in AD 597.

A contemporary of St Columba was Aedán mac Gabráin. The king of Dalriada, he died 11 years after Columba, having earlier extended his kingdom in much the same way that Kenneth I mac Alpin (Cinaed I mac Alpin) was to do more than two centuries later.

A son of Aedán, Eochaid Buide succeeded his father, while the next Dalriada king was Domnall Brecc, whose sorry reign ended in AD 642 with his death in battle at the hands of Owen (Ywain), the king of Strathclyde. Still farther south, the Northumbrians of northern England became a force under King Oswy, while Oswy's nephew, Talorcan, briefly ruled the land of the Picts. A king who made a more lasting impression than Talorcan was Bridei, the Picts' ruler who defeated the Northumbrians at Nechtanesmere near Forfar in AD 685.

In AD 728, following the peaceful reign of Nechtan, the Picts fought a civil war that

238 The Historie of Scotlande.

auginkting the fee with fundoes fayze reuenewes to the better mayntenance thereof.

Malcolme thus hauing purchased refte from further troubles of warre, gouerned the realme a certain time after in good ozder of iuftice, & cau=

The boke called Regia maieftas. fed a booke to be fet fozth, called *Regiam maiefta=rem,* conteyning the lawes & ozdinances, wherby the realme fhoulde be gouerned : and affigning fozth in the fame what fees alfo fhould be giuen vnto the Chauncellour, Secretarie, Conftable, Merfhall, Chamberlayne, Juftice, Treafozer, Regifter, Comptroller, & other the officers of his houfe. Such pziucely doings and noble bertues were found in this Malcolme foz a feafon, that if the fame had continued with him in his later

age, there had neuer reygned any king in Scot-land, that might haue bene thought to haue paf-fed him in woozthy fame : neuertheleffe his excel-lent qualities were ftayned at length by that re-pzochfull bice of bile auarice. Foz as it oftetimes happeneth, couetoufneffe and age layde holde on him bothe at once. He then beganne to repent in that he had bene fo liberall in giuing away his landes to his Barones, and to recouer the fame agayne, hee furmifed fayned mater by bntrue fuggeftions agaynft diuers of the chiefeft No-bles, putting fome to death and banifhing other, that he might by this meanes enioy theyz landes and goodes as confifcate to the crowne foz theyz fuppofed offences.

Malcolme waxeth auari-tious.

Couetoufneffe and age arri-uing togkther.

Malcolnes crueltie to purchas richs

brought to the fore the mighty Oengus, a warrior-king who, in AD 741, captured the Dalriada capital Dunadd, to become king of the Scots. Later, kings such as Constantine (Constantin), a second monarch named Oengus and his son, Eogánán, all reigned over the kingdoms of the Picts and Dalriada. By the end of the eighth century, however, there was a new power on the loose in Scotland.

Capturing island after island, the Vikings eventually made moves to conquer mainland territories, by which

ABOVE: An extract from Volume one of Holinshed's History of Scotland
LEFT: Scales of Justice monument

time the new kingdom of Alba or Alban had been formed by Kenneth I mac Alpin. Although little is known of this king, it seems probable that in AD 840 he freed Dalriada from its subjugation by the Picts. Continuing to impose his will on his kingdom, after seven years of struggle Kenneth had created Alba and all but consigned the Pict nation to the history books.

EARLY RULERS OF WALES

People have lived in Wales for 21,000 years or more and the early settlers came from near and far. During the Neolithic period of the late Stone Age, émigrés sailed north from Brittany, from other parts of France and from Spain. Later, in the Bronze Age, the Beaker people arrived. So-called because of their pottery designs, from the early years of the second millennium BC they occupied areas of Wales.

Then came the Celts. These Iron Age peoples spread out from Central Europe from 500–400 BC. Travelling extensively, two bands of Celts arrived in Wales: the Brythons (or Britons) and the Goidels (or Gaelic peoples, who came via Ireland).

Centuries then passed before the next main wave of settlers washed over Wales in the shape of the Romans. Spearheaded by Suetonius Paulinus, his invasion force eventually defeated the wily King Caradog. Otherwise known as Caratacus or Caractacus, he was the son of Cunobelin. The ruler of the Catuvellauni of eastern England at the time of the Roman invasion, later he was pushed out west, where he helped take the fight to the Romans as a leader of forces from the Silures tribe of South Wales and the Ordovices tribe from the north before finally being taken prisoner. Unfortunately the fate of Caradog mirrored that of the Welsh peoples. Brave resistance campaigns were mounted, but ultimately the Romans won through. Massacring the druids of Anglesey in AD 61, their conquest of most of Wales was complete by about AD 80.

Establishing forts and building roads, the Romans remained in Wales for the next 300 years. Then, as commanders such as the legendary Macsen Wledig (Magnus Maximus) sailed away, new bands of foreigners arrived to fill the void. From Ireland there came more Goidelic invaders, their arrival sparking a struggle for supremacy between the Goidels and the Brythons that would last until the rise of Cunedda. The king of the Votadini, Cunedda arrived in Wales from northern Britain at the turn of the fifth century. Defeating the Goidels, he created in North Wales what was to become the kingdom of Gwynedd. As the royal house of Gwynedd was established, descendants of Cunedda such as Einion Yrth, Cadwallon and Maelgwyn (also known as Maglocunus) ruled over the region.

Another power in the land from the fifth century was Christianity. No Christian missionary was more esteemed in Wales than Dewi. More commonly known as St David (the patron saint of Wales) he made his mark in the sixth century. The influence of the later Christian missionaries was paralleled by the influence of the pagan tribes of the Anglo-Saxons and it was in this period that the legendary figure of Arthur was said to have flourished.

The battle for supremacy continued with rulers such as Cadwallon of Gwynedd, who fought to assert his kingship until his death. With the help of Penda of Mercia he had killed Edwin and defeated his Northumbrian forces by AD 633, but died in battle himself the following year. Cadwallon's brief taste of power came at a time when the notion of *Cymry* (or 'compatriots') was prevalent. Yet after the eclipse of Cadwallon and his son, Cadwaladr, ap Cadwallon, the highly acclaimed Gwynedd king, the Brythons were never again to wield such power beyond what we know today as Wales.

One hundred and fifty years after the death of Cadwallon, the Mercian king, Offa, ordered the construction of his famous dyke. Effectively marking the border between his kingdom in the east and Wales in the west, Offa's Dyke was built

ABOVE: Copper and flint dagger, Beaker culture
RIGHT: Offa's Dyke

late in the eighth century. It was Europe's longest earthwork, running from Prestatyn in the north to Chepstow in the far south.

In AD 768 while the dyke was still being completed, the Church in Wales fell into line with the orthodoxies of the Roman Church. Meanwhile, in Gwynedd, as in other lesser kingdoms such as Ceredigion (Cardigan), Dyfed, Powys, Morgannwg (Glamorgan) and Brycheiniog (Brecon), rulers came and went. So, in Gwynedd Cadwaladr was succeeded by the likes of Idwal (d. AD 712), Rhodri Molwynog (d. AD 754), Cynan (d. AD 816) and then Ethyllt (or Esyllt).

Alive in the early years of the ninth century, Ethyllt was the father of Merfyn Frych (Merfyn the Freckled). Marrying the daughter of the reigning Powys king, Merfyn had reigned first in Anglesey, then in the Gwynedd kingdom, where his son, Rhodri Mawr (Rhodri the Great), would achieve power and glory. King in the years following Merfyn's death in AD 844, Rhodri succeeded in extending the borders of the kingdom by conquest and marriage, despite the Viking raids that were a recurrent feature of Welsh life during the ninth and tenth centuries.

AED (d. 878)

King of the Picts and Scots (AD 877–78). Aed, sometimes known as Aed the Furious, or Whitefoot, was the son of Kenneth mac Alpin. He was the brother of Constantine I, who he succeeded as king of the Scots and Picts. Aed reigned for barely a year before he was killed, while in the Strathallan region, by his cousin, Giric. The murdered monarch was succeeded by Giric, who may have ruled jointly with Aed's nephew, Eochaid.

))))▶ *Constantine I, Eochaid, Kenneth I mac Alpin*

ALEXANDER I (c. 1077–1124)

King of the Scots (1107–24). One of four sons of Malcolm III to be crowned, Alexander I earned the nickname Alexander the Fierce by taming northern clans. In 1100 a younger sister married England's Henry I, thus Alexander I became the English king's brother-in-law and subsequently his son-in-law when he married one of Henry's illegitimate daughters, Sibylla.

Ascending the throne in 1107, following the death of his half-brother, Edgar, his realm included central and eastern lands south of the Spey river and South Scotland where, grudgingly, he allowed his brother, David, to hold sway. A devoutly Christian monarch, he supported the Scottish Church in its efforts to fight the combined threats posed by paganism and the English archbishops at Canterbury and York. The king's 17-year reign ended with his death in 1124. Scotland's crown passed to Alexander's younger brother, David I.

))))▶ *David I, Henry I, Malcolm III*

ALEXANDER II (1198–1249)

King of the Scots (1214–49). The only legitimate son of William the Lion, who he succeeded in 1214, Alexander's early reign was dominated by raids on England, with King John retaliating by invading Lothian. Later, Scotland's sovereign married John's daughter, Joan, but the union produced no children. Queen Joan died in 1238, one year after Scotland and England had signed the Treaty of York. Alexander took his second wife, Marie de Courcy, in 1239. Their son succeeded the throne as Alexander III in 1249.

Born at Haddington in Lothian, the son of William the Lion and Ermengarde de Beaumont, Alexander II ascended the throne on the death of his father in 1214, at the age of just 16. Three years later he signed an Anglo-Scottish treaty and on 19 June 1221 the seal was put on this treaty with Alexander's marriage to England's Princess Joan, the eldest daughter of John and the sister of the new English monarch, Henry III. A Christian king, Alexander promoted the Scottish Church, founded abbeys and built castles. The man King John called the 'red fox cub' was also said to have ordered the brutal maiming of 80 men who had been witnesses to the murder of a Caithness bishop; each man had his hands and feet hacked off.

Alexander II strove to assert his authority in the north (Caithness and Moray), west (Argyll) and south-west (Galloway), made a vain bid to purchase the Hebrides and the kingdom of Man from Norway and, in 1237, put his name to the Treaty of York, an attempt to end border disputes. The new borderline between Scotland and England stretched from Gretna in the west to just north of Berwick in the east. The agreement saw Alexander renounce his claim to Northumbria and Westmoreland in exchange for money and other territories.

Ten years later, while on his way to attack Viking settlers on the Western Isles, Alexander II fell ill with a fever. Dying on the island of Kerrera on 8 July 1249, he was buried at Melrose Abbey.

))) *Alexander III, Henry III, John*

ALEXANDER III (1241–86)

King of the Scots (1249–86). Only eight years old when he inherited Scotland's crown from his father, Alexander II, two years later the boy-king married Princess Margaret of England. Fighting Haakon of Norway at Largs in 1263, in 1281 his daughter married Haakon's grandson, Eric II. The passing of the king's first wife in 1275 was followed by the deaths of two sons and his daughter Margaret, the mother of his successor, Margaret the Maid. Alexander died in 1285, five months after his marriage to Yolande.

Born at Roxburgh in 1241, by the time Alexander was 10 years old he was king of the Scots and married to Margaret, the eldest daughter of Henry III. The wedding took place in York on 26 December 1251. Sending an army to attack Norse settlers in the Hebrides, in 1263 the Scots engaged a large Norwegian force at the west-coast port of Largs. Three years later the Treaty of Perth saw Norway hand over control of the Hebrides to Scotland's king.

Alexander fell out with his English in-laws in 1278, but good relations were restored when Alexander agreed to pay homage to his brother-in-law, Edward I. In 1283 relations with Norway improved when Alexander's daughter, Margaret, married King Eric II. Then, just as the Scots were beginning to reap the benefits of their sovereign's largely successful rule, the king was killed. On 18 March 1286, while riding home from Edinburgh to his second wife, Yolande (also known as Joleta) of Dreux, the king's horse fell, throwing its royal rider to his death. With all three of Alexander's children and his first wife having predeceased him, this fatal accident brought to the throne the late king's infant granddaughter, Margaret.

))) *Edward I, Henry III, Margaret*

BELOW: Alexander III is rescued from the fury of a stag

ALFRED THE GREAT (AD 849–99)

King of Wessex (AD 871–99); son of Ethelwulf.
One of the best-loved figures in English history,
Alfred was the fourth and last of his father's sons to reign
in Wessex. A devout Christian, famous for defeating the
Danes and remembered in legend as the king who burnt
the cakes, Alfred fortified his kingdom and was a
lawmaker and educator. He succeeded his brother
Ethelred I, in AD 871, but seven years later a major
Danish offensive forced him to flee his kingdom and bide
his time until he could gather forces enough to counterattack. His time came: he beat the 'Great Army' of Danes
at Edington in AD 878. He also overran London in AD
886. Married to Ealswith, his crown passed to their son,
Edward the Elder.

Alfred was born at Wantage in Oxfordshire in
AD 849, when his father had already ruled the kingdom

of Wessex for almost a decade. Ethelwulf had consolidated the West-Saxon dynasty established by his own father, Egbert. Egbert had once ruled over a kingdom that included the modern-day counties of Sussex, Surrey, Kent and Essex, while even Mercia in the east came under his command. Later, Ethelwulf's death saw the Wessex crown pass in quick succession to Alfred's elder brothers: Ethelbald, Ethelbert and Ethelred I.

In AD 868, Alfred married Ealswith, a Mercian princess. Two years later, on Berkshire Downs, Alfred assisted his brother, Ethelred, in inflicting a heavy defeat on the marauding Danes. However, the 'Great Army' struck back swiftly, bringing Northumbria and East Anglia under their sway and attacking Wessex once again. Alfred had become king of the West Saxons – ascending the throne ahead of Ethelred's young son, Ethelwold – in April AD 871. Within a year he was forced to negotiate a peace settlement with the Danes. After a brief foray into Mercia, however, the Danes returned to Wessex yet again and in AD 878 the invaders launched a surprise attack at Chippenham.

Forced to retreat when a full-scale invasion of Wessex threatened, during Easter AD 878 Alfred sought refuge in the marshlands of Athelney, Somerset. This period in the wilderness has given rise to several tales, including the one in which the disguised king was scolded by a swineherd's wife for burning the cakes she had asked him to tend. Also leading raiding parties from his hideaway in the wilds of Somerset, Alfred then won a crucial victory by defeating the Viking, Guthrum, at Edington, Wiltshire. A short time later the Treaty of Wedmore was agreed: acknowledging Danish rights to rule over territory they had already conquered, the deal secured the independence of Wessex.

With peace now assured, Alfred took to strengthening the defences of his kingdom by creating new burgs (fortified towns) and transforming old Roman towns such as Winchester. In AD 886 Alfred's militia captured London. Seven years later a vast Danish army went on the rampage, but the strong fortifications in Wessex held

firm. In addition to keeping the Danes at bay, the Wessex king ensured the continuation of his dynasty by diplomatic manoeuvrings with rival kingdoms such as Mercia where, for much of his reign, Burhed (his brother-in-law) and Ethelred (his son-in-law) were rulers.

A popular, resourceful leader, who compiled a code of laws, King Alfred also made an important contribution to educating the people of his kingdom. He translated Christian texts, wrote his own original works and was one of the first authors to refer to 'England', the word *Angelcynn* coined by Alfred meaning 'English folk'. His religious faith and passion for learning underpinned the move to raise levels of literacy throughout the land, while a knowledge of Latin became a necessity for officials of court, Church and the justice system. Dying at Winchester on 26 October AD 899, Alfred the Great was buried at Winchester Abbey. Survived by his wife, he was succeded as king by his son.

Edward the Elder, House of Wessex

TOP LEFT: *King Alfred dividing his last loaf with the pilgrim*
LEFT: *King Alfred reading*
RIGHT: *Statue of Alfred the Great, Wantage*

ALPIN (d. c. 834)

King of the Scots of Dalriada; possibly the son of Eochaid. The territory of Dalriada encompassed modern-day Argyll, Kintyre and various west-coast islands and here Alpin reigned for approximately three years. He was killed around AD 834 while on a raiding mission in Galloway. Little is known about Alpin (or Alpín), the Scottish royal who was reputedly the father of Kenneth mac Alpin, the man who later ruled over Dalriada and the former kingdom of the Picts.

⟫➤ *Eochaid, Kenneth I mac Alpin*

ANARAWD AP RHODRI (d. AD 916)

King of Gwynedd (AD 878–916). Son of the celebrated Welsh king, Rhodri Mawr, like his father, Anarawd, reigned for more than three decades. Coming to power in AD 878 following Rhodri's death, Anarawd ap Rhodri established his own royal house, Deuheubarth, centred on the Gwynedd capital, Aberffraw. At Conwy in AD 881 the Gwynedd king notched a notable victory against Ethelred of Mercia. He later acknowledged Alfred the Great as his overlord and before his death in AD 916 Anarawd repelled a number of Viking raids and declared war on his brother, Cadell. He was succeeded by his son, Idwal ap Anarawd.

⟫➤ *House of Deheubarth, House of Gwynedd, Idwal ap Anarawd, Rhodri Mawr*

ANGEVIN DYNASTY (SEE HOUSE OF PLANTAGENET)

ANGLO-DANES

Viking rulers of the British Isles. Viking raids were recorded as long ago as the end of the eighth century when many battles were fought between native Britons and Danish raiders. Lands in all four corners of the British Isles had been seized and many sums paid by native peoples to Norsemen in the form of tribute. Yet it was not until 1013 that Svein Forkbeard became the first Dane to be recognised as king of England.

The eldest son of Denmark's monarch, Harald III ('Bluetooth'), in AD 994 Svein and Norway's Olaf Tryggvason sailed to England at the head of a huge fleet of warships and there besieged London. Eventually peace was exchanged for £16,000, but regular Viking raids continued to afflict English settlements. Svein's sister, Gunhild, was allegedly one of many English-based Danes to be slaughtered in the St Brice's Day Massacre in 1002. The following year Danish militia sought revenge for this atrocity by fighting their way deep into the heart of England. Another attack in 1004 and a third in 1009 led to Danish assaults on 15 counties before Svein Forkbeard broke the back of native resistance.

Crowned in 1013 following Ethelred II's hurried dash into exile, Svein died just a few months later and Ethelred was reinstated as king until his own death in 1016. Succeeded by his son, Edmund II ('Ironside'), the Danish threat showed no signs of abating as Svein's son, Cnut, continued the challenge to Anglo-Saxon rule, which he had helped sustain during his father's lifetime. Overlooked in 1014, two years later Edmund's death saw Cnut add the kingdom of Wessex to the territory ceded him a short time before by King Edmund.

King of Denmark from 1019 and ruler of Norway after 1030, Cnut reigned as England's king until his death in 1035. Succeeded in England by the younger son from his first marriage, Harold I's ('Harefoot') reign was brief. On Harold's death in 1040 he was succeeded by his half-brother, Harthacnut (or Hardicanute). The only son of Cnut and Emma (the widow of Ethelred II), he had been chosen to rule jointly with Harold in 1035, but had forfeited this opportunity by his continued absence from England.

King for just two years, Harthacnut's death brought an abrupt end to the rule of England's Danish kings and the accession of Edward the Confessor heralded the final flourish of the Anglo-Saxon age. However, in 1066, an Anglo-Danish kingship was fleetingly restored when Harold II was crowned. The eldest son of Earl Godwin and his wife, Gytha, Harold's mother was the great-grand-daughter of the one-time king of Denmark, Harold III.

)))➤ *House of Wessex*

BELOW: The Anglo-Danish Kings, Canute, Harold I and II with Edward the Confessor, the Anglo-Saxon King
RIGHT: Harthacanute

ANGLO-DANISH KINGS

1013–1	Svein Forkbeard
1016–35	Cnut
1035–40	Harold I 'Harefoot'
1040–42	Harthacnut
1066	Harold II

ANNE (1665–1714)

Queen of Great Britain (1702–14); daughter of James II and sister to Mary II. Succeeding her brother-in-law, William III, Anne was crowned on St George's Day, 1702. Queen for 12 years, her reign witnessed the great military victories during the War of the Spanish Succession, the creation of the United Kingdom (1707) and the development of party politics. Married to Prince George of Denmark, his death in 1708 was followed six years later by that of Anne. The first sovereign of Great Britain, but the last of the Stuart monarchs, she was succeeded by the first Hanoverian king, George I.

Anne was the second daughter of the then Duke of York and his first wife, Anne Hyde. She was born at St James's Palace, London, on 6 February 1665. As a child her father, James, was a leading figure at the court of his brother, Charles II. Still an infant when featured in Peter Lely's well-known portrait of James's family, Anne was just six years old when her mother died, but she soon gained a stepmother in Mary of Modena, her father's second wife.

At the age of 18 Anne wed the Danish prince, George, and two years later, on her twentieth birthday, her father began his reign as king. It was not long, though, before his Catholic sympathies forced his abdication and exile and a war began between the king and his son-in-law, William of Orange, husband of Anne's elder sister, Mary. When the Glorious Revolution occurred in 1689 Anne agreed to allow William to rule alone if Mary should die first without producing an heir; in return she received £50,000 a year and the exclusive use of the Cockpit, a London mansion that stood on what is now Downing Street.

Anne was desperate for a family and, most importantly, an heir. She fell pregnant at least 18 times, but tragically only one child survived infancy: William, Duke of Gloucester. With his death in 1700, at the age of 11, hope of the continuance of the Stuart line also died.

Mary II had died in 1794 and William had continued to serve as king as agreed. His death in 1702 led to Anne's accession as queen. Crowned at Westminster Abbey on 23 April 1702, the ailing monarch was carried to and from her coronation in a sedan chair. Two weeks later, the first shots were fired in a war with France, a nation then supporting the 'Old Pretender', James Edward Stuart. Continuing until 1713 and costing around £150 million, the War of the Spanish Succession saw John Churchill, Duke of Marlborough, the husband of the queen's long-time friend, Sarah Churchill, win great victories at Blenheim (1704), Ramillies (1706) and Oudenarde (1708).

At home a notable facet of Anne's short reign was the growing influence of the Whigs and the Tories in parliament and the rivalry of these political parties was mirrored by the improved standing of parliament and the holding of regular general elections.

The major event for which Anne's reign is remembered, though, is the Act of Union. This was the formal creation of the United Kingdom of Great Britain: two realms united politically. Placed in the statute books on 6 March 1707 the Act of Union of England and Scotland disbanded the Scottish parliament, although it left unchanged Scotland's legal and ecclesiastical systems.

TOP: Battle of Malaga, the War of Spanish Succession
RIGHT: Anne presents the plans of Blenheim to the Duke of Marlborough

The Act also changed the sovereign's title and Anne became Queen of Great Britain and Ireland.

A passionate Protestant and loyal to friends, Anne was stout and short: she was once described as 'one of the smallest people ever set in a great place'. Anne was a diligent queen, but she was unremarkable and frequently suffered from ill health. She died at Kensington Palace in London on 1 August 1714 and was buried at Westminster Abbey.

)))⟩ *House of Hanover, House of Stuart*

ATHELSTAN (c. 895–939)

King of England (AD 924–39). Athelstan was the son of Edward the Elder, and he forged a reputation to rival that of his illustrious grandfather, Alfred the Great. Ascending the thrones of Mercia and Wessex in AD 924, following the death of his father, in AD 927 Athelstan was recognised as king of England and he also conquered the Danish kingdom of York. At Brunanburh in AD 937 he won a remarkable victory against combined Danish and Scottish forces. A shrewd diplomatist with a worldly approach, he arranged important marriage alliances with foreign dynasties. He was also a notable lawmaker and administrator at home. Athelstan died in AD 939 at the age of 44. He was unmarried and without issue and his death brought Edmund I to the throne.

Athelstan was the first-born child of Edward the Elder and Egwina and was the eldest of at least 14 offspring born to the king. Some doubt has been cast on his legitimacy, as it is unknown whether Edward the Elder was actually married to Egwina at the time of Athelstan's birth. Whatever the case, Athelstan is reputed to have been doted on by his grandfather, Alfred the Great, although the prince was still a young boy at the time of Alfred's death.

Athelstan spent much of his childhood in Mercia, where he was largely brought up by his aunt, Aethelflaed. He was so much regarded as one of their own that on his father's death in July AD 924, having spents 25 years as heir to the throne, the Mercians immediately proclaimed him their king. His ascension to the throne of Wessex took longer as the witan deliberated on his suitability (another possible indication of his illegitimacy). His coronation as king of Wessex eventually took place at Kingston Upon Thames on 5 September AD 925.

Known in his charters as 'King of the English, raised to the throne ... by the hand of the Almighty', it was in AD 927 that Athelstan rose to become the undisputed ruler of England. His authority was acknowledged by the Norse king of York, Sihtric Caech, who no doubt feared the threat that Athelstan's Mercian following might pose to his own kingdom. Terms for peace were agreed and as part of the deal Sihtric married Athelstan's sister on 30 January AD 926. This marriage alliance foundered with the early death of Sihtric, however, and so did the tentative peace that had accompanied it. The people of Sihtric's realm in Northumbria accepted the selection of the late king's son, Olaf, as his successor and Athelstan was forced to make a decisive move against them. Marching into Northumbria in AD 927, his invasion led directly to the submission of the kings of Scotland and Strathclyde as well as the lord of the English enclave of Bamburgh. This profitable campaign then reaped further dividends when Athelstan seized York.

The first king to bring most of England under his control, within four years of his successful sorties in the north Athelstan had made considerable inroads in the west, thus emphasising his status as the most powerful ruler in the British Isles. Athelstan first attacked and pushed back the Britons in South-West England and across the Bristol Channel the leading Welsh kings, such as the Deheubarth ruler, Hywel Dda, were also quick to acknowledge Athelstan's greatness and pay homage to him. Later quelling an attempt at invasion by a fighting force of Scottish, Strathclyde and Irish-Viking men, the English sovereign's last great victory was won on the battlefield of Brunanburh in AD 937.

Athelstan was also highly influential throughout Continental Europe and a series of carefully planned marriages of his family members with European royalty helped England's king establish a network of alliances. Fortunately for him, Athelstan had been blessed with no fewer than seven half-sisters. One wed Otto, a German prince who later became Holy Roman Emperor; a second married the king of the West Franks, Charles II the Simple; while other daughters of Edward the Elder became the wives of foreign dukes such as Hugh the Great, Boleslav II of Bohemia and Louis of Aquitaine.

A renowned administrator and lawmaker, whose many charters bear witness to the sheer volume of new laws introduced in his reign, Athelstan died at Gloucester on 27 October AD 939. Buried at Malmesbury Abbey, the unmarried king's successor was his half-brother, Edmund I.

LEFT: Athelstan, king of the West Saxons

▶ House of Deheubarth, Hywel Dda, House of Wessex

BALLIOL, HOUSE OF

Originally the de Bailleul family of Picardy, France, like the Bruce clan the Balliol émigrés who settled in the British Isles following the Norman Conquest became wealthy and influential members of the Scottish nobility. With estates in both Scotland and England, it was during the twelfth century that the Scots' king, David I, had given lands north of the border to Bernard de Bailleul. Firmly established by the reign of William the Lion, in 1174, at the Battle of Alnwick, Bernard 'The Younger' Balliol tamed the lion. Handed over to England's Henry II, William was then forced to sign the Treaty of Falaise, which acknowledged English suzerainty over Scotland.

A man of substance, Bernard Balliol was the grandfather of John. His father's namesake, the younger John Balliol flourished in the middle years of the thirteenth century, when he was one of the most powerful landowners of the period. Married to Devorguilla (Dearbhfhorghaill), the daughter of Alan, Lord of Galloway, when the minor Alexander III ascended the throne, John Balliol was one of the regents appointed to rule Scotland. Accused of treason in 1255 John was forced to give up his vast estates, but by siding with Henry III against Simon de Montfort he regained his former status.

In 1263 John founded a college at Oxford University as a penance. After her husband's death in 1269 John's widow donated further funds to Balliol College and it still bears the family name more than seven centuries later. Living until 1290 Devorguilla suffered the loss of two sons during her lifetime, but a third boy lived long enough to become king of the Scots.

Nominated as Scottish monarch by Edward I of England, John Balliol endured a short and difficult reign. Caught between the Scottish nobility and the English monarchy, the king, later derided by Scots as Toom Tabard ('Empty Coat'), made his last stand in 1296. Beaten by the English at Berwick in March of the same year, four months later England's forces were established as an army of occupation and at Montrose on 10 July John Balliol was dethroned.

However, the demotion of Toom Tabard did not mark the end of the Balliol dynasty as, in 1332, the former king's son, Edward, succeeded David II as king of the Scots. John Balliol's eldest boy, like his father, Edward Balliol, relied heavily on English support in his bid to win Scotland's crown.

SCOTLAND IN 1290

Beating the king's regent in battle on Dupplin Moor in August 1332, six weeks later Edward was crowned at Scone. No sooner was his coronation concluded, however, than Edward Balliol was forced into exile. Returned to the throne in 1334, the following year he was ousted once more. Continuing to lead various raids in his attempt to regain power, in 1346 he fought his way to Glasgow. But the tide had turned and Edward was doomed never again to rule in Scotland, although the second and last Balliol king of the Scots did not finally renounce his claim to the throne until 1356.

)))➤ *Edward Balliol, John Balliol, David II Edward I, Henry III*

THE HOUSE OF BALLIOL

| 1291–96 | John Balliol |
| 1332–36 | Edward Balliol |

BALLIOL, EDWARD (c. 1283–1364)

King of the Scots (intermittently 1332–56); son of John Balliol. Assuming power in 1332, Edward regained the Scottish crown that had been snatched from his father's head 36 years previously. While in exile, his successful move to dethrone David II was backed by Edward III of England in exchange for land. Victorious at Halidon Hill in 1333, the following year Berwick and Lothian were ceded to England. Driven from Scotland in 1335, prior to the restoration of David II he made sporadic returns to attack successive Scottish regents.

Edward was the eldest son of John Balliol and his wife, Isabelle, and he spent many years living on his family's estates in France. He settled in England in 1324 and six years later he sailed to Scotland at the head of a large fleet of warships in an attempt to reclaim the Scottish throne for the Balliols. He defeated a Scottish force at Dupplin Moor, near Perth, in August 1332, and the following month Edward was crowned at Scone. He was soon forced to beat a hasty retreat from Annan, however, after a surprise attack by a militia led by the regent and the future Scots king, Robert II.

LEFT: John of Balliol's Seal
ABOVE LEFT: Scotland in 1290
RIGHT: Edward III who backed Edward Balliol's move to usurp David II

Edward was not to be deterred, though. By 1334 he was back in Scotland and as English armies won notable victories at the battles of Halidon Hill and Berwick, Edward Balliol must have rejoiced. However, with England then given vast tracts of land, supporters loyal to the deposed king, David II, struck back and, in 1235, a surprise attack at Culblean Hill in the Grampian mountain range caused Balliol to hurry south to seek sanctuary in England. Thereafter, he led various English-sponsored raiding parties, only renouncing his claim to the Scottish throne in 1356.

)))➤ *House of Balliol, Constantine III, David II, Edward III, Robert II*

BALLIOL, JOHN (c. 1250–1313)

King of the Scots (1291–96). John Balliol was the father of the later Scottish sovereign, Edward Balliol. A leading candidate for the Scottish crown after the death of Margaret the Maid in 1290, John Balliol was appointed king of the Scots by the English king, Edward I. In 1295 John Balliol renewed Scotland's links with France, but in 1296 he lost his crown after the sacking of Berwick and the Scots' defeat at Dunbar. Formally stripped of the regalia of kingship in 1296, he was imprisoned in London. He was later placed in papal custody, where he died in 1313.

A son of John and Devorguilla (Dearbhfhorghaill) Balliol, the deaths of his father and elder brothers led to John's inheritance of large estates in both Scotland and England. John was married to Isabelle, the daughter of the Earl of Surrey, and their son, Edward Balliol, was to fight an intermittent battle for the Scots' crown between 1332–56. In 1290, however, John Balliol was one of more

than a dozen contenders for Scotland's throne and as tensions surfaced and infighting broke out amongst the clans, the Scottish lords called on Edward I of England to choose their nation's next monarch. A meeting was called and in November 1291 the English king announced that John Balliol would be Scotland's next sovereign.

Crowned at Scone in 1292, from the first the new king struggled. Torn between his demanding English master and his resentful subjects, in 1294 John Balliol rejected a summons to join Edward on a campaign against England's old enemy, France. He compounded this rejection by signing a treaty with the French. Two years later, in 1296, he declined to pay homage to Edward: the consequences of this insubordination were swift and savage. Marching north with a large army, Edward the 'Hammer of the Scots' struck the first of several blows. In November 1291 Berwick had been the setting for the grand assembly at which Edward I conferred kingship on John Balliol, but five years later the city was rased to the ground by English forces. Continuing northwards, Edward's army reached the eastern seaport of Dunbar, where it inflicted a humiliating defeat on the Scottish king and his supporters.

Stripped of his crown, John Balliol was sent to the Tower of London while Edward I continued his victory procession through the Scottish heartland. Held prisoner in the Tower for three years, eventually John Balliol returned to his ancestral homeland in Picardy, France, where he died in 1313.

► *House of Balliol, Edward Balliol, Constantine III, Edward I*

BLEDDYN AP CYNFYN (c. 1025–75)

King of Gwynedd and Powys (1063–75). Bleddyn was installed as king of the northen regions of Wales by the English king, Edward the Confessor, after the death of Gruffudd ap Llewelyn and he proved to be worthy of the position. He ruled there with his brother, Rhiwallon, and together they ran the provinces of Powys and Gwynedd during one of the most turbulent times in

LEFT: John Balliol surrenders his crown to Edward at Kincardine, Scotland
RIGHT: Brian Bóruma is killed by Brodar, a Dane, after the Battle of Clontarf

British history: the Norman Conquest. The Welsh kings supported the English against the Normans and forced William the Conqueror to take military measures to control the Welsh.

The conquest over, internal wranglings in Wales caused problems as the sons of Gruffudd ap Llewellyn challenged for the throne. At the Battle of Mechain in 1070 they both died, along with Rhiwallon, leaving Bleddyn solely in charge of the two kingdoms. For some time after this Bleddyn was able to turn his attention to the things he cared about most and he earned the love and respect of his people through his generosity and his just rule. This period of respite lasted just three years, however, and in 1073 the Normans made their move into Wales. The ensuing struggle allowed kings of other Welsh provinces to move in on the powerful areas of Gwynedd and Powys and Bleddyn was mudered in 1075.

))⯈ *Edward the Confessor, Gruffudd ap Llewelyn, William I the Conqueror*

BÓRUMA, BRIAN (c. 926–1014)

High king of Ireland (1002–14); son of Cennétig. Brian Bóruma (also known as Brian Boru), a king from southern Ireland, was a great Dál Cais ruler. He seized Limerick in AD 968, then became king of Munster after the murder of his brother, Mathgamain (AD 976). Chief of Cashel by AD 978, he later advanced into Connacht and Leinster. Striking a deal with Máel Sechnaill II in AD 997, the kings agreed to divide Ireland between them. Brian Bóruma took Dublin in AD 999 and was elected as Ireland's high king in 1002. 'Emperor of the Irish' from 1005, he led his warriors into battle at Clontarf in 1014, but was killed a short time later.

Already a political and military veteran (he had won notable victories against Viking opponents at Limerick and Waterford), Brian Bóruma succeeded his elder brother, Mathgamain, as king of the southern province of Munster in AD 976. Munster's new chief launched successful retaliatory raids against his brother's killers, before turning his attentions to the neighbouring kingdoms of Connacht (to the north of Munster) and Leinster (to the east). Eventually he agreed an uneasy truce with the powerful eastern king, Máel Sechnaill II, and after overrunning Dublin's Norsemen Brian Bóruma became high king of Ireland in 1002.

Recognised as such in a ceremony held on the hallowed Hill of Tara in County Meath, Irish kings and Viking leaders beat a path to Kincora, by the banks of the River Shannon, to pay homage there to Ireland's king of kings at his royal residence.

Still allied with Máel Sechnaill II of the southern Uí Neill clan, the self-proclaimed 'Emperor of the Irish' looked to establish a foothold in the far north of Ireland, the territory of the northern branch of the Uí Neill family, but he was unable to conquer the region fully. Leinster also refused to be cowed and in 1014 Leinstermen and their Viking allies waged war on the men of Munster at the near-legendary battle of Clontarf. Although he won the conflict, fought a short distance from Dublin, in the aftermath Brian Bóruma was slain while still in his battlefield tent. He was succeeded initially by men such as Teige and Donnchad, then later by his grandson, Toirrdelbach Ua Briain. Distant latter-day descendants of the great Irish king include the hero of Waterloo, the Duke of Wellington, and Queen Elizabeth II.

▶▶▶ *House of Dál Cais, Máel Sechnaill II, Mathgamain, House of O'Neill*

BRUCE, HOUSE OF

Descendents of the de Brus family of Bruis (Brix), near Cherbourg, France,. It was in the early years after the Norman Conquest that the first members of this clan arrived in the British Isles, where they were granted 43 manors in Yorkshire. Ennobled as Lords of Annandale in South-West Scotland early in the twelfth century, in 1238 Robert de Bruce (nicknamed 'The Competitor') was made heir presumptive to the Scottish crown. Appointed as one of the 15 regents in Scotland in 1255, 35 years later he was a prime candidate to be chosen as monarch in succession to Margaret the Maid. Passed over in favour of John Balliol, in 1294 Robert the Competitor died and the fight to become king of Scotland was carried on by his grandson: Robert the Bruce.

Taking up arms against Edward I, in 1306 Robert Bruce was crowned Robert I at Scone. Famed for his legendary encounter with a spider and for his great victory against the English at Bannockburn in 1314, the following year his brother, Edward, became his heir.

Younger than Robert, Edward then proclaimed himself 'King of Ireland', but was killed in battle in 1318 and so, when Robert I died in 1329, he was succeeded by his young son, David II, who in turn was succeeded by the grandson of Robert I the Bruce: Robert II.

The younger King Robert was Scotland's first Stewart king (the name was changed later to Stuart). He ruled until 1390 and was followed as king of the Scots by his son, Robert III, who handed over the reins of power to a younger brother, Robert, Duke of Albany. The duke was duly appointed as regent, while the brothers' sister, Jean, married Sir John Lyon. The Thane of Glamis, Lyon was a distant ancestor of Queen Elizabeth, the Queen Mother.

▶▶▶ *David I, Edward Bruce, Robert Bruce, Edward I, Edward II, Elizabeth the Queen Mother*

ABOVE: The seal of David II
TOP: Robert the Bruce statue, Stirling
RIGHT: The Battle of Bannockburn

influential Gaelic chiefs such as Donal O'Neill, a month after landing in Ireland he commanded an attack that rased Dundalk to the ground.

Pressing south, the would-be king and his army fought and won successive battles in the counties of Antrim, Meath and Kildare, finally reaching Offaly early in 1316. That same year Edward Bruce made Carrickfergus his capital, while in 1317 his brother, Robert, joined the offensive heading towards Dublin.

Edward's men-of-war remained undefeated in battle, yet there was one foe they could not overcome: famine.

THE HOUSE OF BRUCE

1306–29	Robert I 'the Bruce'
1329–71	David II
1371–90	Robert II 'Stewart'
1390–1406	Robert III

BRUCE, EDWARD (c. 1276–1318)

Brother of Robert the Bruce, Edward fought alongside his famous sibling at the Battle of Bannockburn in 1314. Appointed heir presumptive in Scotland in 1315, that same year he sailed to Ireland and there proclaimed himself king. He fought for three years to assert his claim, but was killed in battle in 1318.

Edward was two years younger than his brother, Robert, but he was a powerful force in Scotland where, as Lord of Galloway and Earl of Carrick, he forged a reputation as a bold, often daredevil, warrior. He launched a failed attempt to take Stirling in 1313, but returned to the city the following year to play a prominent part in the Scots' legendary victory at Bannockburn. In May 1315 he made the short crossing to the Irish port of Larne. Soon bolstered by strong support from Anglo-Irish nobles and

Hurrying back to the north, where food could be found, the army returned to action the following year. However, Edward Bruce was destined never to be the true king of Ireland, nor to succeed to the Scottish throne. Fighting a battle on 14 October 1318, he was slain at Faughart near Dundalk, the town where he had won his first major success on Irish soil just three years before.

⮞ *House of Bruce, Robert Bruce, House of O'Neill*

BRUCE, ROBERT (SEE ROBERT I)

CADELL AP RHODRI (d. AD 909)

King of Deheubarth (AD 878–909). A son of Rhodri Mawr, after his father's death Cadell was created joint ruler, with elder brother Anarawd, of the lands bequeathed them. Cadell reigned over the southern region known as Deheubarth and was given considerable help in defending his territory by Alfred the Great. However, with the English king's passing in AD 899, troubled times befell Wales and the gloom did not lift until the reign of Cadell's acclaimed son, Hywel Dda.

)))➤ *Anarawd ap Rhodri, House of Deheubarth, House of Gwynedd, Hywel Dda, Rhodri Mawr*

CADWALLON AP IEUAF (d. AD 986)

King of Gwynedd (AD 985–86). Cadwallon succeeded his brother, Hywel ap Ieuaf, after his death in AD 985. Little is known about Cadwallon prior to his gaining the throne of Gwynedd and even when he did his reign was so short-lived that not much information can be gleaned. It is likely that he supported his brother in his struggles during his lifetime. Cadwallon was murdered by Maredudd ap Owain, who united the houses of Deuheubarth and Gwynedd.

)))➤ *House of Deuheubarth, House of Gwynedd, Hywel ap Ieuaf, Maredudd ap Owain*

CANUTE (SEE CNUT)

CENNÉTIG (d. AD 951)

King of the Dál Cais. Son of Lorcán and father of Mathgamain and of the celebrated high king of Ireland, Brian Bóruma. The king of North Munster, also known as Cennétig mac Lorcin, he did much to establish the Dál Cais tribe as a powerful, rising force in and around their South Ireland home.

)))➤ *Brian Bóruma, House of Dál Cais, Eóganacht, Mathgamain*

CHARLES I (1600–49)

King of England (1625–49); son of James I. Succeeding his father in 1625, Charles I soon declared war on Spain and France. He later commanded the Royalist (Cavalier) army in the English Civil War (1642–48) and after his defeat by the Parliamentarians (Roundheads) he was tried, found guilty of waging war against his own people and, in January 1649, publicly beheaded. He was married to Henrietta Maria of France and their son, Charles II, succeeded his father as ruling monarch in 1660 after the 11-year Interregnum, known as the Commonwealth.

Charles was born on 19 November 1600 at Dunfermline in Scotland, the second son of James I (VI of Scotland). He became heir to the thrones of England and Scotland when his elder brother, Henry, died of smallpox in 1612. Blossoming late, after his sister's marriage and the death of his mother, Charles became the protégé of his father's favourite, the Marquis of Buckingham. Then, on 27 March 1625, James I died. England's second Stuart monarch was crowned in England at Westminster Abbey on 2 February 1626, but was not crowned king of the Scots until 18 June 1633. He married Henrietta Maria, the sister of the French

ABOVE: A Miniature of Charles I by M. Snelling
ABOVE RIGHT: The 3 pound piece of 1644

monarch, Louis XIII, two months after his accession. The royal couple had a large family with six children reaching adulthood. The eldest of these was the prince who became Charles II. Another son was crowned James II and a daughter, Mary, was mother to William III.

The young monarch declared war on Spain in an attempt to regain lands the Spanish had taken from the Elector Palatine of the Rhine, the husband of Charles's sister, Elizabeth. Marriage to a French princess did not prevent Charles I from going to war with France as well, in 1626. However, from 1625 to 1630 campaigns foundered badly as parliament withheld its support. The king retaliated by ruling from March 1629 to the spring of 1640 without once summoning parliament, a period that became known as the 'Eleven Years' Tyranny'. The question of faith could not be so easily ignored, especially in Scotland, where the imposed introduction of a new prayer book sparked a controversy that, in turn, led to all-out war.

Defeated by the Scots in the campaign that became known as the Bishops' Wars of 1639 and 1640, in the latter year Charles twice recalled parliament in an effort to gain funds for his campaigns. Having been overlooked for 11 years, parliament was unwilling to concede to the king's demands and pressed for a change. A band of dissenters objected to what they believed were the pro-Catholic leanings of the king and the Archbishop of Canterbury, William Laud, but the main demand was that parliament never again be dismissed without its own consent. Attacked on all sides, the king agreed to meet some of parliament's demands, but remained rigidly opposed to others. Dissension became more pronounced and rebellious factions formed. On 4 January 1642, during a visit to the House of Commons, Charles tried to arrest five leading members of these factions, including John Pym. This only served to further antagonise members of the Commons.

Relations between monarch and Commons continued to deteriorate until, on 22 August 1642, Charles I raised his standard at Nottingham to signal the start of the English Civil War. On 23 October, at Edgehill in Warwickshire, neither Royalists nor Parliamentarians were able to secure victory, but in 1643 the king won a battle at Newbury. Then parliament turned the screw, its forces grinding out a key victory on 2 July 1644 at the Battle of Marston Moor in Yorkshire and triumphing again the following year at Naseby in Northamptonshire. From then on, there was no stopping the Roundheads, the well-drilled New Model Army under Sir Thomas Fairfax, pressing home their superiority over Cavalier troops.

Finally abandoning the fight, Charles attempted to curry favour with the Scottish army occupying North-East England, but instead the so-called Covenanter army passed him into parliament's custody. Throughout 1647, Fairfax and Oliver Cromwell negotiated with the defeated king, but in 1648 the Royalists launched another wave of attacks, which ended in August that year with the rout of Charles's Scottish army at Preston. With victory secured, Charles I was put on trial. A believer to the end in the divine right of kings, he refused to acknowledge the legitimacy of the court. Condemned to death by the massed ranks of judges at Westminster Hall, the 'Martyr King' was executed at Whitehall on 30 January 1649 and was buried without ceremony at St George's Chapel, Windsor.

▶ *Charles II, Interregnum, James I, House of Stuart*

CHARLES II (1630–85)

King of England (1660–85); son and heir of Charles I. Charles II succeeded his executed father in 1649, but did not rule until 1660. He fought in the English Civil War and beyond, but was defeated at Worcester in 1651. Famously taking cover by hiding in the 'royal oak', Charles II then went into exile. Following the Restoration, he was crowned in 1661, marrying his wife, Catherine, the following year. During his 25-year reign two Anglo-Dutch wars were fought (1665–67 and 1672–74). The Popish Plot (1678) and the Exclusion Crisis (1679–81) reflected the tensions between Protestants and Catholics, while the Great Plague (1665) and the Great Fire of London (1666) were major disasters. Known as the 'Merry Monarch', Charles II died in 1685 and was succeeded by his brother, James II.

Born at St James's Palace in London on 29 May 1630, the second son born to Charles I and Henrietta Maria enjoyed an untroubled childhood until he was 12 years old. Then, in 1642, the English Civil War commenced. Whisked from his privileged surroundings, the heir to the throne accompanied his father on his early adventures before being sent abroad. Having reached Holland, from there he led a fleet of warships against the Parliamentarians. After his father's execution and the creation of a republic, Charles allied with the

Scots in an attempt to restore the monarchy, but was defeated at the Battle of Worcester.

Fleeing from this rout, Charles was hunted down by Roundhead soldiers, at one time eluding capture at Boscobel, Worcestershire, by hiding in an oak tree. He continued to mount further small-scale attacks, but it was not until the death of the Lord Protector, Oliver Cromwell, and the subsequent resignation of Cromwell's son, Richard, that Charles was invited back to England in 1660 and eventually crowned king on his thirtieth birthday.

Restoring the Stuart line, the new sovereign did not have things all his own way, with religious concerns rising to the fore during his reign. The Popish Plot loomed large in 1678, due to Titus Oates and others feeding rumours that a pro-Catholic group intended to murder the Protestant Charles and install as king his Catholic brother, James. Next came the Exclusion Crisis (1679–81), with arguments raging for and against the idea that James Stuart, as a Catholic, should be barred from succeeding. In addition, two Test Acts curtailed the influence on public life of practising Catholics. As for foreign policy, this was dominated by the wars with the Dutch. The first of these naval conflicts coincided with two domestic disasters: the Great Plague, which ravaged the population with a final outbreak in 1665, and the Great Fire of London which took hold during the hot summer of 1666.

In 1662 Charles II had married Catherine of Braganza, the daughter of John IV of Portugal. However, although the marriage endured, it did not produce any children. In contrast the sovereign's extra-marital liaisons saw various mistresses give birth to 13 or more illegitimate children. Of all the king's affairs, the best-known by far was the one he enjoyed with Nell Gwynne. Doted on by the king to the end of his life, the orange-seller-turned-actress outlived her lover, Charles II, who died on 6 February 1685 at Whitehall Palace, London and was buried at Westminster Abbey. After his death the Stuart line was carried on by his younger brother, James II.

))▶ *Charles I, Interregnum, James II, House of Stuart*

LEFT: Regal Heraldry of Charles II
RIGHT: Armour of Charles II

LEFT: *Charles, the current Prince of Wales, speaks to Chelsea pensioners*
BOTTOM RIGHT: *Investiture of Prince of Wales*
FAR RIGHT: *The crown of Prince Charles*

Buckingham Palace on 14 November 1948. At that time, his mother was heiress apparent to the throne, but in February 1952 George VI died in his sleep and the princess became queen. Crowned at Westminster Abbey, Elizabeth's coronation was attended by her own heir, the four-year-old Charles, while an even younger onlooker was the prince's two-year-old sister, Anne.

Charles was the first Windsor child to break with a long-held tradition of being taught by personal tutors and instead the prince was sent away to school at Hill House, Cheam and then to Gordonstoun, where years earlier his father had been a pupil. The first heir to the throne ever to go to school, on leaving Gordonstoun, a brief stay at a school in the Australian outback known as Timbertop was followed by the prince enroling as an undergraduate at Trinity College, Cambridge.

While still at university, Charles was given the title of Prince of Wales in an investiture ceremony staged at Caernarfon Castle on 1 July 1969. The investiture ceremony coincided with the screening of a television documentary entitled *The Royal Family.* Innovative then, the BBC's cameras recorded the Windsors away from the pomp, circumstance and majesty of royal engagements.

After his investiture and his graduation the new Prince of Wales embarked on a life in the Royal Navy. Then, with the success of the Queen's Silver Jubilee celebrations of 1977 still fresh in the memory, the Windsors' standing in the affections of the British public rose higher still when the engagement of Prince Charles to Lady Diana Spencer was announced. The couple were married on 29 July 1981 in what became known as a 'fairy-tale' wedding, amid the splendour of St Paul's Cathedral, with thousands lining the streets to watch the wedding procession and millions more watching from afar via their television sets. Eleven months later, on 21 June 1982, the Princess of Wales gave birth to Charles's son and heir, William; a second son, Henry, always referred to as Harry, was born on 15 September 1984.

For the next 13 years images of Diana adorned newspapers and magazines, while the world's television

CHARLES, PRINCE (b. 1948)

Eldest son of Elizabeth II. Heir to the throne from 1952, he became Prince of Wales in 1969. He married Lady Diana Spencer in 1981 and the couple had two sons, William and Harry. Charles and Diana were divorced in 1996 and the Princess of Wales died in 1997. The Prince turned 50 in 1998.

The eldest son of Elizabeth II and Prince Philip, Charles Philip Arthur George Windsor was born at

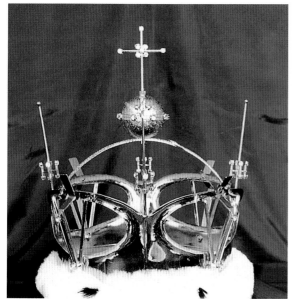

companies covered her every move. She was the darling of the media. Welcome or not, media coverage of a royal figure, fêted as one of the world's most attractive women, became as relentless as it was intrusive, not least when rumours concerning the Wales's troubled marriage were confirmed in 1992 by the announcement of a legal separation, one that would eventually lead to a full divorce four years later. Stories about the private lives of the prince and the princess then made news as much their official engagements or their charity work.

In August 1997 Diana, Princess of Wales (as she became known after her divorce from Charles), was killed in a car crash in Paris. Her death evoked an unprecedented response from the public that was as remarkable as it was unparalleled, the outpourings of grief reaching their zenith on 6 September, the day of her funeral. This difficult time for the Prince of Wales was made tougher still by the furore stirred up by the tabloid newspapers – a furore that engulfed the Windsors following the death of Diana. However, the perception of a royal family out-of-touch with the popular mood was not a new one, any more than the difficulties of living life as heir to the throne were new to Charles.

First-in-line to ascend the throne for most of his life, the Prince of Wales has had to adjust and then re-adjust to a life in the wings. He has not been the first Prince of Wales to live in the shadow of a long-reigning monarch, but he has been the first to do so in an era when the focus on the monarchy and its future has been particularly intense. Now in his fifties, Prince Charles continues to attend to the unending round of official duties that are part and parcel of being a leading royal figure, although like other royals he also has his own pet projects, one of which is the Prince's Trust.

))⟩➤ *Elizabeth II, House of Windsor*

CNUT (c. AD 994–1035)

King of England (1016–35); son of Svein Forkbeard. Renowned for telling the tide to turn, the king better known as Canute succeeded Edmund II in 1016. Earlier he had won the Battle of Ashingdon and been rewarded with possession of all lands north of the Thames. Crowned in 1017, that same year Cnut divided his realm into four distinct earldoms. He was king of Denmark from 1019 and later ruler of Norway. Cnut died in 1035 and was followed as England's king by two of his sons, the half-brothers, Harold I ('Harefoot') and Harthacnut.

The grandson of the Danish king Harald III ('Bluetooth'), Cnut was the second son born to King Svein and his first wife, Gunhild. Years later, as Svein sought to dethrone Ethelred II, the young prince fought at his father's side. Svein died after serving just six months as king of England: Cnut was about 20 years old at the time. Ethelred had returned from exile to retake England's crown and Cnut once again began plotting his enemy's downfall. After bringing Northumbia back into Danish hands, Cnut began an advance on London in 1016. Ethelred's death brought the Danish challenger into direct conflict with the new king, Edmund II. Fighting for the right to rule, a series of skirmishes followed until the autumn of 1016 when fighting and fate combined to shape Cnut's destiny. At Ashingdon in Essex his men inflicted a heavy defeat on Edmund, who was forced to make substantial concessions to his conqueror. The sons of the two previous English monarchs then divided the country in two, with the Dane reigning over all English lands north of the Thames. It was not long, however, before Cnut was king of all England.

Ascending the throne following Edmund's death on 30 November 1016, Cnut's coronation was held two months later at St Paul's Cathedral, London. Brutally flexing his royal muscle, he ordered the murder of Eadric Streona, the turncoat Earl of Mercia, who had so frequently switched sides in the struggle between the Anglo-Saxons and the Danes. Also sacrificed was Eadwig, a brother of the former king.

RIGHT: Canute and Queen Elgifu presenting a cross to Newinster Abbey
FAR RIGHT: Watching the approach of Danish raiders from the English coast

Later, as courtiers fawned over the powers of the young monarch, Cnut's hard-nosed approach surfaced again: the king ridiculing his flatterers by ordering the sea to obey his commands. In 1017, the year that he married Ethelred the Unready's widow, Emma, the English kingdom was divided up into the four earldoms of Northumbria, Mercia, East Anglia and Wessex, but as Cnut's empire expanded, to encompass Denmark (from 1019) and Norway (from 1028), changes in England were kept to a minimum and subsequently the country enjoyed a rare period of calm.

Cnut died at Shaftesbury, Dorset, on 12 November 1035 and was interred at Winchester Cathedral. He was succeeded by a son from his marriage to Elgifu of Northampton, Harold I. When Harold I Harefoot died, the English crown passed briefly to that monarch's half-brother, Harthacnut, a son of Cnut and Emma.

▶ *Edmund II, Ethelred II*

CONSTANTINE I (d. c. AD 877)

King of the Scots and Picts (AD 863–77); also known as Constantin. The son of Kenneth mac Alpin and the brother of Aed, Constantine became king in AD 863 after the death of his uncle, Donald I. He spent much of his reign fending off a stream of Viking attacks. He was able to extend his realm southwards, claiming Strathclyde in AD 871 or 872 following the murder of his own brother-in-law, Artgal (whose death Constantine may have ordered). By this time the dominant ruler in central and southern Scotland, Constantine I did not always use force to get the better of his enemies and often preferred to buy peace. In AD 875 he was defeated by Halfdan, a Viking enemy of Alfred the Great, who was then launching raids from Northumbria. Two years later Constantine again locked horns with Norse warriors, but was killed in action at Inverdovat on

Tayside. His death sparked a power struggle in Scotland that was to last for more than two decades, but his immediate successor was his little-known brother, Aed, while his son reigned later as Donald II.

))))➤ *Aed, Donald II, Kenneth mac Alpin*

CONSTANTINE II (d. c. AD 952)

King of Scotland (AD 900–43). Constantine II fought against Viking raiders during his reign and was heavily defeated with various allies by Athelstan of England at the Battle of Brunanburh (AD 937). By retaining inherited lands and conquering new territory he became the first Scottish ruler to hold power south of the Forth river. Constantine (also Constantin) reigned for 43 years before abdicating. He was succeeded as king by Malcolm I and his last years were spent in a monastery.

There was no Scottish crown in AD 900, but Constantine's accession ceremony took place on Moot Hill at Scone. With the stone of destiny (which was to become such a potent symbol of Scottish national pride) a centrepiece of the ceremony, the new king was 'married' to the land. His bloodline was recited and members of the nobility swore their allegiance to the new sovereign.

In the often troubled reign that followed, Constantine II had to contend with a series of Viking raids, but in AD 937 he joined forces with Olaf, king of Dublin's Norsemen, and with Strathclyde's ruler, King Owen. However, this alliance of kings was comprehensively routed at the Battle of Brunanburh by Athelstan. This defeat, at the end of a day-long battle fought on an unknown site, led to Constantine II offering his second 'submission' to the victorious Athelstan. Ten years earlier he had bowed down before the English king following his invasion of Northumbria.

Defeat at Brunanburh and his subsequent submission proved to be the last notable events of Constantine's reign as he abdicated in about AD 943. During his reign, though, he had successfully consolidated his kingdom, extending its borders into Strathclyde and Lothian. He lived out the rest of his life in a monastery at St Andrews, Fife.

))))➤ *Athelstan, Malcolm I*

CULEN (d. AD 971)

King of Scotland (AD 996–71); son of King Indulf. Sometimes referred to as Cuílán the Whelp, like his father Culen also came to a bloody end. He was murdered in Lothian in AD 971 by Rhydderch, the king of Strathclyde. Enthroned only five years earlier, Culen was said by some to have been the man who ordered the capture and murder of his predecessor, King Dub, while his own death avenged the earlier murder of Rhydderch's brother and the abduction or rape of the Strathclyde ruler's daughter. After this spate of revenge-seeking was over, Culen was succeeded by the new king of Alba: Kenneth II.

)))➤ *Dub, Kenneth III*

CYNAN AP HYWEL (d. 1005)

King of Gwynedd (AD 999–1005); son of Hywel ap Ieuaf. After the death of Maredudd ap Owain, Cynan retook the throne of Gwynedd. Maredudd had restored the glory of the kingdom after years of war between Hywel and his enemy, Iago ap Idwal, but under Cynan's six-year rule the realm was plunged into chaos once more. Little is known of Cynan, but he was succeeded by Llywelyn ap Seisyll.

)))➤ *Hywel ap Ieuaf, Iago ap Idwal, Maredudd ap Owain*

CONSTANTINE III (d. AD 997)

King of Scotland (AD 995–97). This son of Culen, also known as Constantine the Bald, probably came to power in AD 995 following the death, in suspicious circumstances, of his distant relative, Kenneth II. Sometimes cited as the man behind Kenneth's demise, Constantine III reigned for just 18 months before he, too, was killed. The sixth successive Scottish monarch to die a violent death, his murder may have been ordered by Kenneth III, the man who next ascended the throne.

)))➤ *Culen, Kenneth II, Kenneth III*

TOP LEFT: Constantine I and St Helen
ABOVE: King Indulf, father of Culen

CYNAN AP OWAIN (c. 1140–74)

King of Gwynedd (c. 1170–74). When Owain Gwynedd died his kingdom was divided between his sons, thus intiating sibling rivalry and a period of turmoil in Gwynedd. Little knowledge of Cynan exists, other than that he established enough claim to serve as king for a few brief years. His sons, Gruffudd and Maredudd, succeeded in expelling Rhodri from Anglesey.

)))➤ *Gruffudd ap Cynan*

Siding with Edward I, following the English king's invasion of South Wales, he was rewarded with estates in Wales and England and married Edward's relative, Elizabeth Ferrers. However, Dafydd switched allegiances once more in 1282, siding with Llywelyn and his Gwynedd warriors as they started a short-lived revolt against English targets.

In December 1282 Dafydd ap Gruffydd became Prince of Wales after his brother's death in battle. His reign was brief. After losing Snowdonia to Edward I in May 1283, he was forced to retreat and the following month he was taken prisoner and tried at Shrewsbury in Shropshire. Condemned to die, on 3 October 1283 he became the first man in more than two centuries to be executed in England for taking part in a rebellion.

))))➤ *Edward I, House of Gwynedd, Henry III*

DAFYDD AP GRUFFYDD (d. 1283)

King of Gwynedd (1282–83) and last old-style Prince of Wales; son of Gruffydd ap Llywelyn. Opposing the accession of his elder brother, Llywelyn ap Gruffydd, Dafydd nevertheless supported Llywelyn when he was made Prince of Wales. Later scheming to kill him, Dafydd succeeded his brother as Prince of Wales in 1282. He was then captured by Edward I, found guilty of treason and executed.

Dafydd was the third and youngest son of Gruffydd ap Llywelyn. After contesting the accession of his brother, Llywelyn, he defected. He moved to England where he won the backing of Henry III and with this support he worked to bring about the downfall of Llywelyn as Gwynedd struggled to retain its independence. Defeated by Llywelyn in a skirmish at Bryn Derwin in 1255, he was forgiven by his conqueror and swore loyalty to Llywelyn when he became Prince of Wales in 1267.

When he later was discovered plotting Llywelyn's death, Dafydd was forced to flee and lay low in England.

LEFT: *Edward I seated with bishops and monks*
BELOW LEFT: *Edward I and son*
BELOW RIGHT: *Twelfth-century Welsh manuscript featuring an unnamed
early Welsh king*

DAFYDD AP LLYWELYN (c. 1208–46)

King of Gwynedd (1240–46); son of Llywelyn ap
Iorweth. Recognised as king-in-waiting by Henry
III, the pope and Welsh lords, Dafydd extended his
kingdom by marriage and by seizing lands belonging to
his half-brother, Gruffudd. Although he was knighted by
Henry III, from 1244 the two kings were enemies.

A son of Llywelyn the Great and his wife, Joan,
Dafydd was the acknowledged heir to his father's
territories, but he was forced to fight a successful
battle for supremacy in Gwynedd against his
illegitimate step-brother, Gruffudd, whom he later
imprisoned. Previously his right to succeed had
been backed by an extraordinary gathering of
nobles who, in 1238, travelled to the great
Mid-Wales abbey of Strata Florida to pledge
their loyalty to Dafydd.

He succeeded his father two years later
and his marriage to Isabella de Braose
brought Dafydd more territory. He received
a major blow in 1241, however, when
Henry III and Welsh princes conspired
against him. Continuing to be preyed upon
by the English king, blows were exchanged
in 1245. The fight between the two kings
was brief, though, and Dafydd died on 25
February 1246 at Aber, North Wales. His
death created a power vacuum, not truly
filled until the reign of Gruffudd's son,
Llywelyn ap Gruffudd. He was buried at
the abbey of Aberconwy.

))))▶ *House of Gwynedd, Henry III,
Llywelyn ap Iorweth*

DAFYDD AP OWAIN
(c. 1135–1203)

King of Gwynedd (1170–95);
son of Owain. At first Dafydd
ruled with his brother, Rhodri, but
after Rhodri's death in 1195 Dafydd became sole ruler of
Gwynedd. In 1195 Dafydd was deposed by his grandson,
Llywelyn ap Iorweth.

After his father's death in 1170 Dafydd and his brother,
Rhodri, attempted to assert their authority in Gwynedd by
killing their step-brother, Hywel, and ruling jointly. In the
south and east Dafydd forged a number of alliances as he
reigned over his kingdom. Rhodri was ruler of Anglesey
from 1175, but his death in 1195 inspired Owain's
grandson, Llywelyn ap Iorweth, to make his move. Taking
his uncle captive during a battle at Aberconwy in North-
West Wales, Llywelyn banished Dafydd from his own
kingdom. The defeated king retiring to Shropshire. Married
to Emma, a half-sister of Henry II, he died in 1203.

))))▶ *House of Gwynedd*

DÁL CAIS, HOUSE OF

 In the ascendancy in Ireland during the first half of the tenth century, the Dál Cais remained a major influence until the early years of the twelfth century. With its roots in Munster, the 'Seed of Cas' first announced itself as a force to be reckoned with under the leadership of Rebachán mac Mothlai (d. AD 934) and its influence did not wane until the death of Muirchertach Uá Briain in 1119.

Following the reign of Rebachán, a key figure in establishing this southern clan was Cennétig, the son of Lorcáin. It was Cennétig who led his people to the brink of greatness. Previously one of a number of minor sub-kingdoms in Southern Ireland, under Cennétig the Dál Cais began to eat away at the long-held authority of the Eóganacht confederacy. Following Cennétig's death, his eldest son, Mathgamain, made further gains until his murder in AD 976.

He was succeeded by his younger brother, Brian Bóruma (Boru), and it was under his dynamic leadership that the most dramatic advances were made. Already a rising star in the land when he became king of Munster, in little more than a quarter of a century as the Dál Cais king, Brian Bóruma claimed many notable scalps and several titles. He became king of Cashel (which for centuries had been the Eóganacht seat of power), the acknowledged king of the south and latterly the self-proclaimed 'Emperor of the Irish'. In 1002 his election as his country's high king (or king of kings) established the high-water mark in the rise of the Dál Cais.

Brian Bóruma was killed in the aftermath of his most celebrated battle, at Clontarf in 1014. He was succeeded by a line of rulers who remained potent figures in Irish affairs for more than a century after the death of their mighty ancestor. Remaining a leading light in Thomond,

North Munster, later members of the Dál Cais family bore the names Uá Briain, Briain or O'Brien, their surnames reflecting their descent from Brian Bóruma.

⟩⟩⟩▶ **Brian Bóruma, Cennétig, Eóganacht, Máel Sechnaill II, Mathgamain**

THE HOUSE OF DÁL CAIS

d. AD 934	Rebachán mac Mothlai
d. AD 951	Cennétig
d. AD 976	Mathgamain
c. AD 926–1014	Brian Bóruma
d. 1023	Teige
d. 1064	Donnchad
d. 1086	Toirrdelbach Uá Briain
d. 1119	Muirchertach Uá Briain

DAVID I (c. 1084–1153)

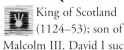 King of Scotland (1124–53); son of Malcolm III. David I succeeded his brother, Alexander I, in 1124 and extended his kingdom farther south than any previous Scottish king. He was defeated by King Stephen at the Battle of the Standard, but gained control by the Treaty of Northumbria. He introduced Norman customs, built many religious houses (hence the nickname 'David the Saint') and was succeeded by his grandson, Malcolm IV.

The youngest son of Malcolm III and his second wife, Margaret, David was a still a child when both his father and mother died in 1093. He therefore spent much of his youth in England, where he became an important and powerful landowner. He also gained the earldoms of Northampton and Huntingdon by virtue of his marriage to the widow Maud. His sister, Edith, (also known as Matilda or Maud), married Henry I, while another sister, Mary, wed the Count of Boulogne and gave birth to a daughter, who married the man who

would later become King Stephen of England. However, despite his many English connections, David returned to his native country during the reign of his elder sibling, Alexander I, and the continued the tradition of all heirs to the Scottish throne by ruling southern Scotland.

David shared many of his brother's qualities and as king was a modernising force in Scottish affairs. He introduced new, Norman, methods to Scotland's government and to the judiciary and he encouraged trade, agriculture and education. Under David many churches and abbeys were built and monastic orders flourished. Anglo-Normans were appointed to bishoprics old and new and Norman families settled in Scotland, among them the de Brus (later Bruce),

de Bailleul (Balliol) and fitzAlan (or Fitzalan) clans.

David also generally managed to maintain good relations with England. During the civil wars between Stephen and Matilda he recognised Matilda's claim to the English throne and in 1138 he was beaten by Stephen at the Battle of the Standard, which was fought on Cowton Moor, near Northallerton. Eleven years later, though, he gained English lands stretching from Tyneside to the Tees.

David died in May 1153, outliving his son and heir by a year. The throne passed to his grandson, Malcolm IV.

))))➤ ***House of Balliol, House of Bruce, Henry I, Malcolm IV, Matilda, Robert I, Stephen, Alexander I***

LEFT: Brian Bóruma after the Battle of Clontarf
TOP: The Norman Priory on Holy Island, Northumberland
RIGHT: David I

DAVID II (1324–71)

King of Scotland (1329–32, 1341–71); son of Robert the Bruce. David II was married at the age of four and succeeded his father just one year later, in 1329. Deposed by Edward Balliol in 1332, David reclaimed his crown in 1341. Defeated, injured and captured at the Battle of Neville's Cross, he was allowed to return to Scotland as a condition of the Treaty of Berwick. Although he married twice, he died without an heir and was succeeded by Robert II.

At Berwick on 16 July 1328 David, the four-year-old son of Robert the Bruce and his second wife, Elizabeth, was married to Joan, the seven-year-old daughter of England's former king, Edward II, and younger sister of Edward III. Succeeding his father the following summer, David's coronation was staged at Scone on 24 November 1331. With power in the hands of the regent, Thomas Randolph, Earl of Moray, a successful coup in 1332 by Edward Balliol saw the latter become king. David settled in France and it was not until 1341 that he was restored to the Scottish throne.

David retained his country's traditional allegiance with France and in 1346 he attacked England while Edward III was away fighting French forces. Despite this distraction, the Battle of Neville's Cross on 17 October 1346 was a personal disaster for David II, who was injured and taken prisoner by Edward's men. David remained in England for more than a decade. In 1357 the Treaty of Berwick was negotiated, guaranteeing a decade of peace between Scotland and England. In addition the Scots regained their sovereign in exchange for a king's ransom of 100,000 marks. A crippling sum that the Scots struggled to pay even as their pro-English king negotiated a deal with Edward III, one that would have seen the heir to England's throne become heir to Scotland's, too.

Queen Joan died on 7 September 1362 and her widowed husband later married Margaret Drummond. However, no legitimate heir resulted from either marriage and so, on David's death, the crown passed to his step-sister's son, who became Robert II.

>> *Edward Balliol, House of Bruce, Edward III, Robert II, House of Stewart*

DEHEUBARTH, HOUSE OF

With its capital at Dinefwr, the medieval kingdom of Deheubarth ('south part') was the traditional southern ally of Gwynedd. The realm covered much of southern and western Wales, incorporating the south-western regions of Dyfed, Ceredigion (Cardigan) and

Ystrad Tywi (south of Carmarthen to the Gower), while occasionally reaching into Brycheiniog (Brecon) in the south-east.

Once part of Rhodri Mawr's vast empire, after his death in AD 878 the region was ruled over by its own line of kings. Rhodri Cadell reigned until

TOP LEFT: David II
ABOVE: Hywel Dda
RIGHT: A celtic cross on the Island of Iona

AD 909 and Hywel ap Cadell to AD 950. The latter, better known as Hywel Dda, merged his Seisyllwg territory with Dyfed in AD 904 to create Deheubarth. At the end of the eleventh century Rhys ap Tewdwr, son of Tewdwr the Great, forged an alliance with the Gwynedd king, Gruffudd ap Cynan. Previously living in exile in Brittany, Rhys made a triumphant return home, winning back Deheubarth.

Inextricably linked with Gwynedd since the ninth-century heydays of Merfyn and his son, Rhodri Mawr, in the twelfth century the then king of Deheubarth, Rhys ap Gruffudd, accepted the English title 'Lord Rhys' and the role of Justice of South Wales. After his death the Deheubarth line lived on through men such as Maredudd and his son, Rhys ap Maredudd, while later descendants included Owain Glyndwr and Henry VII.

))))➤ *House of Gwynedd, Maredudd, Rhodri Mawr, Early Rulers of Wales*

THE HOUSE OF DEHEUBARTH

AD 918	Cadell
c. AD 880–950	Hwyel Dda
d. 986	Owain ap Hywel
d. 999	Maredudd ap Owain
d. 1005	Cynan ap Hywel
d. 1033	Rhydderch ap Iestyn
d. 1035	Maredudd ap Edwin
d. 1044	Hywel ap Edwin
d. 1055	Gruffudd ap Rhydderch
d. 1093	Rhys ap Tewdwr
1090–1137	Gruffudd ap Rhys
d. 1291	Rhys ap Maredudd

DONALD I (d. AD 862)

King of the Scots (AD 858–62); son of Alpin. Donald (or Domnall) succeeded his brother, Kenneth I mac Alpin, and reigned for about four years. His appearance was unfavourably described by some medieval writers, who looked more favourably on his record as ruler instead. Consolidating the gains won by his predecessor, he died near Scone. Perhaps struck down by illness, or possibly murdered, Donald I's death saw power pass to Kenneth mac Alpin's son, Constantine I.

))))➤ *Kenneth I mac Alpin, Constantine I*

DONALD II (d. AD 900)

King of Scotland (AD 889–900); son of Constantine I. Also referred to as Domnall II, Donald II was the first man to be described by chroniclers as Rí Alban (King of Scotland). Although he was monarch for 11 years, little is known about his reign. He was succeeded by his cousin, Constantine II.

Facts concerning the reign of Donald II are scarce, but some historians believe that he succeeded the co-rulers Eóchaid and Giric, the latter being sent into exile by the new king. However, if Donald successfully established himself as chief of the Scots and the Picts, he made little impact further north, as his reign coincided with the rise to power of the Orkney-based Viking known as Earl Sigurd the Mighty.

Donald was possibly murdered at Dunnottar, near Stonehaven on Scotland's east coast; legend has it that the body of the first king of Scotland was buried on the island of Iona.

))))➤ *Constantine I*

DONALD III (c. 1031–99)

King of Scotland (1093–97); son of Duncan I. Twice Scotland's king, Donald III (known as Donald Ban) succeeded his murdered brother, Malcolm III. He was deposed by his nephew, Duncan II, but six months later (after Duncan had been murdered) Donald was restored to the throne. He reigned for three more years and then in 1097 a second nephew, Edgar, usurped the throne and blinded and imprisoned Donald III, who died a short time later.

The younger brother of Malcolm III, Donald, had ascended the throne left vacant by Malcolm's murder. Donald had been in exile at the time of his brother's death and on hearing of it he leapt into the breach. He was already an old man, however, and found that retaining power was more difficult than seizing it. His right to the throne was soon challenged by Duncan, Malcolm's son by his first wife, and in 1094 the younger man successfully ousted Donald. However, later that year Duncan was murdered, most likely on the orders of Donald. The death of his usurper allowed Donald to reclaim the throne.

Dividing his kingdom in two, Edmund, a half-brother of Duncan, was appointed to help him govern. But then in 1097 yet another son of Malcolm III and Margaret, stole Donald's crown. This time there was no way back. Cruelly blinded and imprisoned by the new king, Edgar, the forlorn figure of Donald Ban died in 1099. He is believed to have been laid to rest on Iona – the last in a long line of Scottish kings to be buried on the Inner Hebridean island.

))))▶ *Duncan I, Duncan II, Malcolm III*

DUB (d. c. AD 966)

King of the Scots (AD 962–c. 966); son of Malcolm I. Dub (also known as Dubh or Duff) succeeded the murdered King Indulf in AD 962, but came to a grisly end himself just four years later. Kidnapped by a band of assassins Dub's corpse was discovered in a ditch at Kinross on the banks of Loch Leven. He was succeeded as king of the Scots by Culen, the shadowy son of Indulf and the man alleged to have ordered the murder of King Dub.

))))▶ *Culen, Malcolm I*

DUNCAN I (c. 1010–40)

King of Scotland (1034–40); grandson of Malcolm II; also known as Donnchad I. King of Strathclyde, Duncan succeeded his grandfather as king of the Scots in 1034. He was defeated twice in battle by his cousin, Earl Thorfinn of Orkney, and besieged Durham before being killed by his famous successor, Macbeth. Later

Duncan's sons, Malcolm III and Donald III Ban, ascended the Scottish throne.

Duncan I was the son of Crinan, the Abbot of Dunkeld, and Bethóc, the daughter of Malcolm II. He succeeded Owen the Bald as king of Strathclyde in 1018. Married to a cousin of the Earl of Northumbria, Duncan I became king of the Scots after the murder of his grandfather by rivals in the Scottish royal family. His accession signalled the end of tanistry in Scotland. An often divisive system, choosing a future king from within the royal ranks became a thing of the past once Duncan, Malcolm's nominated heir, succeeded to the throne unopposed.

Young and ambitious, the new king's forays to north and south gained him little, with even his siege of Durham in 1139 proving unsuccessful. Heading north in 1040, in Moray the king met his nemesis: Macbeth. Caught up in a feud that had claimed lives in both men's families, Duncan's raid on Macbeth's home territory ensured that still more blood would be spilt. The exact setting of the skirmish that took place is unknown. Pitgaveny to the north of Elgin or a site nearer Forres have both been suggested, but wherever the setting was, Duncan I was mortally wounded there leaving Macbeth as the new king.

))))➤ *Macbeth, Malcolm II*

DUNCAN II
(c. 1060–94)

King of Scotland (1094); son of Malcolm III by his first wife, Ingeborg. Duncan II spent his childhood as a hostage in England; after 22 years in exile he returned to his native land to claim the Scottish crown worn for so long by his father. The English king, William II, provided Duncan with an army and with this support behind him, the challenger succeeded in

overthrowing his uncle, Donald III Ban, in May 1094. However, he enjoyed the briefest of reigns. On 12 November 1094, just six months after he became king, Duncan II was murdered and Donald, the likely orchestrator of his death, became Scotland's sovereign for the second time.

))))➤ *Normans, Donald III*

DYFED, HOUSE OF

An independent kingdom in South-West Wales. Once the homeland of the Demetae people and later a setting for the fabled tales known as *The Mabinogion*, Dyfed was ruled over by its own line of kings until the death of Llywarch ap Hyfaidd in AD 904. With his passing, the kingdom was absorbed into the new kingdom of Deheubarth by Hywel Dda, the husband of Llywarch's daughter, Elen.

))))➤ *House of Deheubarth, Hywel Dda*

EADWULF (d. AD 913)

King of Bernicia (AD 888–913). Eadwulf ruled the area of Bernicia, which lay between the rivers Tyne and Tweed, during the reign of Alfred the Great and forged a good relationship with the king of Wessex throughout his campaigns against the Vikings. It is likely that Eadwulf pledged allegiance to and acknowledged the overlordship of Alfred.

))) ➤ *Alfred the Great*

EDGAR THE PEACEFUL (c. AD 943–75)

King of England (AD 959–75); son of Edmund I. Known as Edgar the Pacific (or Peaceful), he became king of Northumbria and Mercia before succeeding his elder brother, Edwy, as king of Wessex and all England in AD 959. Untroubled by Danish raids, Edgar was an able ruler who encouraged the monastic reforms of Dunstan. He was crowned for the second time

in AD 973 and the same year leading British kings paid homage to Edgar at Chester. He fathered three sons, including his successor, Edward the Martyr, and Ethelred II ('the Unready').

The second son of Edmund I by his first wife Elgifu (or Elgiva), and great-grandson of Alfred the Great, Edgar was still a babe-in-arms when his father died. Growing up during the reigns of his uncle, Edred, and his brother, Edwy, he was still a young prince when, late in the year AD 957, both Mercia and Northumbria swore their allegiances to him.

On 1 October AD 959 Edwy died and Edgar ascended the throne as king of Wessex and all England. The transfer of power from brother to brother was smooth, with the new monarch effecting few changes in personnel or policy during tranquil years refreshingly free from war. In this climate religious reformers such as Dunstan, Ethelwold and Oswald, all subsequently canonised, were given greater freedom.

Dunstant was appointed Archbishop of Canterbury in AD 960 and 13 years later he was the man who devised

BOTTOM LEFT: King Edgar with Cuthbert and Ethelfleda
LEFT: The barge of Edgar

EDGAR (1074–1107)

King of Scotland (1097–1107); son of Malcolm III and great-grandson of England's Edmund II. Edgar was Scotland's ruler for 10 years, after he overthrew Donald III in 1097. He is reputed to have been a generous ruler, and a strong supporter of the Church, but he abandoned the island of Iona and lost the Western Isles.

Edgar was the fourth son of Malcolm III and Margaret. He first came to the fore in 1095, when the English king, William II, declared himself to be Scotland's overlord and Edgar to be the country's king. In 1097, with an army paid for by William II and led by his uncle, Edgar the Atheling, Edgar won a decisive battle at Rescobie, to the east of Forfar. Defeating, overthrowing and blinding the reigning Scottish sovereign, Donald III, Edgar claimed the throne and remained there for the next decade. Links with England were maintained during this period and, in November 1100, his sister Matilda married the newly crowned English king, Henry I. On the negative side Iona, the ancestral burial ground of Scottish kings, was given up, while Norway's Magnus Barelegs captured the Western Isles.

Edgar died in 1107 and was buried at Dunfermline. He was succeeded by his younger brother, Alexander I.

))) *Alexander I, Donald III, Edgar the Atheling, Henry I, William II*

the lavish spectacle of the king's second coronation. This was staged at Bath Abbey on 11 May AD 973 and the magnificent spectacle stressed the holy status of the sovereign who, with his wife, Elfrida, was anointed and crowned. A short time later, an equally grand ceremony attracted an impressive cast of British kings to the banks of the River Dee at Chester. Gathered there to cement alliances, Kenneth II of Scotland and other crowned heads from Wales and the far north pledged to support the English king who, legend has it, they rowed along the river from palace to monastery and back.

Edgar's first wife, Ethelfleda, had given birth to his son and heir, Edward, while his second marriage to Elfrida (also known as Elfthrith), produced two sons. The eldest boy, Edmund, died in AD 971, but the younger son was later crowned Ethelred II. Having reigned for 16 years, Edgar died on 8 July AD 975 and was buried at Glastonbury Abbey.

))) *Ethelred II*

EDMUND I (AD 921–46)

King of England (AD 939–46); son of Edward the Elder; known as Edmund the Magnificent. Edmund I succeeded his half-brother, Athelstan, in AD 939. A warrior-king, who lost and then won back the Five Boroughs, he took Northumbria and York and invaded Strathclyde. His first wife, Elgifu (Elgiva), was the mother of two future kings: Edwy and Edgar. He later married Ethelfleda. Edmund was killed while helping to arrest an outlaw and was succeeded by his brother, Edred.

Edmund was the grandson of Alfred the Great and the first-born child of Edward the Elder by his third marriage. In AD 937 Edmund fought alongside his step-brother, Athelstan, at the Battle of Brunanburgh. Two years after this triumph he became king. Eighteen years old when crowned at Kingston Upon Thames on 16 November AD 939, his first task as king was to defend the large confederation of subkingdoms over which he claimed sovereignty. Led by Olaf Guthfrithson, Dublin's king and ruler of the Norse kingdom of York, the invasion force of AD 940 swept into the Midlands towards Leicester. There, faced with a formidable army, Edmund was forced to sue for peace and, in so doing, to surrender into Danish hands a swathe of land running from Northumbria south to Watling Street. Worse was to follow as Olaf drove on to conquer more northern territories.

However, the English king rallied in AD 942, beating into submission both Olaf Guthfrithson's cousin, Olaf Sihtricson, and his brother Raegnald II. The Five Boroughs were taken back and English forces marched into Northumbria and took York in AD 944. Finally, in AD 945, Strathclyde was overrun and handed over to England's ally, the Scots' king, Malcolm I. Yet Edmund I had little time to bask in the glory of his military victories. At Pucklechurch, Gloucestershire, on 6 May AD 946, the king and his entourage tried to arrest the outlaw, Liofa. A scuffle ensued and in the confusion Edmund I was stabbed. Dying of his wounds, he was buried at Glastonbury Abbey and was succeeded as king by his younger brother, Edred.

➤ *Athelstan, Edred*

EDMUND II (c. AD 993–1016)

King of England (1016); son of Ethelred II; known as Edmund Ironside because of his bravery in battle. Edmund reigned for just seven months in 1016. He was succeeded by Cnut after the Danish leader defeated him in battle at Ashingdon.

Edmund was the son of Ethelred II and his first wife Elgiva. After his father had been reinstated as king in

1014 the two men fell out, but were eventually reconciled before Ethelred's death on 23 April 1016.

Ascending the Wessex throne, Edmund II was crowned at St Paul's Cathedral. However, his kingship was immediately challenged by Cnut, the son of Svein Forkbeard, who had briefly deposed Edmund's father three years ealier. In the meantime Cnut had re-established Viking control in the northern Danelaw as he continued the struggle between the Danish kings and their Anglo-Saxon counterparts. His next move was to besiege London.

Edmund successfully managed to relieve the city, where he enjoyed considerable support, but he soon lost the initiative he had gained, by suffering a heavy and decisive defeat at Ashingdon, Essex. The two warrior kings then came to an agreement by which they would divide England between them: Edmund would rule over Wessex and Cnut was to claim sovereignty in all areas north of the Thames. The arrangement did not last long because on 30 November 1016 Edmund II died. He was buried alongside his grandfather, Edgar, at Glastonbury. Married to Ealdgyth from 1015, Edmund was survived by his wife and their two infant sons, Edmund and Edward. Cnut succeeded him without any opposition.

))))➤ *Cnut, Ethelred II*

EDRED (c. AD 923–955)

King of England (AD 946–55); son of Edward the Elder; also known as Eadred. He succeeded Edmund I and established a wealthy, united kingdom despite the Viking threat led by Eric Bloodaxe. After his death the crown passed to his nephew, Edwy.

A grandson of Alfred the Great, Edred was the second son of Edward the Elder's third marriage. Handed the reins of power following the death of his brother, Edmund I, on 26 May AD 946, he was crowned at Kingston Upon Thames on 16 August that year. Failing in his attempt to defeat the marauding Vikings under Eric Bloodaxe in AD 948, Edred was able to take comfort from the Northumbrian support he then enjoyed. Later losing this support as a power struggle flared up between Olaf

LEFT: Edmund II Ironside
ABOVE RIGHT: Edred

Sihtricson and Eric, it was not until AD 954, the year of Eric Bloodaxe's death, that control of Northumbria reverted to an Anglo-Saxon ruler.

He died after a long illness on 23 November AD 955 at about the age of 32. Edred passed away at Frome in Somerset, but was interred at Winchester. Edred had never married and was succeeded by his young nephew, Edwy.

))))➤ *Edmund I, Edwy, Eric Bloodaxe*

EDWARD I (1239–1307)

 King of England (1272–1307); son of Henry III; known as 'Longshanks', 'The Father of the Mother of Parliaments', 'The English Justinian' and 'The Hammer of the Scots'. This great and long-serving monarch succeeded his father in 1272. He pushed through many administrative and legal reforms and is remembered for his military victories in Wales and in Scotland, the latter leading him to seize the historic Stone of Scone. Edward fathered 18 children and was succeeded by his son, Edward II.

The eldest child of Henry III and Eleanor of Provence, Edward, was born at Westminster, London on 17 June 1239 and grew up at a time when England was relatively united. In October 1254 the 15-year-old prince married Eleanor of Castile. A decade then passed before Simon de Montfort and his supporters led a rebellion that was to see the emergence of a strong, new defender of the Plantagenet dynasty. A key figure at the Battle of Evesham in 1265, 'Lord' Edward, as he was then known, was the undisputed power behind the throne by the time he set off on crusade in 1270. He was away from England for four years, during which time he learned of his father's death (in 1272) and was wounded at Acre. He did not return to England immediately and it was not until 19 August 1274 that he and his wife Eleanor were crowned in a joint coronation ceremony held at Westminster Abbey.

It was not long before Edward proved himself to be a shrewd politician. Early in his reign he commissioned an in-depth review of his realm, which became the documents known as the Hundred Rolls. This was the most comprehensive summary of English life produced since the Domesday Book of William I had been completed almost two centuries before. The Hundred Rolls contained a mass of information, particularly about the distribution and ownership of land at the beginning of the reign. Also in the first years of his reign Edward introduced a number of statutes in parliament, including two Statutes of Westminster (1275 and 1285) and the Statute of Wales (1284). Completing the judicial reforms of his father, in his long reign Edward I established the office of conservator of the peace (a forerunner of the modern Justice of the Peace) and created the Chancery Court, where aggrieved citizens could seek legal redress.

Set on taming over-mighty nobles at home, but ever eager to lead an army on foreign soil, the king soon had designs on Wales. In 1277 he marched on to Welsh soil and attacked the defiant Gwynedd king, Llywelyn ap Gruffudd, inflicting a heavy defeat. Five years later, however, the Welsh warriors struck back. The death of Llywelyn, the construction and revamping of castles in the north and west and new laws and administrative appointments confirmed English dominance and in two separate campaigns Edward I eventually overran the country.

Edward also mounted a series of campaigns to bring Scotland under his control. In March 1296 English troops launched a series of attacks against their old enemy in the north. Beginning with the storming of Berwick and continuing on to victory at the Battle of Dunbar, the superiority of the English king's army forced the overthrow of John Balliol, the man Edward himself had placed on the Scottish throne just five years previously. In the Highlands and the northern territories resistance to the 'Hammer of the Scots' remained fierce, while to the south first William Wallace and then Robert the Bruce carried the fight to the English. Success for the Scots, notably at Stirling Bridge in 1297, was countered by English success the following year at the Battle of Falkirk. And so the war in Scotland rumbled on, continuing long after Edward's death in 1307.

LEFT: Edward I on his throne

The son of a Frenchwoman and the long-time husband of a Castilian, England's king was too pre-occupied with asserting control in the British Isles to achieve much success in Europe. Inheriting Gascony, Edward acquired the French region of Agenais in 1279 and held court at Bordeaux in 1289. Although he began a costly war with France in 1294, the campaign halted before it had really even begun.

Edward married twice. His first wife, Eleanor of Castile, was just a child at the time of the royal wedding in October 1254. She later became the mother of 15 of Edward's children and died in November 1290. Nine years later the king wed his second wife, Margaret, at Canterbury Cathedral. Forty years Edward's junior, in the last years of the old king's life the daughter of the French king, Philip III, gave birth to two sons and a daughter.

Edward passed away on 7 July 1307 at Burgh-on-the-Sands, near Carlisle. The old warrior-king died while on his way to launch yet another attack on Scotland. Buried at Westminster Abbey, the English crown passed next to his eldest surviving son, Edward II.

⫸ *John Balliol, Edward II, Llewelyn ap Gruffudd, Robert I*

Mariage du Roi d'Angleterre et d'Isabelle de France

EDWARD II (1284–1327)

King of England (1307–27); son of Edward I.
Edward was created Prince of Wales in 1300
and succeeded his father as England's king in 1307.
During his reign Piers Gaveston and the Despensers,
father and son, rose to the king's favour and suffered
the consequences. Thomas of Lancaster and Queen
Isabella turned against the king. Lacking his father's
soldierly qualities, Edward II was defeated by the Scots
at the famous Battle of Bannockburn in 1314 and
eight years later the king was overthrown by Isabella
and her lover, Roger Mortimer. Edward was forced
to abdicate, but was murdered in the same year.
The country breathed a sigh of relief when his son,
Edward III, was crowned king.

Edward II was born at Caernarfon on 24 April 1284; he
was the thirteenth child born to Edward I and his first
wife, Eleanor of Castile. With three of his older brothers
dead, however, Edward found himself left as heir to the
English throne at the age of only four months. He was

formally invested with the title Prince of Wales at the age
of 16, and seven years later, on 7 July 1307, the prince
became king on the day his father died. He was crowned
at Westminster Abbey on 25 February 1308 in a joint
ceremony with his wife, Queen Isabella. The couple had
wed in Boulogne a month before the coronation. The
eldest daughter of the French king, Philip IV, but later
known in England as the 'she-wolf of France', Isabella
gave birth to two sons, including Edward III, and two
daughters, among them, Joan, who married David II
of Scotland.

At the time of Edward II's accession royal policy
was dominated by the struggle with the Scots. However,
the new king lacked his father's enthusiasm, not to
mention his aptitude, for war, and after a half-hearted
attempt to complete the action to which his father had
been travelling at the time of his death, Edward II
quickly lost interest in the Scottish campaign. He had
indulged his friends while he was prince and continued
to do so as king. Among these favourites none was more
favoured than Piers Gaveston, with whom the king is
reputed to have had a sexual relationship. But Gaveston's
time in the king's inner circle was destined to be brief.
Captured in Scarborough in 1312, he was found guilty
of treason and summarily executed, much to the anguish
of the king. Central to Gaveston's downfall was Thomas,
Earl of Lancaster – a man who would play a central role
in later events.

After the death of Gaveston, the king was forced
to respond to the worsening situation in Scotland.
Leading an army to Bannockburn in 1314, the king and
his men suffered a devastating and ignominious defeat
at the hands of Robert Bruce. In England, too, storm
clouds were gathering as the king's cousin, Thomas of
Lancaster, became still more powerful. Two other
influential figures to emerge at this time were the
Despensers. Lords in the Welsh Marches, the son, Hugh,
had followed his namesake father into high office, but as
the ambitious Despensers rose to power they made many
enemies, Edward's queen among them. In August 1321,
an aggrieved group of nobles led by Lancaster marched
on London. The king managed to draw the rebels' sting,
but relief was only temporary: seven months later the two
sides went to war.

The king took control in Wales and won the Battle of Boroughbridge in Yorkshire in March 1322. Lancaster was caught and executed one week after the conflict: one of many rebel nobles to lose their lives in the bloody aftermath of this battle. Despite the swift and merciless punishment of the rebels opposition to Edward II remained. So, while the king's forces continued to engage Robert Bruce in Scotland, his English enemies regrouped behind Queen Isabella, her lover, Roger Mortimer, and this rebel couple's most

valuable asset: the heir to the throne, Prince Edward. The rebels set sail from France in September 1326 and, on landing in England, they attracted enough support to force the king to head west. But the net was closing in on the third Plantagenet king and the force of his turncoat queen and her lover proved too much for him. The killing of the king's men preceded his own dethronement, torture and execution.

Edward was captured on 16 November 1326 and after his forced abdication the following January he remained in prison until he was finally put to death on 21 September 1327. Popular legend has it that he was executed by having a red-hot poker plunged into his rectum. Edward II died at Berkeley Castle in Gloucestershire. Two months later, the body of the former sovereign was buried at Gloucester Abbey, the funeral shamelessly attended by his widow and his eldest son, who had been crowned Edward III nine months previously.

)))➤ *Edward I, Edward III, Robert I*

TOP LEFT: The Marriage of Edward II to Isabelle of France
ABOVE: Seal of Edward II

Edward was appointed Keeper of the Realm on
26 October 1326. Proclaimed king on 25 January 1327,
he was crowned eight days later at Westminster Abbey. A
year later he married his French bride, Philippa of
Hainault, at York Minster.

Edward was quick to make his mark as monarch, and
in 1330 the young king sanctioned the arrest of Roger
Mortimer. Mortimer had been a leading figure in the
downfall of Edward's father and also his mother's lover,
thus his execution eliminated a potential rival to the
throne. With this danger removed, attention turned
towards the continuing problem posed by Scotland. Just
two years old when his father was routed by the Scots at
Bannockburn, one of Edward's first duties as king was to
sign the Treaty of Northampton in 1328. Still smarting
from conceding sovereignty to the Scots just before
Robert Bruce died leaving a minor as his heir, the English
king was further stung by subsequent border raids. So,
taking up arms, he laid siege to Berwick in 1332 and the
next year he won a notable victory at the Battle of
Halidon Hill.

He next turned
his attention to
France. In 1337
Edward III and his
allies went to war
against the French
king, Philip IV.
Among the early
conflicts of the
Hundred Years War,
the naval Battle of
Sluys in 1340 was
won by the English.
Then the English
longbow archers loosed their deadly arrows at Crécy in
1346. A year later Calais was besieged and the French
troops were dealt another crushing blow, at Poitiers in
1356. This victory tasted all the sweeter thanks to the
capture of King John of France and so, with David II
of Scotland a hostage in England, Edward III's winning
hand contained not one, but two, kings. Pressing home
the advantage, further attacks on the French resulted in
the Treaty of Brétigny in 1360, by which Edward III

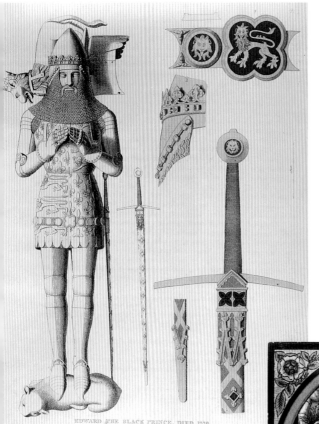

EDWARD THE BLACK PRINCE, DIED 1376.
from his Tomb in the Chapel of the Holy Trinity Canterbury Cathedral.

EDWARD III (1312–77)

King of England (1327–77); son of
Edward II. Crowned in 1327 after the
overthrow of his father, Edward proved to be
one of the greatest medieval monarchs. He
assumed the title king of France at the outset
of the Hundred Years War, in which his son,
Edward, the Black Prince, played his part in the
victories at Crécy and Poitiers; these lands won in France
were later lost. At home the nobility were tamed and
peace restored, but the Black Death ravaged the country,
killing over a million. Monarch for 50 years, Edward III
was succeeded by his grandson, Richard II.

Edward was the eldest son of Edward II and Isabella;
he was born on 13 November 1312 at Windsor Castle.
He was just 13 years old when his doomed father was
captured by enemy forces led by his mother; as a result

LEFT: Edward from his tomb in the chapel of the Holy Trinity, Canterbury Cathedral

BELOW LEFT: Victorian tile showing Philippa pleading with Edward III

withdrew his claim to the French throne in exchange for Calais and Aquitaine, provinces that covered approximately one quarter of France.

The successes in France harked back to the glory days of the early Plantagenets, but they had been gained only after Edward III had endured a crisis of confidence at home. Set on waging war abroad, the king had taxed his subjects to the hilt. Edward was a popular ruler, whose foreign sorties had been well supported, yet there was a limit to the amount of money and service he could demand. Forced to back down between 1339 and 1343, Edward survived this minor crisis, but within a few years there came a more serious problem: plague. Reaching England in 1348, the Black Death spread relentlessly, wiping out around one third of the population.

The king's daughter, Joan, was one victim of the 'great mortality', but despite this sad loss Edward III's large family continued to grow. In an attempt to gain support while trying to overthrow his father, Edward's mother had agreed that he would marry Philippa of Hainault. He acquiesced to her wishes and the couple produced no fewer than 12 children. Such a large family secured the Plantagenet dynasty, as it enabled Edward III to arrange marriages to ensure much-needed support from magnates ambitious for power. Edward's eldest child, also christened Edward, was born in 1330 and became Prince of Wales in 1343. Known to history as the 'Black Prince' because of the armour he wore, he was a warrior from a young age. He was only 16 years old when he took part and in the Battle of Crécy, it was the 26-year-old Black Prince, who took all the accolades for the victory at Poitiers.

Four years later the king was at the height of his powers; his popularity in the land was matched only by that accorded his fighting son. In the age of chivalry, he had founded the Order of the Garter (1348), had won great victories in France and had brought the nobility over to his side. Yet after 1360 events conspired against Edward III and the last 17 years of his long reign were punctuated with depressing losses and personal setbacks. The plague returned and the English hold on Aquitaine

grew less secure. France clawed back so much territory that by 1374 England retained less French land than at any time since the outset of Edward's reign. The forlorn king was badly mauled by parliament in his last days.

There were personal tragedies, too. Seven of his children had already died when the old king suffered two further losses. In August 1369 Queen Philippa died, then in June 1376 the sovereign mourned the death of his son and heir, Edward the Black Prince. Finally, the 64-year-old king, who had reigned for half a century, passed away. Dying at Sheen Palace on 21 June 1377, he was buried at Westminster Abbey. Edward III was succeeded by his grandson, Richard II.

)))➤ *Edward II, Richard II*

EDWARD IV (1442–83)

 King of England (1462–70, 1471–83); son of Richard, Duke of York. Edward IV succeeded the Lancastrian Henry VI. His first reign lasted eight years, after which he was briefly deposed while Henry was reinstated. Edward's second reign lasted 12 years. Rising to prominence during the Wars of Roses, after becoming the first Yorkist king he defeated and killed Richard Neville, Earl of Warwick (known as 'the Kingmaker'). The father of the Princes in the Tower, Edward IV was succeeded by the eldest prince, Edward V, who never made it to his coronation.

Born in the French city of Rouen on 28 April 1442, Edward was the eldest son of Richard, Duke of York, and his wife, Cecily. At the time of Edward's birth, Henry VI was on the throne, but his gradual frailty opened the door of power to men such as the king's cousin, the Duke of York. York was twice appointed Protector of the Realm, when Henry VI was deemed unfit to rule. After participating in battles against Lancastrian troops loyal to Henry's wife, Queen Margaret, Edward's father claimed the crown. Edward was finally acknowledged as heir to the throne in October 1460, but two months later the Duke of York and his younger son, Edmund, were killed at the Battle of Wakefield. The Yorkist cause was not to be denied, however, and on 28 June 1461 at Westminster Abbey the duke's son, Edward, who had fought alongside his father, was crowned Edward IV.

With Henry VI, Margaret and their son, Prince Edward, all still alive, however, the young king was heavily dependent on men such as his cousin Richard Neville, Earl of Warwick, and his younger brother, George, Duke of Clarence, for support and advice. His hold on the throne was tenuous and constantly under threat. These two men had proved to be loyal lieutenants during Edward's rise to power, but later they both turned to plotting against him. Despite the capture of the former king, Henry VI, in 1465, the house of Lancaster continued to fight against the Yorkists. Early progress by the Lancastrian rebels was not sustained and in early 1470 Warwick, Clarence and their supporters were driven into exile. Surprised, however, by a new rebellion in September, it was Edward's turn to flee the country. With the king in Burgundy, the Earl of Warwick assumed control and reinstated Henry VI as his puppet king.

Meanwhile Edward IV prepared to make his comeback. Persuading his brother-in-law, the Duke of Burgundy, to provide him with an army of 1,500 men, he returned to England. Triumphing in April 1471 at Barnet (where Warwick was killed), he then marched west to Tewkesbury where, on 4 May, the Yorkist king won a battle, took Queen Margaret captive and killed her son. The execution of the unfortunate Henry VI soon afterwards completed Edward IV's purge of the leading Lancastrians. Only Clarence remained at large; his treachery was forgiven until further schemings a few years later resulted in charges of treason. Sentenced to death, legend has it that Clarence was drowned in a butt of malmsey wine on 18 February 1478.

Restored as king in 1471, Edward IV was reunited with his wife, Elizabeth. Whilst in in sanctuary at Westminster Abbey she had given birth to the couple's

LEFT: *Manuscript showing Edward IV*
TOP RIGHT: *The chronicle of Jean de Wavrin is presented to Edward IV*

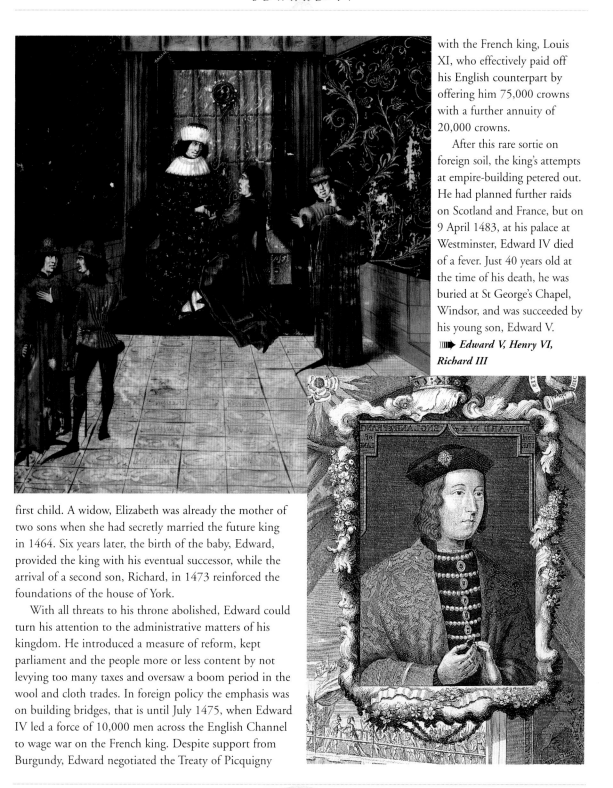

with the French king, Louis XI, who effectively paid off his English counterpart by offering him 75,000 crowns with a further annuity of 20,000 crowns.

After this rare sortie on foreign soil, the king's attempts at empire-building petered out. He had planned further raids on Scotland and France, but on 9 April 1483, at his palace at Westminster, Edward IV died of a fever. Just 40 years old at the time of his death, he was buried at St George's Chapel, Windsor, and was succeeded by his young son, Edward V.

))))▶ *Edward V, Henry VI, Richard III*

first child. A widow, Elizabeth was already the mother of two sons when she had secretly married the future king in 1464. Six years later, the birth of the baby, Edward, provided the king with his eventual successor, while the arrival of a second son, Richard, in 1473 reinforced the foundations of the house of York.

With all threats to his throne abolished, Edward could turn his attention to the administrative matters of his kingdom. He introduced a measure of reform, kept parliament and the people more or less content by not levying too many taxes and oversaw a boom period in the wool and cloth trades. In foreign policy the emphasis was on building bridges, that is until July 1475, when Edward IV led a force of 10,000 men across the English Channel to wage war on the French king. Despite support from Burgundy, Edward negotiated the Treaty of Picquigny

EDWARD V (1470–c. 1483)

King of England (1483); son of Edward IV.
Edward V has gained his place in history through
the dark dealings going on around him during this period
rather than through any virtue of his own. As one of the
'Princes in the Tower', Edward never had the
chance to prove himself. He succeeded his
father at the age of 12, but the unfortunate
child-king was never crowned. He actually
ascended the throne on 9 April 1483, but by
25 June 1483 he had been deposed. Sent to
the Tower of London with his younger
brother, Richard, neither boy was ever
seen again in public. Killed by persons
unknown, Edward V was succeeded by
his 'wicked uncle' Richard III.

Edward was born on 4
November 1470 while his
mother, Elizabeth, was
seeking sanctuary at
Westminster Abbey. A
few days before his birth
his father, Edward IV,
had been deposed when
the Lancastrian king,
Henry VI, was replaced
on the throne. The
following spring,
however, Edward IV
returned to regain the
throne successfully, the
queen and her new son
came out of hiding and the
king began showering titles
on the prince. Already Duke
of Cornwall, the boy became
Prince of Wales and Earl of
Chester and other earldoms
and honours were lavished on
the young Edward, who was the fourth
of 10 children. Only one other son
survived infancy, the similarly ill-
fated Richard, but his eldest sister,
Elizabeth, became wife to Henry VII,

while the youngest, Bridget, became a nun, entering
Dartford Priory when she was just seven years old.

With his father firmly re-established as king, the life of
the younger Edward was filled with all the ceremonial
trappings associated with his position as heir to the
English throne, a status that had been formally recognised
in July 1471, when 47 lords of the realm swore an
oath of allegiance to the eight-month-old baby.
Among those gathered to bear witness to Edward's right
to accession was his uncle, Richard, Duke of Gloucester.
Two years later, and not yet three years old, Edward
was taken to his new home at Ludlow Castle where
he came under the watchful eye of his uncle and
governor, Earl Rivers.

Meanwhile, as the young Prince of Wales enjoyed
his childhood years in Shropshire, another uncle,
George, Duke of Clarence, stepped out of line
for the last time. Accused of treason, Edward
IV himself read out the charges levelled
against his younger brother. Gloucester's
role in Clarence's trial was less clear-
cut, but Henry Stafford, Duke of
Buckingham, played his part by
pronouncing the death sentence.
Clarence was executed in February
1478. Five years later the king
himself died.

On hearing the news of his
father's passing, the 12-year-old
Prince Edward left Ludlow for
London, where his coronation
was scheduled for 4 May. Richard,
Duke of Gloucester, also hurried
south from his Yorkshire estate.
Gloucester intercepted the royal
party and took his nephew
under his wing. Together they
continued their journey to
London. Gloucester, an astute
and power-hungry man, had
moved quickly and with his
nephew in his control,
the duke was holding
all the aces. Realising

the danger in which she and her sons now found themselves, the late king's widow took the younger son, Richard, and again sought sanctuary at Westminster Abbey. Gloucester, Buckingham and Prince Edward arrived in the capital and Gloucester chose the Tower of London as the new king's residence: although the Tower functioned as a prison for much of its history, it was also a place of royal residence so there was nothing unusual about this choice. In no time at all, Gloucester had created himself Protector of the King and Realm; all that remained for the moment was to postpone the new king's coronation until June.

As the day of the coronation loomed, Gloucester made his next move: he sought out and kidnapped Prince Edward's brother, Richard. With both princes under his command, Gloucester's plan was almost complete. He began alleging that Edward IV's marriage to Elizabeth Woodville had been invalid because the former king had been engaged to another woman at the time of his wedding. Through means of this challenge to their legitimacy, Gloucester succeeded in nullifying the claims both princes had to the throne. Now the Protector, Richard of Gloucester, only had to arrange for Edward V to be deposed, an event that duly occurred on 25 June 1483. The very next day Buckingham formally invited Gloucester to become Richard III and the reign that never was, that of Edward V, had become history. But what became of the two 'Princes in the Tower'? They were seen again briefly in September of that year, but after that no one saw or heard from them again. Did their uncle, Richard of Gloucester, have them killed? Or did his successor, Henry VII, arrange their murder to prevent challenges to the new, Tudor, line? Although many theories have been proposed about the fate of the princes, none has yet been proved and the fact remains that we will probably never know. In 1678 the bones of two young boys were discovered is a secret hole in a wall in the Tower of London. It is likely that these were the remains of Edward V and his brother. The reigning monarch at the time, Charles II, ordered that these bones be interred at Westminster Abbey.

))))▶ *Edward IV, Richard III*

ABOVE: A portrait of King Richard III from William Shakespeare's play

EDWARD VI (1537–53)

King of England (1547–53); son of Henry VIII by his third wife, Jane Seymour. Edward VI was nine years old when he succeeded his father and on his ascension the Duke of Somerset became Lord Protector.

Somerset won the Battle of Pinkie against the Scots, but was later deposed, executed and replaced by the Duke of Northumberland. A Protestant like his father, Edward allowed Archbishop Cranmer to introduce two Books of Common Prayer. On the young king's early death the succession temporarily passed over his half-sisters, Mary and Elizabeth, and went to Lady Jane Grey.

Edward was the first and only child born to Henry's third wife, Jane Seymour. Married in 1536, Queen Jane gave birth to the next king of England on 12 October 1537. Henry VIII was delighted and ordered celebrations on a grand scale, but joy at the birth of a son and heir was soon diminished by Jane Seymour's death at Hampton Court, 12 days after the arrival of baby Edward. A motherless child, during the next nine years his father remarried three times and the young prince and his older half-sisters, the future queens, Mary and Elizabeth, only enjoyed a more settled home life when Henry wed his sixth wife, Catherine Parr.

For the most part, though, Edward grew up surrounded by adults, with some of the kingdom's leading academics appointed to teach him. A committed Protestant, piety and a serious outlook were the main characteristics of the young royal, who nevertheless enjoyed playing the lute, while hunting, riding and other outdoor pastimes also kept him amused.

Ascending the throne on 28 January 1547, in the first months after the death of Henry VIII, Edward VI was guided by his uncle, Edward Seymour, Duke of Somerset. Appointed Lord Protector of the Realm, Somerset began by fighting in Scotland, where he won the Battle of Pinkie on 10 September 1547, but his fortunes soon declined as unrest grew. France declared war on England, while at home a population hit by religious upheaval, rising inflation and radical changes to land enclosure laws vented their anger by rioting and rebellions such as that led by Robert Kett in July 1549. Three months later Somerset's time as Protector was ended by a coup mounted by John Dudley, Earl of Warwick, later Duke of Northumberland. Somerset was imprisoned and then released, but he was later found guilty of treason and beheaded.

As heads rolled, the English Reformation, which had begun during the reign of Henry VIII, continued to take effect, overseen by Thomas Cranmer, who had become Archbishop of Canterbury during the reign of Henry VIII. In 1549 he masterminded the publication of the First Book of Common Prayer. A seminal work written in English, not Latin, it was superseded by a second volume. This was issued in 1552, just months before Edward VI became terminally ill. Struck down in the winter of 1552–53 by pneumonia (or possibly tuberculosis), the 15-year-old king died at Greenwich Palace on 6 July 1553. Buried in Westminster Abbey, he was briefly succeeded by the daughter-in-law of the Earl of Northumberland: Lady Jane Grey.

))))➤ *Elizabeth I, Lady Jane Grey, Henry VIII, Mary I*

ABOVE: Latimer preaching to Edward VI at Paul's cross, 1458
RIGHT CENTRE: Marriage of Edward VII to Alexandra

and went to Ireland for military training. He was 20 years old when his father, Prince Albert, died in December 1861. Two years later the Prince of Wales married his Danish bride, Princess Alexandra. After their wedding the young couple moved into Marlborough House, a London mansion that became the birthplace of four of the six children born between 1864 and 1871. Alexandra devoted her time to raising her children and charity work. She stood by her husband despite his well-publicised affairs that caused one wit to comment that he 'preferred men to books, and women to either'.

Edward spent most of his life waiting in the wings, and he was 59 when he ascended the throne on 22 January 1901. Crowned Edward VII at Westminster Abbey on 9 August 1902, the new king proved to be a capable monarch. Edward was particularly interested in the military and was a strong francophile; some commentators believe that he was instrumental in arranging the Entente Cordiale, the unofficial alliance forged by Britain and France in 1904.

When not engaged on royal duties, the popular king continued to enjoy the good life, not least horse racing. 'The sport of kings', Edward's horse, Minoru, won the Epsom Derby in 1906. That same year the Liberals returned to power, while the Labour Party won its first seats in the Commons. Under the leadership of Prime Minister Campbell-Bannerman, the Liberal government placed a strong emphasis on social reform introducing free school meals, old-age pensions and labour exchanges.

EDWARD VII (1841-1910)

King of England (1901-10); son of Queen Victoria. The only British monarch of the Saxe-Coburg-Gotha or Wettin dynasty, Edward succeeded his mother in 1901 after six decades as Prince of Wales. The Edwardian age witnessed the end of the Boer War, alliances with Japan, France and Russia, the arrival of the Labour Party and the revival of the Liberal Party. Edward VII died in 1910 and was succeeded by his son, George V.

Just a year younger than his sister, Victoria, Albert Edward was born at Buckingham Palace on 9 November 1841. The eldest son of Queen Victoria and Prince Albert, he was followed into the royal nursery by three brothers and four sisters. He was a spirited, friendly boy, known to his family as 'Bertie'. On reaching maturity the Prince of Wales began to make his way in the world, embarking on a tour of North America. Back in Britain he moved into a new home, enjoyed a stint at university

Meanwhile, the king's health steadily deteriorated and on 6 May 1910 he died at Buckingham Palace. Edward VII was buried at St George's Chapel, Windsor. Survived by his wife, Queen Alexandra, he was succeeded by his eldest surviving son, George V.

)))➤ *Queen Victoria, George V*

EDWARD VIII (1894–1972)

King of Great Britain (1936); son of George V. Edward succeeded his father in January 1936, but, torn between the crown and the woman he loved, he abdicated after just 11 months as king and before he had even been crowned. His duties were taken on by his brother, who became George VI, and in 1937 Edward married Wallis Simpson three months after being given the title Duke of Windsor.

Born at White Lodge, Richmond Park, on 23 June 1894, the first child of the then Duke and Duchess of York was christened Edward Albert Christian George Andrew Patrick David. The last four names are, of course, those of the patron saints of the countries that make up the United Kingdom, and it was by the last of these, David, that he was known to his family. Gaining four brothers and a sister before he was 11 years old, as a boy he spent much of his time on the Sandringham estate, where York Cottage was home. Educated by private tutors before enroling at naval college, after a short time at sea the prince went to Oxford University. From there he moved on to a life in the Officers' Training Corps. Then came the horrors of World War I. Pressing for active involvement Edward became an army officer and served throughout the 'Great War' of 1914–18 and for a year beyond.

With his military service at an end, the 25-year-old, unmarried prince set out on the next phase of his life as heir to the throne. Slight and dapper, Edward had an easy charm and soon became popular as he travelled from country to country as a royal ambassador. Relations were less easy with his father, as the king viewed with disdain his eldest son's liking for parties and the company of married women such as Wallis Simpson, who the prince first met in 1930.

Raised in Baltimore by her widowed mother, in 1916 Wallis Warfield (as she then was) married her first husband, a naval officer. This marriage lasted until December 1927 and the following summer she married her second husband, Ernest Simpson. Transferring to London, it was there that she met the Prince of Wales. Then the heir to the throne, on 20 January 1936 George V died and the prince succeeded his father as Edward VIII.

Edward was six years old when his great-grandmother, Queen Victoria, died and he ascended the throne at the age of 39. In government circles there were many who admired the personable approach of the new sovereign, but there were also men who had serious reservations about a man so obviously besotted with Wallis Simpson, a married woman and divorcée. In the course of the next 10 months, the king's personal life increasingly became a public issue. At the beginning of November 1936 Edward VIII attended the state opening of parliament for the first and only time: the storm clouds were gathering over his choice of partner. British magazines and newspapers had consistently turned a blind eye to the king's love affair, but by late 1936 their approach seemed set to change, especially as Mrs Simpson had just been granted a decree nisi.

Before long a series of discussions took place behind the scenes as politicians tried to prevent the constitutional crisis that would follow the marriage of a British sovereign to a twice-divorced woman. The king made his position very clear and informed the prime minister, Stanley Baldwin, that he was determined to marry Wallis Simpson. The crisis had begun. Baldwin and his advisers investigated various possibilities. One option open to Edward was to enter into a marriage that gave his wife no royal title, property or rights of succession and would disqualify any children from acceding to the throne. But the idea of a morganatic marriage had to be abandoned and the Irish government even went so far as to state that such a marriage would mean that Edward VIII would no longer be recognised in Ireland as the British sovereign.

With the king standing his ground, alternatives were scarce. Then, on 10 December 1936, the king put his name to a document that began with the words, 'I, Edward the Eighth, of Great Britain, Ireland, and the British Dominions beyond the Seas, King, Emperor of India, do hereby declare My irrevocable determination to renounce the Throne for Myself and for My descendants...'.

After signing this Instrument of Abdication, the second Windsor king spoke to the nation in a radio broadcast, and then he was gone. Travelling by car to Portsmouth, from there he sailed into a long exile abroad.

Succeeded by his younger brother, who became George VI, the 42-year-old former sovereign was created Duke of Windsor in March 1937. Three months later the duke married his duchess, Wallis Simpson. The subject of allegations that he was a Fascist sympathiser, he spent the war years as governor and commander-in-chief of the Bahamas (1940–45). Later settling in Paris, the duke died there on 28 May 1972, but was buried at Frogmore, Windsor. Survived by the duchess, she lived on in the French capital until her death on 24 April 1986.

))))▶ *George V, George VI*

Edward was born at Islip, Oxfordshire, when his father Ethelred II, was England's reigning monarch. After the king's death in 1016 Edward and his younger brother, Alfred, sailed to Normandy, the homeland of his mother, Emma. Edward spent his childhood years in the duchy where his uncle Richard, the grandfather of William the Conqueror, was duke. In this age of marriages between the royal families of Europe, Edward, the son of Ethelred, was also the stepson of Cnut, whom Emma had married after the death of Ethelred. Cnut became king of England in 1016 after the death of Edward's half-brother, Edmund II. Remaining in Normandy during the reigns of Cnut (1016–35) and Cnut's son, Harold I, (1035–40), Edward became a welcome guest at the English royal court once again when his half-brother, Harthacnut, was crowned king of England. Then, on 8 June 1042, Harthacnut died.

Ascending the throne left vacant by his half-brother's death, it was only right and proper that the devoutly Christian Edward was crowned on Easter Sunday 1043 in a grand coronation service held at Winchester Cathedral.

EDWARD THE CONFESSOR (c. 1003–66)

King of England (1042–66); son of Ethelred II ('the Unready'); half-brother of Edmund II and stepson of Cnut. England's last Anglo-Saxon king succeeded his half-brother, Harthacnut, in 1042. His nickname was granted to him because of his piety and his lasting monument was Westminster Abbey. Edward the Confessor was married to Edith, but the couple remained childless and on the Confessor's death the throne was inherited by the queen's brother, who became Harold II. One of the most famous successions in English history, it was this that instigated the Norman Conquest that was to change the face of Britain for ever. Had Edward produced an heir, history might have been very different. Edward the Confessor was canonised in 1161.

Edward's accession had been readily accepted, but the new king was soon faced with difficulties. The danger of invasion by King Magnus of Norway remained a threat until 1047 when Magnus's successor, Harold Hardrada made peace with England.

In 1045 Edward had married Edith, a daughter of
Earl Godwin. Later the king became unpopular with some
nobles for appointing men from Normandy to important
posts, but neither the Norman presence, nor a year in exile
in the company of his wife and four sons (including the
future king Harold II), could halt the rise and rise of Earl
Godwin and his family. At home,
therefore, Edward the Confessor had to
cope with the problems posed by three
powerful earls: Leofric of Mercia (the
husband of the famous Lady Godiva),
Siward of Northumbria and Godwin of
Wessex. All of them resented the Norman
influence that Edward brought to England
from his time at the court of Normandy.

As the king grew older and no heir
appeared to confirm the line of
succession, potential candidates jostled
for position behind the throne. Briefly,
the Confessor's chosen heir had been
Edward the Atheling, son of Edmund II,
but after his death in 1057, the mantle
passed to Edmund's grandson, Edgar the
Atheling. Among the other contenders
to succeed Edward the Confessor were
Godwin's sons, Harold and Tostig,
Harold Hardrada and William, Duke
of Normandy.

On 5 January 1066, just eight days
after the consecration of his beloved
Westminster Abbey, Edward the
Confessor died. He was buried at
Westminster the day after his death. In
the immediate aftermath of his funeral
the late king was formally succeeded by
his wife's brother, Earl Godwin's eldest
son, Harold, whom he had apparently
promised the throne while on his
deathbed. Queen Edith herself lived
on until 1075, when her body was laid

to rest alongside her husband. Canonised by Pope
Alexander III in 1161, eight years later the mortal
remains of Edward the Confessor were reburied with
great reverence and humility by Henry III in a new
shrine at Westminster Abbey. Across the Channel,
however, William of Normandy was preparing to
challenge the right of Harold to succeed a throne
that had also been promised to him by Edward
the Confessor.

))))➤ *Cnut, Edmund II, Ethelred II, Harthacnut, William I*

EDWARDVS REX . ANGLIÆ

DIEU ET MON DROIT

EDWARD THE ELDER (c. AD 870–925)

King of Wessex (AD 899–924); son of Alfred the Great. Edward the Elder succeeded his father as king of Wessex in AD 899 following a succession struggle with his cousin, Ethelwold. A successful king who reigned for 25 years he battled against the Danes to regain lost lands. Hailed as overlord by other British kings, he was the father of Athelstan (his successor), Edmund I and Edred.

The eldest son of Alfred and Ealhswith, Edward ascended the Wessex throne on his father's death on 26 October AD 899 and was crowned at Kingston Upon Thames on 8 June AD 900. Earlier he had fought and defeated his cousin, Ethelwold, in a fight for the throne. The son of Ethelred I, who as a child had been passed over in favour of Alfred the Great, Ethelwold remained a thorn in the king's side for some years until he was killed in battle. This was just one of many military victories enjoyed by Edward the Elder during his 25-year reign and he emulated his father by inflicting a series of defeats on the Danes throughout the period AD 910–18.

Regaining possession of the Danelaw in the East Midlands and Essex, Edward also forced the East-Anglian Danes into submission. In the west, Edward's cause was aided and abetted by his formidable sister, Ethelflaed. Known as the 'Lady of the Mercians', she fortified her kingdom's borders in the face of attacks from the Welsh, Danish and Norwegian forces, while her battlefield triumphs included her seizure of Derby in AD 917. The following year Edward received the submissions of the Welsh kings of Dyfed and Gwynedd. Then, in AD 923, Constantine II of Scotland and Raegnald, crowned head of the newly established kingdom of York, added their acknowledgements of Edward's position as British overlord.

Married three times, Edward's marriages to Egwina, Elfleda and lastly to Eadgifu produced many children in the years before his death. Dying in Mercia at Farndon, Cheshire, on 17 July AD 925, he was buried at Winchester in Wessex. He was succeeded by his eldest son, Athelstan. He was also survived by his third wife, Queen Eadgifu, who lived long enough to witness the coronations of her sons, Edmund I and Edred and her grandsons, Edwy and Edgar.

)))➤ *Alfred the Great, Athelstan, Constantine II, Edmund I, Edred*

EDWARD THE MARTYR (c. AD 962–78)

King of England (AD 975–78); son of Edgar the peaceful. Succeeding his father in AD 975, Edward reigned for just three years. Probably murdered by his stepmother, Elfrida, he was succeeded by his half-brother, Ethelred II.

The son of Edgar and his first wife, Ethelflaeda, Edward became king of Wessex after his father's death on 8 July AD 975. Crowned at Kingston Upon Thames, Edward was to endure a difficult time as monarch: his troubled reign a marked contrast to the calm of Edgar's years on the throne.

Probably hot-headed and blunt, possibly quick to make enemies, there is little doubt that the teenaged king suffered a violent death. Dying on the night of 18 March AD 978 Edward was murdered by a band of assassins, who intercepted him as he headed for Corfe Castle in Dorset. As he had been travelling there to meet his young half-brother, Ethelred, and his step mother, Elfrida, inevitably she was implicated in Edward's murder. However, no charges were ever brought and, as quickly as Edward's body was buried at the Dorset settlement of Wareham, Elfrida's young son was crowned Ethelred II. Luckless in his short life, in death Edward came to be seen as a saint. Later known as Edward the Martyr, one year after his murder the body of the boy-king was reburied at Shaftesbury Abbey.

)))➤ *Edgar the Peaceful, Ethelred II*

EDWY (d. AD 959)

King of England (AD 955–59); son of Edmund I. Also known as Eadwig the Fair, he succeeded his uncle, Edred, in AD 955. His coronation was marred by a brawl and his reign was marked by the rising power of his brother and successor, Edgar.

The eldest son of Edmund I and his first wife, Elgifu, Edwy was still in his teens when he became king. The latest in a series of Wessex monarchs to be crowned as minors, his coronation took place in January AD 956 at Kingston Upon Thames. The ceremony itself passed off without incident, but the post-coronation banquet was interrupted by a heated argument. This argument began after the young king decided to steal away from the formal banquet to amuse himself in the company of two women, his wife-to-be, Elgifu, and her mother, Ethelgiva. What happened next is uncertain, but the more sensational accounts suggest that the powerful cleric, Dunstan, was sent by Archbishop Oda to call the king back to the banquet. Flying into a fury at seeing the juvenile king wrapped in the arms of two women, his crown dismissively cast to one side, Dunstan was said to have manhandled both Edwy and the women.

Whether this is what actually happened, the coronation incident preceded a reign as short as it was eventful. Dunstan slipped away into exile, while Edwy wed Elgifu. King in Wessex, Mercia and Northumbria at the time of his accession, in AD 957 the Mercians

FAR LEFT: Edward the Elder
CENTRE LEFT: Edward the Martyr
ABOVE RIGHT: Edwy

and the Northumbrians adopted Edwy's brother, Edgar, as king of their realms. Worse was to follow for the young king as his marriage to his blood-relative, Elgifu, was annulled by Archbishop Oda in AD 958. Then, in September AD 959, his ex-wife died, her death followed on 1 October by that of Edwy. Monarch for less than four years, he was succeeded by his brother, Edgar.

)))➤ *Edgar, Edmund I*

ELIZABETH I (1533–1603)

Queen of England (1558–1603); daughter of Henry VIII by his second wife, Anne Boleyn. Elizabeth was the half-sister of Edward VI and Mary I, who she succeeded in 1558. Known as 'Gloriana', 'Good Queen Bess' and the 'Virgin Queen', Elizabeth turned out to be was the last Tudor monarch. Her long reign was notable for the defeat of the Spanish Armada, the imprisonment and execution of Mary, Queen of Scots, and the discoveries made by seafarers such as Sir Francis Drake and Sir Walter Raleigh. Elizabeth I was succeeded by James I (James VI of Scotland).

Born at Greenwich Palace on 7 September 1533, the early life of the daughter of Henry VIII and Anne Boleyn was clouded by disappointment and loss. Desperate for a male heir, Elizabeth's birth so distressed her father that he declined to attend her christening. Then, before she was three years old, she lost her mother, who was beheaded in May 1536. The young princess was to witness increasing change in the country over the next two decades and more. She came to be on good terms with two of her step mothers, Catherine Parr and Anne of Cleves, who travelled with the 20-year-old Elizabeth to and from Mary's coronation. Imprisoned in the Tower of London a short time later, when she was suspected of being involved in a rebellion led by Sir Thomas Wyatt, on 15 November 1558 the death of Mary I saw Elizabeth ascend the throne.

Crowned at Westminster Abbey on 15 January 1559, she came to power at a difficult time, her accession following an 11-year period in which a regency, a nine-day queen and the religious turmoil of Mary's brief reign had undermined the Tudor dynasty. Her own safety, the important matter of religious faith and the issue of succession: these were some of the major concerns facing the new queen. Then there was the threat posed by Mary, Queen of Scots, the English queen's Catholic cousin, who was to remain a thorn in Elizabeth's side for more than a quarter of a century. Yet she survived and ultimately thrived to become one of the most enduring and endearing of all English monarchs.

In the early years of her reign threats came from every angle. Mary, Queen of Scots, was a potential challenger and Lady Margaret Douglas (like Mary Stuart a descendant of Margaret Tudor) and relatives of Jane Grey (herself a descendant of Henry VIII's youngest sister, Mary) were others. Then, in late 1562, Elizabeth suffered a near-fatal attack of smallpox. Made head of the Church of England just three years earlier, her subsequent excommunication by Pope Pius V made an assassination attempt on the Protestant queen all the more likely. Inevitably there were plots. A highly ambitious one fronted by Roberto Ridolfi was uncovered in 1571, while the Babington Plot was foiled by agents working for the Principal Secretary of State, Sir Francis Walsingham. Here the detection methods ranged from the sophisticated (for example, deciphering of codes) to the barbaric (for example, the rack). Finally, there was the major threat posed by Philip II of Spain.

ABOVE: The Armada Jewel Locket
ABOVE RIGHT: Elizabeth I at prayer

The former husband of Mary I, the Spanish king became a sworn enemy of the English queen. Yet earlier Philip had seen Elizabeth as a potential wife. He was not alone in thinking this; many pressed their suit, yet none were chosen. Other foreign princes were linked with Elizabeth as were English suitors such as Robert Dudley, Earl of Leicester, and Sir Christopher Hatton. Dudley was nicknamed 'Eyes' by the queen, while Hatton was 'Lids', but neither man won Elizabeth's hand in marriage.

Philip II was another to be disappointed as the 'Virgin Queen' remained a spinster to the end of her life.

Once rejected by England's queen, Philip II of Spain returned to his native country determined to wreak revenge on the queen and restore the country to its Catholic status. In 1587 the Catholic Mary, Queen of Scots had been executed after a long period of imprisonment and Sir Francis Drake had led a raid on Cadiz singeing, 'the King of Spain's beard' as he did so. These events spurred Philip to action and in 1588 he ordered the galleons of the Spanish Armada to set sail for England. What happened next soon passed into English legend and made a national hero of Drake. Approaching the enemy ships anchored off Calais in the dead of night, the English fleet unleashed a collection of fire ships. Lashed together and filled with explosives these flaming vessels caused the Armada to panic. A battle then ensued and the remaining Spanish ships were forced to sail north towards Scotland taking the threat of invasion with them.

Judged by some to have mixed strong rule with a laissez-faire approach verging on indecisiveness, Elizabeth managed to out last potential usurpers, ruling over England at a time when Drake, Shakespeare and Raleigh were some of her illustrious subjects. So it was that the death of the last Tudor monarch was viewed by many as the end of the golden Elizabethan age. Living to a greater age, 69, than all of her many royal predecessors, she also enjoyed the longest reign of any English monarch since the days of Edward III. Dying at Richmond Palace on 24 March 1603, Elizabeth I was buried at Westminster Abbey and was succeeded by James I.

)))➤ *Edward VI, Henry VIII, James VI, Mary I, Mary Queen of Scots*

ELIZABETH II (b. 1926)

Queen of Great Britain (since 1952); the eldest daughter of George VI and Queen Elizabeth the Queen Mother. Succeeding her father in 1952, the queen became the longest-reigning British monarch of the twentieth century. Much-travelled and hard-working, she has remained popular in the 'media age' despite intense criticism of the royal family. A grandmother and mother of four children, her eldest son 'Prince Charles' is heir to the throne.

Born on 21 April 1926 at 17 Bruton Street, London, the first child of the Duke and Duchess of York was not expected to become queen. At the time of her birth her

69-year-old grandfather, George V, had been king for 15 years while waiting in the wings was his son and heir Edward, Prince of Wales. Next in line in 1926 was Elizabeth's father, Edward's younger brother, Albert. Ten years later, the situation would remain unchanged, but in the meantime 'Lilibet', as Elizabeth was known to her

family, was joined in the royal nursery by a sister, Margaret, who was born on 21 August 1930. Enjoying a relatively normal childhood, in 1936 the lives of the two sisters changed dramatically.

The year of three kings, 1936, began much the same as any other. On 20 January, however, George V died. Succeeded by his eldest son, Edward VIII, on 10 December 1936 the new king abdicated so that he could be free to marry the twice-divorced Wallis Simpson. Elizabeth's father stepped into his shoes and Elizabeth found herself heiress apparent.

Crowned as George VI, her father's 16-year reign was dominated by World War II (1939–45), which shook the world to its foundation and changed so much (including the public's opinion of the monarchy). Refusing to leave Britain during the conflict, the popularity of the royal family at this time was further increased by Elizabeth's stint as an officer in the Auxiliary Territorial Service.

The wedding of Princess Elizabeth and Prince Philip in November 1947 helped lift the gloom of post-war Britain. Enjoying the next four years as a married princess, she became queen following the death of George VI on 6 February 1952. By then the mother of Charles (born 14 November 1948) and Anne (15 August 1950),

allow the media to intrude on the private life of her very public family. Nevertheless, aware of changing attitudes, she grasped the nettle and sanctioned the making of a 1969 BBC documentary called simply *The Royal Family*.

Eight years later, the Windsors were once again under the spotlight as the Silver Jubilee celebrations showed the great affection many British people felt for the queen. A mass of street parties also gave a foretaste of the scenes that would accompany the wedding of Prince Charles and Lady Diana Spencer in 1981.

both children attended the queen's coronation at Westminster Abbey on 2 June 1953. A short time later, Elizabeth II embarked on the first of the many royal tours that were to become such a feature of her reign, this round of trips and 'walkabouts' make her the most-travelled British monarch of all time.

However, popular though these early excursions proved to be, they took place in an era when the sun had long since set on the old British Empire. Such a contraction of power, coinciding with an increased boldness in society, inevitably led to questions being asked about 'The Establishment' and to doubts being expressed about the place in a twentieth-century democracy of a royal family, a family viewed by many during the 1960s as being out of touch with everyday life.

By the middle of that decade, the queen had become the mother of four children: Charles, Anne, Andrew (born 19 February 1960) and Edward (10 March 1964). A hard-working sovereign, whose professionalism was rarely doubted, Elizabeth II had long been reluctant to

LEFT: Elizabeth and Margaret

TOP: The Queen and the Duke of Edinburgh arrive at Ascot

RIGHT: The Queen at the naming of HMS Ocean

Since then Elizabeth II has weathered several storms, the most recent coming in the wake of the death of Diana, Princess of Wales, in 1997. However, the queen, like the Queen Mother, retains a degree of popular respect accorded few other members of the royal family. A woman of great wealth and instantly recognised all around the world, Elizabeth II celebrates her Golden Jubilee on 6 February 2002. Enjoying the longest reign since that of Queen Victoria, only two English/British monarchs have reigned longer: Henry III (56 years) and George III (59 years). The fourth British sovereign of the House of Windsor, the queen's heir is her eldest son, Charles, Prince of Wales.

⫸ *Prince Charles, Queen Elizabeth the Queen Mother, George II, House of Windsor*

ELIZABETH, THE QUEEN MOTHER (b. 1900)

The wife of George VI. Born Elizabeth Bowes-Lyon, she married the second son of George V in 1923 and became the Duchess of York. Queen Consort from December 1936, when her husband became George VI, she was a popular figure during World War II. The mother of two daughters, her husband's death in 1952 led to the accession of her eldest girl as Elizabeth II. Thereafter known as Queen Elizabeth the Queen Mother, the doyenne of the Windsor dynasty celebrated her 100th birthday in 2000.

Born in London on 4 August 1900, the ninth child of Claude and Cecilia Bowes-Lyon was named Elizabeth Angela Marguerite. Descended on her father's side from Scottish royalty and on her mother's side from the Duke of Wellington, when Elizabeth was three years old Claude Bowes-Lyon became the 14th Earl of Strathmore and Kinghorne.

Spending her childhood at the family home in Hertfordshire and at Glamis Castle in Angus, Scotland, she spent most of World War I at Glamis, where she helped care for the wounded soliders who were brought there. Eighteen years old at the end of the 'Great War', in which one brother had been killed and three wounded, less than five years after the Armistice was agreed, Lady Elizabeth married Prince Albert, the second son of George V.

Soon given the title the Duchess of York, she gave birth to a baby girl, Elizabeth, in April 1926. Then, in August 1930, the Duke and Duchess celebrated the arrival of a their second daughter, Margaret. However, the Yorks did not have long to enjoy a quiet family life as in December 1936 Edward VIII abdicated to be succeeded by his younger brother, Albert, Duke of York.

Taking the title George VI, the duchess became Queen Elizabeth the Queen Consort. Crowned jointly with her husband at Westminster Abbey on 12 May 1937, just two years were to pass before the outbreak of World War II. Immediately, there was much talk of evacuating the royal family, but the Queen Consort's reply was unequivocal: 'The princesses could never leave without me and I could

LEFT: The engagement portrait of Elizabeth Bowes Lyon
TOP RIGHT: The Queen Mother and previous queens

never leave without the king and, of course, the king will never leave.' Seamingly an easy decision to make, it also proved to be a popular one.

Attending the wedding of Princess Elizabeth and Prince Philip, Duke of Edinburgh, in November 1947, just over four years later the Queen Consort was hit hard by the death of George VI on 6 February 1952. A widow at the age of 51, later she carved out a new role for herself as Queen Elizabeth the Queen Mother.

A great-grandmother, who lived through all but seven months of the twentieth century, the ever-popular 'Queen Mum' celebrated her 100th birthday in 2000. Living a long life that has encompassed two World Wars and the reigns of six different sovereigns, she was a baby during the last days of Queen Victoria and a child during the reign of Edward VII. Later, of course, she became the

daughter-in-law of George V, the brother-in-law of Edward VIII, the husband of George VI and the mother of Elizabeth II.

))))▶ *Elizabeth II, George VI*

EOCHAID (d. c. AD 879)

King of the Scots (AD 878–79); grandson of Kenneth mac Alpin and son of the Strathclyde ruler, Rhun. Succeeding his father as king of the Britons of Strathclyde, Eochaid may or may not have become king of the Scots following the murder of Aed in AD 878. Possibly sharing the duties of kingship with Giric in the Scots' kingdom, the fortunes of Eochaid after the accession of Donald II in AD 879 are not known.

))))▶ *Donald II, Aed, Kenneth mac Alpin*

ERIC BLOODAXE (d. AD 954)

King of York (intermittently AD 939–54). Eric Bloodaxe was the archetypal Viking warrior and possible gained his name from the legendary slaughter he inflicted on members of his own family, particularly his brothers. Eric was the favourite son of Harald Finehair, the king of Norway, and he inherited the throne of this country from his father in AD 933, when the former abdicated. Eric's bloody reign resulted in his own deposition, though, and so he set off to see what other lands he could conquer. After spending some time on Orkney, where he established himelf as king, Eric seized the opportunity offered by the death of Edmund to lay claim to the Viking kingdom of York. He was assisted in this by the province's archbishop, Wulfstan, while the Witan selected Edred as king. There followed a succession of battles between the Anglo-Saxon and Viking claimants to York and others threw in their lot as well, including the Viking Olaf Sihtricson. Eric was thrown out of York and Olaf permitted to rule there under the overlordship of Edred. The tables soon turned, however, and Eric was reinstated, prompting further retaliatory action from Edred. The scuffles continued until Eric was killed by soldiers waiting in an ambush. He was in his sixties at the time and was probably war-weary. His wife and two of their sons escaped back to Orkney, where they continued to rule.

))))▶ *Edred*

ETHELFLAED (c. AD 868–918)

'Lady of the Mercians' (AD 911–918). Ethelflaed was the first-born child of Alfred the Great and at the age of 18 she married Ethelred of Mercia. She proved to be an able administrator and as her husband's health began to fail she took on increasing responsibility for the running of the kingdom. Ethelflaed was truly her father's daughter and she led campaigns not only against the Welsh, but also against the marauding Vikings. Initially she tried to negotiate with the latter, but when they launched an attack on Chester, the queen defended her husband's realm through the construction of fortifications. When Ethelred died in AD 911, Ethelflaed continued to run the kingdom as she had done before. The young Athelstan, son of her brother, Edward the Elder, had spent much of his youth in the court of Mercia and therefore under the influence of Ethelflaed. Her expectation that he would succeed her was eventually fulfilled after her daughter, Elfwynn, had briefly assumed the throne of Mercia.

))))▶ *Alfred the Great, Ethelstan, Edward the Elder*

ETHELRED II (d. AD 911)

Lord of the Mercians (AD 883–911). Firm knowledge of this less-famous Ethelred II is scant. He is likely to have been Mercian or West Saxon by birth. Doubt surrounds his royal status and although some records accord him the title of king, he is more frequently referred to as the Lord of the Mercians. He probably acknowledged the overlordship of Alfred the Great and he was married to Alfred's daughter, Ethelflaed. Ethelred indulged frequently in border battles with the Welsh and was responsible for the fortification of Worcester and Gloucester. On Alfred's death, the security of Ethelred's position declined and in his last years much of the administrative responsibility of the kingdom fell to his wife.

))))▶ *Alfred the Great, Ethelflaed*

ETHELRED II (THE UNREADY)
(c. AD 966–1016)

King of England (AD 978–1013, 1014–16); son of Edgar; known as ('the Unready'). Succeeding his half-brother, Edward the Martyr, Ethelred was king of England from AD 978. His two reigns were marked by regular Viking attacks. Deposed by Svein Forkbeard in 1013, he was restored to the throne in 1014 following Svein's death. His second wife, Emma, later married Svein's son, Cnut, while Ethelred II was the father of Edmund II Ironside (who succeeded him) and Edward the Confessor.

The second son of King Edgar's second marriage, at the age of 10 or 11 Ethelred's half-brother, Edward the Martyr, was killed while on his way to meet Ethelred's mother, Elfrida. Soon Ethelred succeeded Edward, while his mother later became a nun. Ascending the English throne on 18 March AD 978, the young king was crowned by Archbishop Dunstan at the Wessex stronghold of Kingston Upon Thames one month later, on 14 April.

Known to posterity as Ethelred the Unready, the king's nickname was a play on words ('Unrede' meaning 'no counsel') coined in the twelfth century by writers looking back at his time as king. From AD 979 raids by Vikings were a recurrent theme. Initially, the raiders plundered coastal communities, then left as quickly as they had come, but increasingly Danish attackers were paid off with bribes known later as Danegeld. But still the attacks continued and three years after Byrhtnoth of Essex had died a valiant death at Maldon in AD 991, London was besieged by Norway's Olaf Tryggvason and Denmark's King Svein. However, once again a Viking force was paid off. In 1002, it was the turn of

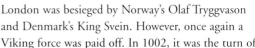

LEFT: King Edward.

Ethelred to go on the offensive as he ordered the murder of every Dane in England. Taking place on 13 November 1002, just a few months after the king had married his second wife, Emma of Normandy, the St Brice's Day Massacre did not go unnoticed in Scandinavia and in 1003 and 1004 hard-hitting Danish attacks were carried out in England.

As more campaigns were launched, the Anglo-Saxons responded by introducing new initiatives, but English resistance was broken in 1013. Beginning in the north, Svein Forkbeard advanced towards the heartland of Ethelred's kingdom. London was defended by Thorkell the Tall, a Viking warrior who had switched sides, but when he was beaten, Ethelred II conceded defeat.

Then, on 3 February 1014, the new king, Svein Forkbeard, died and Ethelred returned to England from Normandy and was accepted as ruler once more. The next year was peaceful, but in 1015 Svein's son, Cnut, made his bid for Ethelred's crown. Yet, just as Cnut made inroads into Anglo-Saxon territories, Ethelred II the Unready fell ill. He died on 23 April 1016 and was buried at St Paul's Cathedral.

The father of many children by his two marriages, he was succeeded by Edmund II, the eldest surviving son of his first marrriage to Elfgiva. Ethelred II was also survived by his second wife, Queen Emma, and their sons, Alfred, and the future monarch, Edward the Confessor.

))))➤ *Edward the Confessor,*
Edmund II, Svein Forkbeard

GEORGE I (1660–1727)

King of Great Britain (1714–27); son of the Elector of Hanover and great-grandson of James I. The first Hanoverian king, George succeeded Anne in 1714, but continued to spend much of his time in his German electorate. In the United Kingdom the huge national debt and the South Sea Bubble posed major problems, while the king's enemies included the Jacobites, Robert Walpole and his own son, George. Before his accession he had married, then divorced and imprisoned his wife, Sophia, the mother of two of his children including the king's eventual successor George II.

Born at Leineschloss in Hanover, Germany, on 7 June 1660, George was the eldest son of the man who eventually became the Elector of Hanover and his wife, Sophia. Sophia's mother was the eldest daughter of James I of Scotland. However, this connection with the British royal family would have meant little to the young George Louis. Growing up on his family's estates, he eventually left Hanover to fight in foreign wars. It was while in England in 1680 that he met Anne, his second cousin

and eventual royal predecessor. The meeting was not a success, however, and all thoughts of a possible marriage match were promptly forgotten.

When George married in November 1682 it was to another cousin, Sophia Dorothea. She gave birth to a boy, called George, and a girl, also called Sophia Dorothea, but in all other respects the marriage was a failure. Both partners embarked on affairs and in 1694 Sophia's lover, Count Philip von Königsmark, was killed. Almost certainly murdered (possibly on George's orders), Sophia was then dealt another crushing blow as her embittered husband divorced her and sent her to a castle, where she spent more than three decades under virtual house arrest, forbidden either to see her children or to remarry.

Four years later the death of George's father saw him become the new Elector of Hanover, while in 1701 the English parliament passed the Act of Settlement. This Act established George's mother as heiress presumptive. The granddaughter of James I, she was thus the appointed successor to Queen Anne. However, her death just weeks before that of Anne robbed Electress Sophia of the chance to be addressed as Queen of Great Britain and Ireland and, with her passing, right of accession was transferred to her son, George.

Ascending the throne on 1 August 1714, George I was 54 years old when he became the United Kingdom's first Hanoverian monarch. Unable to speak more than a few words of English, his coronation service – which took place on 20 October 1714 at Westminster Abbey – was conducted in Latin. George was similarly handicapped during discussions with his ministers, although his son acted as a translator in the early years. The relationship between the two Georges was a stormy one, however.

The king's tempestuous relationship with his eldest child was a personal problem, but the threat posed by the Jacobites in the first months of the king's reign was a national one. Gathered around the flag of the 'Old Pretender', James Edward Stuart, the son of the last Stuart king, James II, the Jacobites had seized and then retained control of much of Scotland by 1715. Forced to act, the king's men defeated the Stuart army at Sheriffmuir. With the threat of invasion averted the attention of the royal family turned again to the worsening feud between George I and his son, the Prince of Wales.

part with their money, huge profits were promised, but in 1720 the company went under. Bankruptcies resulted and vengeance was in the air among investors, much of it directed at a government that had backed the scheme in exchange for funds to clear the national debt, which had reached more than £51 million by 1719. As the crisis deepened, George I was called back from yet another stay in Hanover and Robert Walpole, the new First Lord of the Treasury and Chancellor of the Exchequer, set about repairing the damage done to the government. A Whig politician, who had fallen out with the king in 1717 when his brother-in-law, Charles Townshend, had been sacked as secretary of state, Walpole never looked back after his return to power, retaining the senior treasury post for 21 years.

As for the king, the bursting of the South Sea Bubble proved to be the last major event of his reign. He died at Osnabrück in Hanover on 22 June 1727. Buried at his home town church, he was succeeded by his son, George II.

))))➤ *George II, James I*

In 1716 the king set off for Hanover, but not before drastically reducing the authority of the prince. The following year the rift deepened still further as the king came down hard on the younger George following a violent disagreement with his father's chamberlain. Placing the prince under house arrest, George I took his son's children from him and had him banished from St James's Palace. Typically, the Prince of Wales responded by setting up home at Leicester House, where a rival court soon attracted men such as the politician, Robert Walpole.

Meanwhile, a national crisis erupted in 1720 with the bursting of the South Sea Bubble. So-called because of the fall of the South Sea Company, this finance firm had been set up in 1711. Persuading rich and poor alike to

RIGHT: The golden age of George I

GEORGE II (1683–1760)

King of Great Britain (1727–60); son of George I. George succeeded his father as king of Britain and Elector of Hanover in 1727. Later, during the War of Austrian Succession, he became the last British king to lead troops into battle at Dettingen. At home, Pitt replaced Walpole as prime minister and the Jacobites under 'Bonnie Prince Charlie' won the Battle of Prestonpans, but lost at Culloden. With successes in India and Canada, the reign of the second Hanoverian king ended just as the British Empire was beginning to emerge. George II was succeeded by his grandson, George III.

The son of George I and his wife, Sophia Dorothea, George Augustus was born at Herrenhausen, Hanover, on 30 October 1683. Three-and-a-half years later, George Augustus gained a sister, Sophia, who later became the wife of the king of Prussia. Of greater impact on the young George was the imprisonment of his mother by his father on suspicion of adultery. This ensured that her two children would be placed in the care of their grandmother, Sophia, Electress of Hanover. In 1701, the British Act of Settlement ceded the right of accession to the House of Hanover and gave George British citizenship. Later he received various titles and was invested with the Order of the Garter, all before he had even become heir to the British throne.

With his father's accession in 1714, still more titles were bestowed on George, including the traditional one of Prince of Wales. Uprooting from Hanover, the 30-year-old prince attended his father's coronation and settled at St James's Palace with his wife, Caroline, and their first four children. Despite the bulging eyes typical of the Hanoverians, he cut an elegant figure as a young man and, although far from clever, had a fair memory. In addition, he could speak English, which gave him an advantage over his father and so the younger George acted as a translator at early meetings of the Privy Council.

Such co-operation between king and prince was short-lived and the reign of George I was frequently punctuated by the two men's squabbles. On 22 June 1727 the king died and was succeeded

BOTTOM LEFT: Georges I and II with Queen Caroline
RIGHT: George II

by the Prince of Wales, whose joint coronation with his wife, Caroline of Ansbach, took place four months later, on 11 October, at Westminster Abbey.

By then 43 years of age, George II had fathered nine children, although two had died young. The oldest of the survivors was Frederick Louis, who inherited the title of Prince of Wales. The new monarch's chief minister at the time of his accession was Robert Walpole. War with Spain in the early part of George's kingship, ended in 1729 with the signing of a peace treaty and so, for a time, Britain was not distracted by armed conflict.

However, just as the first years of the reign were peaceful ones, the last 21 years were studded with conflicts, not all of which were fought abroad. By 1739, Britain was at war with Spain again. This time it was the so-called War of Jenkins' Ear, which resulted from an incident at sea in which a Captain Jenkins had an ear cut off. France, too, was an enemy, the Anglo-French conflict creating royal history made in 1742 as George II became the last British sovereign to lead his subjects into battle. He was victorious at Dettingen, but the War of Austrian Succession lasted six more years until peace was confirmed in 1748 by the Treaty of Aix-la-Chapelle.

With the return of the Jacobite threat in the 1740s, the king's troops were once again forced to fight on home soil. No longer led by the Old Pretender, the new leader of the Stuart faction was the charismatic Bonnie Prince Charlie. Initially successful, the Young Pretender's forces marched from Scotland as far south as Derby before the latest Jacobite opposition was crushed in bloody fashion on 15 April 1746 at Culloden Moor near Inverness. The 'Bonnie Prince' escaped with his life, eventually finding refuge in Italy, where he died in an alcoholic haze in 1788, but many other Jacobites were killed during and after the battle.

The English army at Culloden was led by the king's youngest surviving son, William Augustus, Duke of Cumberland. A military man known as the 'Butcher' in the wake of the massacres in Scotland, in contrast to the king's eldest son, Frederick Louis, he was a loyal supporter of his father. Then in 1751 Frederick died.

The death of the Prince of Wales led to Frederick's 12-year-old son, George, being declared heir to the throne. There were also changes on the political scene as Robert Walpole's chief rival, William Pitt, rose to prominence. Given early encouragement as one of the Prince of Wales's Leicester House Set, Pitt's talents were to keep him in the political limelight right up to his death in 1778.

In 1755, Britain waged war on France once more and so for the last five years of George II's life, Britain would be engaged in various conflicts around the globe. The early results of this newly aggressive approach were poor, but later outstanding generals such as Robert Clive and James Wolfe won great victories. Clive of India triumphed at Plassey in 1757, while Wolfe's defeat of the French at Quebec two years later secured possession of Canada for Britain. This momentous victory proved to be the last major event of George II's reign.

Outliving both his wife, Caroline of Ansbach, and his eldest son, the king died at Kensington Palace on 25 October 1760, just five days short of what would have been his 77th birthday. Buried at Westminster Abbey he was, at his insistence, laid to rest alongside his beloved Caroline, their coffins touching and with the adjacent sides removed. George II was succeeded by his grandson, George III.

◗◗◗➤ *George I, George III*

GEORGE III (1738–1820)

King of Great Britain (1760–1820); grandson of George II; nicknamed 'Farmer George'. Succeeding his grandfather in 1760, George III lived longer than any British monarch, while only Victoria has reigned longer. His reign saw Britain lose the War of American Independence, but Nelson at Trafalgar and Wellington at Waterloo secured victories that helped defeat the French emperor, Napoleon Bonaparte. Ultimately deranged by illness, George III was succeeded by the eldest of his 15 children, who reigned as Prince Regent from 1811 and as George IV after his father's death.

The first Hanoverian king to be born in England, George William Frederick was the son of Frederick, Prince of Wales, and his wife, Augusta. The couple's second child, he was born at Norfolk House in London on 4 June 1738 at a time when his father, Frederick, was not on speaking terms with his grandfather George II. George was one of nine children fathered by the Prince of Wales and when he died in January 1751 the 12-year-old George succeeded him as heir to the throne, becoming king on 25 October 1760, the day that George II died.

Crowned George III at Westminster Abbey on 22 September 1761, two weeks earlier he had married a little-known princess, Charlotte of Mecklenburg-Strelitz. A year later the couple had their first child, the future

George IV. Other offspring were born at regular intervals thereafter: Queen Charlotte eventually gave birth to 15 children, among them the future William IV.

For several years after his accession, George III relied greatly on personal favourites to represent him in the minefield of politics. Initially, his shield was the prime minister, John Stuart, Earl of Bute, while later Lord North spent 12 years as premier. Both were subjected to virulent attacks at the hands of politicians and satirists alike, but neither of these Conservative prime ministers was at the helm when Britain was forced to come to terms with a humiliating defeat in 1783, for that was the year in which the American Revolution finally reached its end with the irrevocable loss of the distant colonies. Lord North had been in charge from the outbreak of hostilities in 1775 until 1782, a seven-year period in which the signing of the Declaration of Independence in 1776 had been followed by major military defeats at Saratoga (1777) and Yorktown (1781).

With the American colonies lost, William Pitt the Younger took over as prime minister. Just 24 years old when he was appointed in 1783, except for one three-year spell (1801–04), he remained in office until his death in 1806. This remarkable stint at the top of the political ladder coincided with a significant period in British history. The French Revolution began in 1789, Britain declared war on France in 1793 and the conflict lasted until 1802.

TOP LEFT: George III plays chess with Napoleon
RIGHT: New Yorkers pull down the statue of George III

One year earlier the Act of Union had formally joined England and Ireland. In 1803 Britain returned to the fight against the French emperor, Napoleon Bonaparte, and two years later, with Horatio Nelson at the helm of the *Victory*, Britain routed the French fleet at Trafalgar.

Yet, while politicans such as Pitt attempted to shape Britain's destiny during such eventful times, George III slipped away from the centre of the political stage. Afflicted by porphyria from 1764, recurring bouts of the illness took their toll on his health and on 11 February 1811 the king's powers were transferred to the Prince Regent, George's eldest son, George, Prince of Wales.

Previously a man who had taken the business of kingship seriously, George III had developed such a passion for agriculture that he had become known as Farmer George. He had a similar passion for music and had patronised the arts and sciences, while his impressive collection of books was central to the later foundation of the British Library. But after 1811 the king's deteriorating health reduced the old king to a shadow of his former self. A pitiful figure, blind, deaf and insane, George III can have known little of what occurred outside the walls of Windsor Castle, where he spent his declining years.

He would not have known of the assassination in May 1812 of Spencer Perceval, who became the only prime minister to be murdered (shot dead by a bankrupt with a grudge), nor would he have known of the Duke of Wellington's famous victory at Waterloo in Belgium on 18 June 1815, a triumph that paved the way for the successful conclusion of the Napoleonic Wars. The king would also have been unaware of the marriages of his children, Ernest (in 1815), Mary (1816) and Edward, Elizabeth and Adolphus (all in 1818) the year in which Queen Charlotte died.

Fourteen months later the royal family mourned the death of George III. Dying at Windsor Castle on 29 January 1820, he was buried at St George's Chapel, Windsor. Eighty-one years old when he died, George III was succeeded by his eldest son, the Prince Regent, who was later crowned George IV.

))))➤ *George II, George IV*

GEORGE IV (1762–1830)

King of Great Britain (1820–30); (Regent 1811–20); son of George III. Succeeding his father first as Regent in 1811, then as king, George had been a playboy prince who ran up vast debts and so he became an unpopular monarch. During his short reign Catholics were given greater rights and the first railway was opened. George IV was succeeded by his younger brother, William IV.

Born at St James's Palace on 12 August 1762, the eldest son of George III and Queen Charlotte, George's early promise soon evaporated when the Prince of Wales reached the age of maturity. A constant source of frustration to his father, his debts continued to mount up. Pressing for more money in 1783, the prince's request was turned down, but four years later his financial affairs were discussed again by parliament. This time, it was agreed that £10,000 would be provided by the king, while parliament would clear his debts and would cover the

BOTTOM LEFT: Cartoon showing George IV
RIGHT: The Lord of Misrule, Wellington and George IV
BOTTOM RIGHT: Thoughts on Matrimony, George IV considers potential marriage partners.

considerable cost involved in finishing the heir to the throne's new home, Carlton House. Still the extravagant spending continued and by 1811, the year that marked the start of George's spell as Prince Regent, his total debts amounted to the enormous sum of £500,000.

The son of a king who had been a faithful husband to his wife and an often-doting father to 15 children, George IV was very different to George III. Falling for his first older woman when he was still a youth, his love life took him from affair to affair. Then, in 1785, he secretly married Maria Fitzherbert, a woman who had already been married twice before. However, the marriage was declared invalid as George had not sought or been given permission to marry. Ten years later, though, he was legally married to Caroline of Brunswick. A first cousin of George, she met her future husband in the spring of 1795. A few days later the couple were wed, but the marriage of convenience intended to help repay the prince's mountain of debts produced just one child, Charlotte, and very little else except separation and bitterness.

Appointed Prince Regent on 5 February 1811, the early years of George's regency were dominated by the closing chapters of the Napoleonic Wars, which culminated in Wellington's famous victory at Waterloo in 1815. However, basking in this reflected glory, did not improve the regent's popularity in the country at large and George was the target of an assassination plot in 1817, a year also marred by the death of his daughter, Charlotte.

Finally ascending the throne following his father's death on

Darlington railway line (both in 1825), while four years later an Act was introduced that removed many of the centuries-old restrictions on the civil rights of Roman Catholics. As a result, from 1829 Catholic citizens could at last hold some public offices. This was the last major piece of legislation passed during the king's lifetime. George IV died on 26 June 1830 aged 67. He was succeeded by his younger brother, William IV.

The king died at Windsor Castle and was buried at St George's Chapel, Windsor. The castle at Windsor was one of several royal buildings to undergo extensive and expensive refits during the reign of George IV. Buckingham Palace was another. Rebuilt by John Nash, this architect also redesigned Brighton Pavilion, the now-famous mansion fusing elements of Indian and Chinese architecture, which was sold to the town's commissioners early in the reign of Queen Victoria.

)))⮕ *George III, William IV*

29 January 1820, the coronation of George IV on 19 July 1821 was a typically lavish and spectacular event. It was also one touched with farce, the new king's estranged wife vainly attempting to enter Westminster Abbey in order to be crowned queen. It was almost her final public appearance as she died just three weeks after the coronation ceremony. Caroline of Brunswick, however, had enjoyed one last victory over her husband. Appearing before the House of Lords to defend herself against charges of adultery and scandalous behaviour, eventually in November 1820 the government spiked what was known as the Bill of Pains and Penalties. This very public defeat for George IV prompted celebrations across London that lasted for three whole days.

The king later embarked on a series of royal tours that took in Ireland, a country devastated by famine in 1821–23, Hanover and Scotland. Meanwhile, in England the short reign of George IV was notable for the legalisation of unions and the opening of the pioneering Stockton to

GEORGE V (1865–1936)

King of Great Britain (1910–36); son of Edward VII; nicknamed the Sailor King. The first Windsor monarch, George V succeeded his father in 1910. On the throne throughout World War I and during the Great Depression, his reign was also notable for the creation of the Irish Free State, the first Labour government and the granting of the right to vote to women. He was the father of Edward VIII, who succeeded him, and George VI.

Born at Marlborough House, London, on 3 June 1865, George Frederick Ernest Albert was the second son of Edward, Prince of Wales, and his wife, Alexandra.

A grandson of Queen Victoria, George spent most of his childhood on the royal estate of Sandringham, which had been bought by the royal family in 1862. When he was 15 years old, George and his older brother, Albert (Eddie to his family), became naval cadets at Dartmouth in Devon. Before long the two young royals had fully adjusted to their new life. His life aboard *Britannia* fostered a love of the sea in George that never left the man who would come to be known as the 'Sailor King'. However, after rising to the rank of commander, he became ill with typhoid. He recovered, but when Albert died of pneumonia in 1892 George was forced to abandon his naval career.

In 1893 his life changed again when he married his late brother's fiancée, Princess Mary of Teck. The Duke of York, as he then was, soon became father to a large family of five boys and a girl. The first two sons became the twentieth-century kings Edward VIII and George VI, while daughter, Mary, eventually became known as the Princess Royal. Of the other sons, Henry was made Duke of Gloucester and George, the Duke of Kent, and John died while still in his teens.

George had been 35 years old when his father had ascended the throne in 1901. George succeeded Edward VII nine years later on 6 May 1910. Recognised now as the first monarch of the house of Windsor, George V began his reign as the second king of the Saxe-Coburg-Gotha dynasty. The change of name occurred in 1917, just as World War I was about to drag on into a fourth year, and was prompted by a fierce public loathing for all things German. George V's decision to adopt the very English name of Windsor for his royal house did not impress the king's cousin, the German ruler, Kaiser Wilhelm, but did endear the monarchy to the British people.

BOTTOM LEFT: George V with Mary and their children
RIGHT: Toby jug figure of George V

George V reigned for 26 years, yet even after the peace treaty known as the Armistice was signed on the eleventh hour of the eleventh day of the eleventh month of 1918, the memory of the 'Great War' cast a long shadow over the decades that followed. Breaking out in 1914, this 'war to end all wars' killed and maimed millions of soldiers, the war-dead including the British tommies' who laid down their lives in bloody battles such as the Somme (1916), Paschendaele (1917) and the Marne (1914 and 1918). Yet the 1914–18 war was not the only conflict of the period. In Dublin the Easter Rising of 1916 sparked a nationalist revolt in Ireland that continued to preoccupy politicians and fighting men before, during and after World War I until finally the Irish Free State (comprising 26 southern counties) was created in January 1922.

The immediate post-war years were politically momentous, as the suffragette movement campaigned for equal rights for women. Lady Astor became the first female MP in 1919. Then in 1920 women over the age of 21 were allowed to vote. Four years earlier, the general election of 1924 had led to the formation of Britain's first Labour government under Ramsay MacDonald. A short-lived administration, after just 10 months the Labour Party was swept from office. However, the return of Stanley Baldwin's Conservatives could not prevent the General Strike of May 1926. Then, came the widespread misery of the Thirties. Brought on by the worldwide economic recession that followed the Wall Street Crash of 1929, by 1932 some three million British citizens were out of work. The Great Depression eventually lifted, but by then George V was dead.

Bluff and ruddy-faced, but well-liked during a period when revolution toppled the monarchies of other European powers, George V was a jocular man given to occasional volcanic explosions. He enjoyed living the life of a country aristocrat, while two abiding interests were sailing and stamp collecting. Dying at Sandringham on 20 January 1936, the first Windsor sovereign was buried at St George's Chapel, Windsor, and was succeeded by his eldest son, Edward VIII.

)))➡ *Edward VIII, Edward III*

LONG MAY THEY REIGN

GEORGE VI (1895–1952)

King of Great Britain (1936–52); son of George V. Succeeding his elder brother, Edward VIII, when the latter abdicated in 1936, the reign of George VI was dominated by World War II. A naval officer during World War I, in 1923 he married the 'woman of the century': Queen Elizabeth, the Queen Mother. George VI was succeeded by his eldest daughter, Elizabeth II.

Born Albert Frederick Arthur George on 14 December 1895, his birthplace was the family home of York Cottage on the Sandringham estate in Norfolk. The son of George V and his wife, Mary, when Albert was born his great-grandmother, Victoria, was still queen. However, by the time he was 14 years old, his father was king and he was second-in-line to the throne. Called Bertie on the Sandringham estate where he passed much of his young life, he was a sickly boy, who was also afflicted with a stammer.

Following his elder brother, Edward, to the naval colleges at Osborne and Dartmouth, George was not a gifted student, preferring instead to play the fool and sports such as cricket. Indeed, it is said, he once achieved an unlikely hat trick when, with three successive deliveries, he bagged the wickets of three British sovereigns: Edward VII, George V and Edward VIII.

However, by 1913 white flannels had been cast off in favour of a naval uniform as the future king enroled as a midshipman. When World War I broke out in August 1914, George played his part, seeing front-line service at the Battle of Jutland in 1916. By then a sub-lieutenant, later the prince transferred to the Royal Naval Air Reserve before becoming a pilot in 1918 with the newly formed Royal Army Flying Corps (later renamed the Royal Air Force).

With World War I finally at an end, George once again followed a path taken earlier by his brother, Edward, by spending a year as a university student. Becoming Duke of York in 1920, it was in that same year that he renewed acquaintances with his future wife, a woman who would later come to be synonymous with the best of British royalty. Then known as Lady Elizabeth

Bowes-Lyon, in the second half of the twentieth century the world would know her simply as the Queen Mother. The young couple were married in 1923, their first child, Elizabeth (later Elizabeth II), arriving in April 1926, and their second, Margaret, in August 1930.

Content with a place in the shadows, the duke went about his royal duties diligently and without fuss. A devoted family man, a move to Royal Lodge at Windsor saw George develop an interest in gardening. In 1936, however, such simple pleasures were forced to take second place as the monarchy lurched from one crisis to another. The turbulent year for the Windsors began with the death of the duke's father, George V, and ended with his own accession as George VI. For a shy man, who disliked public speaking, such a sudden elevation came as a huge shock. However, once his elder brother, Edward VIII, had decided to abdicate on 10 December 1936, George was forced to adjust. He did not make the transition any more easily than his father, who had also acceded as a second son, but he persevered to become a popular king. Crowned in a joint coronation ceremony with his wife, the new Queen Elizabeth, the service on 12 May 1937 was covered by the BBC. Formed just 12 years before, it broadcast a special wireless (radio) programme to honour the occasion.

Then, at the close of the 1930s, a decade that had begun with mass unemployment, ended with more misery: the outbreak of World War II. This time there was to be no mainstream role for George. However, he did make many trips to visit front-line troops stationed abroad and the king and queen together visited London's East End to see the damage caused by enemy bombs – Luftwaffe bombs also struck Buckingham Palace in 1940. At the beginning of the war plans had been made to send the royal family to a safe country such as Canada, but neither George VI nor Queen Elizabeth would hear of such a thing and so the Windsors stayed, emerging from the conflict more popular than ever before and a symbol of national resolve.

With war finally at an end, in November 1947 Buckingham Palace was the setting for a celebration: the wedding reception of Princess Elizabeth and the Duke of Edinburgh. Meanwhile, the Labour government of Clement Attlee introduced a radical programme of social reforms that included the formation of the National Health Service and the nationalisation of coal mines, railways, electricity and gas services. For the king, though, the immediate post-war years were a mixed bag; he became a grandfather following the births of Princess Elizabeth's first children, Charles and Anne, but was dogged by recurring illness.

On 6 February 1952 aged 56, he passed away in his sleep at Sandringham. Buried at St George's Chapel, Windsor, he was succeeded by his eldest daughter, who was later crowned Elizabeth II, while the late king's widow soon came to be known the world over as Queen Elizabeth the Queen Mother.

)))➡ *Edward VIII, Elizabeth II, Queen Elizabeth the Queen Mother*

GREY, LADY JANE (1537–53)

Queen of England (1553). A distant cousin of Edward VI, Lady Jane Grey briefly succeeded him. She was proclaimed queen on 10 July 1553, but was deposed and imprisoned by Mary I on 19 July. The protégée and later daughter-in-law of John Dudley, Duke of Northumberland, like Northumberland and her husband, Lord Guildford Dudley, England's 'Nine-Day Queen' was executed.

Born in October 1537, as a young girl Lady Jane Grey received a fine education and had a good command of Greek, Hebrew and Latin. She was one of three daughters born to Henry Grey, Marquees of Dorset and Duke of Suffolk, and his wife, Frances, who was the daughter of Henry VIII's youngest sister. That sister, Mary, had first been married to Louis XII of France, but when the old man died she had secretly wed Charles Brandon, 1st Duke of Suffolk. Later, the couple were forced by the king to pay a huge financial price for Henry's forgiveness. While Brandon's death in 1545 saw Henry Grey inherit his title, it was the influence of a more powerful

nobleman that would lead to the fleeting rise and then fall of Lady Jane Grey. That man was John Dudley, formerly the Earl of Warwick, but from 1551 Duke of Northumberland.

The son of Henry VII's one-time finance minister, Dudley had been a notable army commander, but by the time of Edward VI's minority he had emerged as a leading political figure eager to feather his own nest still further. Replacing the disgraced Edward Seymour, Duke of Somerset, he soon won the confidence of Edward VI. Then, in 1553, with the king in the grip of the illness that was to kill him, the ambitious, sometimes ferocious duke began to promote the cause of Jane Grey, who had become his daughter-in-law when marrying his son, Lord Guildford Dudley, on 21 May 1553.

By this time – less than seven weeks before Edward VI's death – the king's health had so deteriorated that a 'device' to determine the identity of his successor was amended to establish Lady Jane Grey as heir to the throne. Even for a man of Dudley's power this was a daring manoeuvre to make as Edward's Catholic half-sister Mary remained the lawful successor to her childless brother. Others, too, had far stronger claims than Lady Jane, among them Edward's other half-sister, Elizabeth. However, Dudley won the support of the dying king for his Protestant protégée and with it the approval of 26 peers of the realm. So, under the cover of securing English Protestantism, Dudley's bloodless coup was successful and on 10 July 1553, four days after Edward VI had died, the 15-year-old Lady Jane Grey was hailed by her supporters as Queen Jane.

Immediately caught up in the whirlwind that blew her into London in the company of her mother, the girl who had once been viewed as a possible wife for Edward VI was proclaimed queen. However, her reign was to be just as ill-starred and as short as that of the Empress Matilda, who had made her bid for the English crown four centuries before. And so, even as Jane entered the capital, the supporters of Princess Mary were preparing to strike. Then, just a few days later, Mary rode to London in the company of her half-sister, Elizabeth, to assume her rightful place as sovereign and to end the brief reign of Lady Jane Grey.

Retribution was inevitable and followed soon enough. Dudley was arrested, charged and executed, although Mary I showed some clemency in waiving charges against lesser lights. The new queen was also reluctant to condemn to death Lady Jane Grey, the young woman who just a short time before had called on English men and women to 'disturb, repel and resist the feigned and untrue claim of the Lady Mary, bastard daughter of our great-uncle Henry the Eighth'. But in the end, Mary I did sanction Jane's execution.

Imprisoned in the Tower of London for seven months after her arrest, Lady Jane Grey was executed on 12 February 1554. Taken to Tower Green, she was beheaded just a few hours after she had bade a poignant farewell to her husband, Lord Guildford Dudley, before he had placed his head on the executioner's block. A short and sad chapter in the story of English royalty ended with the joint burial of the ill-starred couple at the Tower's Chapel Royal of St Peter-ad-Vincula.

))))▶ *Edward VI, Mary I*

TOP LEFT: Lady Jane Grey
LEFT: Tower of London

GRUFFUDD AP CYNAN (c. 1055–1137)

King of Gwynedd (1081–1137); son of Cynan ap Iago. The only Welsh king known to have inspired a biography written during the Middle Ages, Gruffudd reigned twice in Gwynedd. Dying in 1137 he was succeeded by his son, Owain ap Gruffudd.

Spending his early years in Dublin, in 1075 he sailed to Wales where he made an unsuccessful attempt to seize power in Gwynedd by attacking Rhuddlan Castle in North Wales. However, six years later, with the support of men such as Rhys ap Tewdwr, he killed and succeeded the Gwynedd ruler, Trahearn, at the Battle of Myndydd Carn. Continuing to lead an eventful life, during which he was imprisoned in a Norman gaol, later he became an ally of the Norman king, Henry I.

After his capture by Norman forces, he was ransomed in 1094. Driven westwards, he returned to Dublin in 1098. Back in Wales again the following year, Gruffudd

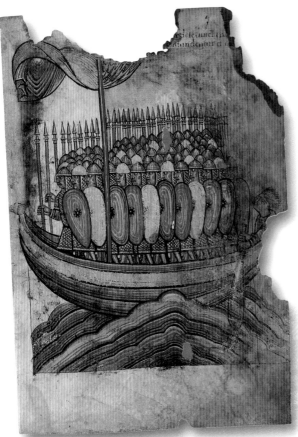

made his peace with Henry I. Initially a client-king based in Anglesey, before his death in 1137 he extended his power throughout Gwynedd. Succeeded by his son, Owain, his daughter, Gwenllian, was the wife of the Deheubarth king, Gruffudd ap Rhys.

➤ *House of Deheubarth, Norman Dynasty*

GRUFFUDD AP LLYWELYN (c. 1000–63)

King of all Wales (1039–63); son of Llywelyn ap Seisyll. One-time king of Dyfed, Gwynedd and Powys, in 1055 Gruffudd claimed Deheubarth to become the first man to rule throughout Wales. Twice doing battle with Earl Harold Godwinson (later Harold II), in 1063 Gruffudd was defeated and killed by the future English king.

The son of Llywelyn ap Seisyll and his wife, Angharad, he took control in Gwynedd from Iago ap Idwal, whom he murdered in 1039. That same year he underlined his power by defeating the Mercians at Rhyd-y-groes (or Crossford) on the banks of the River Severn. Launching his assault on the kingdom of Deheubarth, in 1042 he fought and won a battle with the Deheubarth king, Hywel ap Edwin. Defeating and killing Hywel in a second skirmish in 1044, still Gruffudd could not fully establish his rule in the southern kingdom. Losing in battle to Gruffudd ap Rhydderch in 1045, a whole decade would pass before the Gwynedd king gained his revenge on his opposite number in Deheubarth.

Gruffudd also blazed a warlike trail across the border. He beat the men of Herefordshire at Leominster in 1052, before returning to Wales, where in 1055 he finally won control in Deheubarth. Another victory came Gruffudd's way that year, when he joined forces with Elfgar of East Mercia to attack Hereford, while the following year Leofgar, the Bishop of Hereford, was at the head of a small band of men when he was killed close to Glasbury-on-Wye. Reprisals followed, but Gruffudd continued to make gains before a peace deal was agreed. This recognised Gruffudd's supremacy in Wales, while the Welsh king pledged his loyalty to Edward the Confessor. The deal was sealed by Gruffudd's marriage to Elfgar's daughter, Eldgyth.

In 1058 Gruffudd was on the warpath once more, but then following Elfgar's death in 1062 the mighty English noble Earl, Harold Godwinson, attacked Gruffudd at his court at Rhuddlan Castle in North Wales. The Gwynedd ruler lived to fight another day, but as Harold and his brother, Tostig, conquered Gruffudd's kingdom, the king himself was killed. Murdered by his former supporters on 5 August 1063, according to some accounts they sent his severed head to Harold Godwinson, the soon-to-be-crowned Harold II, who then married Gruffudd's widow, Eldgyth. Once described as the 'head and shield and defender of the Britons', Gruffudd's death led to a succession struggle in Gwynedd that was eventually won by Trahearn.

))))▶ *Llewelyn ap Seisyll*

FAR LEFT: Manuscript showing Norman warriors
BELOW LEFT: Gruffudd, son of Llewelyn
BELOW: Harold II

GRUFFUDD AP RHYDDERCH
(d. 1055)

King of Deheubarth (1033–55); son of Rhydderch ap Iestyn. A feared warrior-king, he defeated Gruffudd ap Llywelyn to claim Deheubarth, but was later killed and succeeded by Gruffudd who thus became the first king of Wales.

Campaigning fiercely in the east and south-east of his kingdom, his greatest victory came in 1045 when he defeated Gruffudd ap Llywelyn. This victory forced the Gwynedd king to give up control of most of Deheubarth. However, in 1047 the northern king struck back. Aided and abetted by an English army led by Svein, a son of Earl Godwin of Wessex, Gruffudd ap Llywelyn's men slaughtered 140 of Gruffudd ap Rhydderch's family and retainers. The Deheubarth king escaped with his life, but in 1055 Gruffudd ap Llywelyn headed south once more, defeating and killing Gruffudd ap Rhydderch to become the first king of all Wales.

))))▶ *Rhydderch ap Iestyn, Gruffudd ap Llywdyn*

GRUFFUDD AP RHYS (d. 1137)

King of Deheubarth (1116–37); son of Rhys ap Tewdwr. In exile after his father's death, Gruffudd did not rule in Deheubarth until he was granted limited powers there by Henry I. Killed in a rebellion, he was succeeded by his sons, Anarawd and Cadell ap Gruffudd.

Following the death in battle of his father in 1093, Gruffudd fled Deheubarth and spent his early childhood in Ireland while the Normans continued their occupation of central and southern Wales. Not returning to his native kingdom until 1113, three years later he made a vain attempt to wrest control of his kingdom from Henry I. Submitting to England's monarch, in return for his support Gruffudd was given a manor by Henry, who also allowed him to remain as the nominal head of Deheubarth.

Killed in the rebellion that followed the accession of England's King Stephen in 1135, his death in 1137 may have been hastened by the treachery of his second wife.

⫸ *Cadell ap Gruffudd, Gruffudd ap Cynan, Henry I, House of Gwynedd, Rhys ap Tewdr*

GUTHFRITH I (d. AD 895)

King of York (AD 883–95). Little is known about this Dane who was elected to be king by the Church leaders of the Viking area of Jorvik. It is possible that he had come to England as part of the 'Great Army' of the leader, Halfdan, but he may have arrived in York later on. Before Guthfrith, the people of York were subordinate to the kings of other regions, without a leader of their own, but towards the end of the ninth century, it was decided that they should pick one of their own to run the province. Guthfrith was already a Christian and this is likely to have swayed the election in his favour. Halfdan had driven out the monks of Durham; Guthfrith's reign saw their return. It was also marked by improved relations between the Vikings and the Angles. On his death, Guthfrith was buried in York Minster.

LEFT: Henry I
ABOVE: Edward I
ABOVE RIGHT: Llwelynap Gruffudd

GWYNEDD, HOUSE OF

One of the leading Welsh kingdoms during the Middle Ages, Gwynedd's heartlands were Anglesey and Snowdonia in North-West Wales, but from the ninth century onwards its borders extended occasionally to the east and down to the south of Wales.

With their origins stretching back to the days of the Romans, by the sixth century the Gwynedd kings were well established. However, it was only after Rhodri Mawr (Rhodri the Great) succeeded his father, Merfyn Frych, in AD 844 that Gwynedd became a national power. Extending his kingdom to take in all but the south-east and south-west tips of Wales, by AD 872 Rhodri had taken control of approximately two thirds of a country still regularly attacked by Vikings based in Ireland and on the Isle of Man.

After Rhodri's death in AD 878, Gwynedd's large kingdom was divided in two, Cadell reigning in Deheubarth in the south with his elder brother, Anarawd, reigning in Gwynedd in the north. The two kingdoms then remained more or less separate entities, although Gwynedd rulers such as Gruffudd ap Llywelyn and Owain Gwynedd reigned briefly over much of Wales.

Llywelyn ap Iorweth (Iorweth the Great) and Llywelyn ap Gruffudd (Llywelyn the Last) were similarly successful in the thirteenth century, but the overwhelming force of the English king, Edward I, finally ended the era of Gwynedd and its long line of kings.

Dafydd ap Gruffudd enjoyed six months as king of Gwynedd, but with his execution in October 1283, the kingdom he had so briefly ruled over was no more. Formally broken up the following year by the Statute of Rhuddlan, from 1294 Gwynedd disappeared to be replaced by three English-style counties: Anglesey, Caernarfonshire and Merioneth.

HALFDAN II (d. AD 910)

King of York (*c.* AD 902–10). Halfdan is belived to have been a joint ruler of the Viking kingdom of Jorvik (York), with Eowils, but little is really known of his reign, or indeed his status. There remains doubt about whether he a king at all. However, what is clear is that this was a troubled time in Northumbria and in AD 909 Ethelflaed, the 'Lady of the Mercians', removed the relics of St Oswald from the area, for safekeeping. This was the period in which Edward the Elder attempted to bring the northern Danes under his control – a time characterised by invasion and battle.

))))➤ *Edward the Elder, Ethelflaed*

HANOVER, HOUSE OF (1714–1901)

The ruling British dynasty from the moment George I succeeded his cousin, Queen Anne, right up to the death of the sixth and last Hanoverian monarch, Victoria.

George I ascended the throne on 1 August 1714, just a few weeks after the death of his mother, Sophia, the Electress of Hanover. Until her death, she had been the likely successor to the last Stuart sovereign, Anne, Sophia having filled that role since 1701 when the Act of Settlement passed by the English parliament ensured that there would be a Protestant monarch after Anne's death. The Act declared that if Anne died leaving no legitimate heir to the throne, then the head of the House of Hanover would succeed her, because Sophia and her son, George, were direct descendants of James VI and I.

A Stuart king, James's eldest daughter, Elizabeth, had married Frederick, the Elector Palatine of the Rhine, in 1613. Later, the couple became the parents of a large family that included a daughter, Sophia, who in time married the Elector of Hanover and gave birth to the son who was later crowned George I.

The great-grandson of James I, like his Stuart ancestor the first Hanoverian monarch arrived in England as a middle-aged man, one who had ruled in a very different political environment. George I also had to face the Jacobite threat that had troubled the later Stuart monarchs, but his prickly relationship with his eldest son and heir proved to be a hereditary Hanoverian problem.

When George I died he was succeeded by his eldest son, George II. Born in Hanover, he became the last British monarch to lead an army into battle, while his brother, the Duke of Cumberland, brutally cut down Bonnie Prince Charlie's Jacobites at Culloden. Frederick, the eldest son of George II, was a thorn in the king's side, but he died before his father, who was later succeeded by Frederick's son, George III.

The first Hanoverian sovereign to be born in Britain, no British king before George III ever lived to so great an age or reigned for so long. A lover of music, books and agriculture, Farmer George was a committed king, who was greatly depressed when the American War of Independence was lost in 1783.

Later the outbreak of the French Revolution led to Britain waging war on the new republic of France. Beginning in 1793

ABOVE: George III
RIGHT: The Brighton Pavilion, a Hanoverion splendour.
FAR RIGHT: Victoria and four previous generations

THE HOUSE OF HANOVER

1714–27	George I
1727–60	George II
1760–1820	George III
1820–30	George IV
1830–37	William IV
1837–1901	Victoria

and ending in 1802, the peace was short-lived as in 1803 the Napoleonic Wars commenced. These lasted 12 years in all, yet by the time the efforts of Nelson, Wellington and others had defeated Napoleon Bonaparte, George III had been overtaken by insanity.

His son, George, was appointed Prince Regent in 1811, a position he held until his father's death in 1820, when he ascended the throne as George IV. A playboy, who had frittered away a fortune, the fourth Hanoverian king was an unpopular figure, whose 10-year reign ended with his death in 1830.

George IV's younger brother, William IV, was already 64 years old when he became king. A naval man, like his elder brother he died without producing a legitimate heir and was therefore succeeded by his niece, Victoria.

Queen for 63 years, Victoria reigned at a time when Britain was galvanised by the Industrial Revolution. The Victorian era was also the age of empire, Britian's colonies at this time in her history stretched over one quarter of the world's land mass. Married to Prince Albert, after his early death the queen shunned public life for many years, but later re-emerged to be proclaimed Empress of India.

A mother of many children, who married spouses from far and near, Queen Victoria died in 1901, precisely 200 years after the English parliament had passed the Act of Settlement, the very Act that had paved the way for the accession of the first Hanoverian sovereign. The last monarch of the House of Hanover, Victoria was succeeded by her eldest son, Edward VII, the only British monarch to reign as a member of the House of Saxe-Coburg-Gotha.

EVENTS OF THE HANOVERIAN ERA

1715	Jacobite Rebellion
1739	Battle of Jenkins' Ear
1740	War of Austrian Succession begins
1743	Battle of Dettingen
1746	Battle of Culloden
1748	Treaty of Aix-la-Chapelle ends the War of the Austrian Succession
1763	Treaty of Paris ends the Seven Years War
1775	Battle of Bunker Hill in the American Revolution
1783	Britain recognises the independence of its former colonies in North America
1803	Outbreak of the Napoleonic Wars
1805	Battle of Trafalgar
1815	Battle of Waterloo
1853	Crimean War breaks out
1899	British refusal to withdraw troops from Transvaal border sparks Boer War

HAROLD I (c. 1016–40)

King of England (1037–40); son of Cnut; known as 'Harefoot'. Harold I was appointed regent for his absent half-brother, Harthacnut, when his father died in 1035. The following year Alfred, son of Ethelred the Unready, was blinded and killed. Harold was proclaimed king in 1037, but died three years later and was succeeded by Harthacnut.

The second son of Cnut and Elgifu of Northampton, in 1035 Harold succeeded his father as regent while Harthacnut remained in Denmark where he was king. Ruling England on behalf of his half-brother, Harthacnut, it was also agreed that Harold's stepmother, Queen Emma, would control Wessex. However, this arrangement lasted less than two years, Harold's cause helped considerably by Harthacnut's continued absence.

Acknowledged as king in 1037, his accession led to Emma's departure for Flanders, her flight probably hastened by the brutal treatment handed out the previous year to her son Alfred. The eldest of her two sons by Ethelred II the Unready, Alfred had travelled to see his mother in 1036, but had been taken prisoner, brutally blinded and left to die from his injuries.

Meanwhile, as Harold I assumed full control, Harthacnut sailed to meet his mother, Emma, at Bruges. Arriving there with his fleet late in 1039, still he made no move to claim the English throne. On 17 March 1040, the unmarried and childless Harold died at Oxford and Harthacnut succeeded unopposed. His half-brother's body was buried at St Clement Dane's Church in London, but legend has it that Harthacnut gave instructions for it to be dug up and thrown into a nearby marsh.

⟫➤ Cnut, Harthacnut

RIGHT: Harold is killed by William the Conqueror
BOTTOM RIGHT: Solemn audience accorded to Harold II

HAROLD II (c. 1020–66)

King of England (1066); brother-in-law of Edward the Confessor. Harold II was England's last Anglo-Danish king. The son of Godwin, Earl of Wessex, he succeeded Edward the Confessor in January 1066. The leading English noble before his accession, he was king for just nine months. Killing his brother, Tostig, and Harald Hardrada at Stamford Bridge in September 1066, less than three weeks later Harold II was killed at the Battle of Hastings. Possibly shot in the eye by an arrow, Harold's death was followed later by the coronation of his Norman conqueror: William I.

Born in 1020 or thereabouts Harold was the son of Godwin, Earl of Wessex, and Gytha, a great-granddaughter of King Harald Bluetooth of Denmark. One of several sons in a large and powerful English family, Harold was also the brother of Edith, who married Edward the Confessor in 1045. Gaining lands and titles, soon after his sister's marriage Earl Harold ruled over much of eastern England.

Falling from favour when his father and family were sent into exile by the king in 1051, Harold returned in 1052 intent on restoring his family's fortunes. It was part of a large force that converged on London and a pitched battle was averted when a hasty peace deal was agreed. The following year Harold's star continued to rise when his father's death saw him become Earl of Wessex; Berkshire and Somerset also coming under his rule. In 1055, Harold's brother, Tostig, was made Earl of Northumbria.

Consolidating his position as the leading English nobleman during the next decade, this was a period in which the question of who would succeed Edward the Confessor was often asked. There

HAROLD HAREFOOT

attack followed, but soon the city was forced to negotiate a peace treaty. A few days then passed before Harold II arrived in the north of England. At the head of his army, England's king attacked his Norwegian counterpart at Stamford Bridge, near York on 25 October 1066. The fighting continued until Harald Hardrada, Tostig and many Norwegian warriors were dead. Harold had secured an important victory but there was little time to savour this success; news soon came through that a large Norman army had landed on England's south coast.

Immediately marching his battle-weary troops back to London, he stopped in London just long enough to recruit more men. In Sussex by 13 October 1066, the following morning Duke William struck the first blow of the Battle of Hastings. In the fighting that followed the king's brothers, Gyrth and Leofwine, were slain. Then, as dusk descended, Harold himself was fatally wounded by an enemy arrow (which may or may not have struck him in the eye). His men fought on, but by nightfall, William of Normandy had won a momentous victory.

His wife, Eldgyth, and his son, Harold, outlived the last Anglo-Danish king, who also left behind a large number of illegitimate children, whose mother, Edith Swan-Neck, reputedly buried the body of Harold II at Waltham Abbey in Essex.

)))))▶ *Edward the Confessor, William I*

were several strong contenders including William, Duke of Normandy, and Edgar the Atheling, but when the old king died on 5 January 1066, he was succeeded by Earl Harold, who was crowned the following day at Westminster Abbey.

Aware from the outset that he would face challenges to his rule, he expected his brother, Tostig, to retaliate following his dismissal as earl of Northumbria the previous year; the king of Norway Harald Hardrada was another likely opponent, as was William of Normandy. However, the first four months of his reign were peaceful. Tostig landed at Sandwich in Kent in May 1066, having earlier launched raids along England's south coast. However, as he sailed up the east coast his attacks petered out, but he would soon return. Meanwhile, Harald Hardrada was planning his attack and Duke William was recruiting more and more men to his invasion force.

In September 1066, Harald Hardrada landed on the East Yorkshire coast and marched his troops the short distance to York. An

HARTHACNUT (c. 1019–42)

King of England (1040–42); son of Cnut.
Harthacnut was king of Denmark from 1028 and succeeded his father as king of England in 1035. Detained in Denmark, his half-brother, Harold, acted as regent in England until 1037 when he declared himself king. Harthacnut succeeded Harold I Harefoot when the latter died in 1040 without a son and heir. Reigning only two years before his own death, Harthacnut's passing led to the accession of a second half-brother: Edward the Confessor.

The son of Cnut and his second wife, Emma, the widow of Ethelred II the Unready, he was still a boy when he became King of Denmark in 1028. Two years later his half-brother, Svein, ascended the throne of Norway, while in 1035 Cnut's death saw him recognised as his father's successor in England.

However, Harthacnut was pre-occupied with the threat posed to Denmark by the new Norwegian ruler, King Magnus. As a result, his half-brother, Harold gradually asserted control in England until finally proclaimed King Harold I in 1037. However, just as Harthacnut was poised to launch an invasion attempt, Harold's early death on 17 March 1040 gave Harthacnut a second chance to become the English monarch.

Sailing to England at the head of an impressively large fleet of 62 warships, on his arrival he was duly crowned at Canterbury Cathedral on 18 June 1040. Two summers later, though, Harthacnut was dead, his short reign clouded by the hostility and murders that followed the imposition of taxes intended to pay for the upkeep of the king's vast armada of ships.

Dying on 8 June 1042, while enjoying himself at a wedding feast in Lambeth, London, the unpopular Anglo-Danish king was buried at Winchester and was succeeded by his half-brother, Edward the Confessor, the younger son of Queen Emma and Ethelred II the Unready.

➤ *Cnut, Edward the Confessor, Ethelred II*

HENRY I (1068–1135)

King of England (1100–35); son of William I.
Succeeding his brother, William II, as England's king in 1100, Henry I successfully defeated and imprisoned his eldest brother, Robert, to claim Normandy six years later. An able ruler, he was the brother-in-law of the Scots' king, Edgar. His son, William, drowned and his daughter, Matilda, became heir to the throne. Henry's successor was his nephew, Stephen.

Born at Selby, Yorkshire, in September 1068 or thereabouts, he was the youngest son of William the Conqueror and Matilda. Given an excellent education, his intellectual prowess gave rise to the respectful nickname Beauclerc (meaning 'fine scholar'). Only 13 or 14 years old at the time of his mother's death, she left her much-loved son her English land. However, when his father died in 1087 Henry was left a mountain of money, but his promised kingdoms went to his two elder brothers. Nineteen years old when his brother, William II, was crowned king of England, he spent the next 13 years fighting for or against William and his eldest brother, Robert, Duke of Normandy. Eventually, because of this, Henry was excluded from the line of succession to the English throne.

Henry was not deterred by this rebuff and on 2 August 1100 he struck. In the south of England that day, by luck or design he was ideally placed to take advantage of William Rufus's death while hunting in the New Forest. Perhaps the king was killed by a wayward arrow or maybe Henry had arranged for his brother to be killed. Either way, the moment he knew William was dead he hurried to Winchester, safe in the knowledge that his other brother, Robert, was still making his way back to Normandy after going on crusade in the Holy Land. Arriving in Winchester he took control of the

ABOVE: Harthacnut, son of Cnut

RIGHT: Henry I with picture of son who died in the wreck of the White Ship

treasury. Next heading for London, on 6 August 1100 he was crowned king at Westminster Abbey.

The first months of the new reign were busy ones. Three months after his coronation Henry I married Matilda (also known as Edith), the sister of the Scots' king, Edgar. He also arranged alliances with France and Flanders, which provided extra security in the likely event of an attack from, his brother Robert. The following year that attack duly came, but all-out war was avoided as Duke Robert returned to Normandy with a settlement worth a sum equivalent to £2,000 a year.

A dynamic, powerful figure with thick black hair, Henry I was reputed to be a king who ruled with a rod of iron, a king who once threw a man to his death from the top of a tower. There was, however, much more to the third Norman king than force and violence, his intellect, drive and clear-headed approach to justice and the administration of his realm made his kingship a notable success. So, as well as earning the nickname Beauclerc, he was also termed the Lion of Justice. Thus, Henry's reign was remarkable for the way in which the judicial system was overhauled: severe punishments were issued and the death penalty was restored for crimes against property. His chief administrator was Roger, Bishop of Salisbury, and it was he who oversaw the collection of revenue by officials, who extended the reach of royal taxation and legislation as never before. Taxation on this scale could not be levied without support, however, and so Henry ensured that loyalty to the crown by powerful magnates was appropriately rewarded.

The king's control was consolidated in other ways, too. A canny man in affairs of state, his many love affairs produced more illegitimate children than have been attributed to any other English king. Yet even illegitimate daughters played a part in securing beneficial alliances and so Henry married off no fewer than eight daughters born out of wedlock. In stark contrast, his first marriage yielded just two children: Matilda and a son and heir, William. With the latter's birth in 1203 the succession issue seemed guaranteed, but a shipwreck in 1120 claimed the life of William and two of Henry's illegitimate children. Coming just two years after the death of the king's wife Matilda, the wreck of the White Ship severely jeopardised the king's ability to secure his line.

He married again in 1122, but his second wife, Adela of Louvain, did not give birth to any children until her second marriage. His options becoming increasingly limited, the king attempted to name his daughter as his successor. But the death of her husband, Henry V of Germany, in 1125 and her subsequent marriage to Geoffrey of Anjou made that an unlikely prospect: most Norman and English earls were hostile to the Angevins. The king did somehow manage to win the barons round and Matilda was accepted as heir to the throne.

Henry I died in 1135 at St Denis-le-Fermont, near Rouen in Normandy. This location was significant for at the time of his death the 67-year-old king was based in his ancestral duchy, where he spent a large part of his reign as English king. That he was able to live in Normandy at all was thanks to his victory at the Battle of Tinchebrai in 1106, a triumph made all the more satisfying by the capture of his brother, Robert, and other powerful lords.

With Robert kept under lock and key at Cardiff Castle, where he was doomed to remain until his death in 1134, and with Normandy under his command despite the threat posed by Robert's son, William Clito, Henry's control in England and his alliances with neighbouring dynasties meant that he was able to turn his attention to the dangers posed to Normandy by Flanders, France and Anjou.

Dying on 1 December 1135 a short time after eating lampreys (a favourite fish dish), the body of Henry I was brought back to England to be interred at Reading Abbey. The only English king to born and buried in England in the long period separating the reigns of Harold II and John, his 35-year reign was the longest since that of Ethelred the Unready more than a century before. Despite his long and successful kingship Henry I was succeeded not by his daughter, Matilda, but by his nephew, Stephen.

)))➧ *Matilda, Stephen, William I, William II*

HENRY II (1133–89)

King of England (1154–89); grandson of Henry I and the first Plantagenet king. Succeeding Stephen in 1154, as English king he also ruled successfully over a vast Continental empire. Thomas Becket was murdered during his reign, which was also notable for military campaigns in Scotland, Wales and Ireland. Henry II 'crowned' his son, Henry the Young King, and

survived a rebellion led by his wife and three sons, including the future kings Richard I, who succeeded him, and John.

The son of Geoffrey, Count of Anjou, and the Empress Matilda, the daughter of Henry I, he was born at Le Mans in Anjou on 4 March 1133. Just two years old when his grandfather, Henry I, died, as a boy the younger Henry was caught up in the fight for the English crown that was fought by his mother and King Stephen. At 14 years of age he made his first attempt at deposing Stephen, yet a short time later he achieved his goal without bloodshed: the ageing king chose Henry as his heir on the understanding that his own son, William, would be allowed to retain his estates.

Following the death of Stephen on 25 October 1154, the crown passed unchallenged to Henry II. The grandson of Henry I, at the time of his accession he was also Count of Anjou, Duke of Normandy and Duke of Aquitaine. So, at the age of just 21, he began his reign as England's first Plantagenet (or Angevin) king at the head of a mighty empire.

One of his first tasks as king was to assert control over a realm, that had been ravaged by civil war for much of his predecessor's reign. In addition, he set about capturing land that had earlier been lost to the Scots and the Welsh. More successful in the north, he regained Northumbria from Malcolm IV and later captured Malcolm's successor, William the Lion. Meanwhile, he sent forces into Wales in 1157, his men waging war there with the kings, Owain of Gwynedd and Rhys ap Gruffudd of Deheubarth.

Henry was also active in Ireland. Postponing a campaign he had planned in 1155, the year Pope Adrian IV had given his blessing for an attack on the heretic Irish Church, he did launch an attack in 1166. Then in 1171 a follow-up campaign ended with Irish kings acknowledging Henry II as Lord of Ireland. At home, the English heartland was untroubled by war until 1173, when the king's wife and three of his sons turned on their father forcing him to take up arms. Henry and his sons were reconciled in 1174, although Henry remained at daggers drawn with his queen and so after 1173 Eleanor of Aquitaine was often imprisoned.

The king's problems with his sons contrasted sharply with the very different problems of his three immediate predecessors. Not one of these men had been succeeded by a son, yet Henry II was cursed with a surfeit of male children. Marrying Eleanor of Aquitaine in May 1152, the couple's first son was born in 1153 just before Henry was crowned King of England. William did not survive infancy, but seven more legitimate children were born, including four sons. Dividing his territory between his sons, it was decided that Richard would be granted Aquitaine, Geoffrey would rule in Brittany, John would reign over Ireland, while the eldest boy, Henry, would inherit England, Anjou and Normandy. To this end Henry II arranged the unprecedented crowning of Prince Henry. The only incidence of an heir being crowned in the lifetime of a living English sovereign, it was this coronation that hastened Thomas Becket's fateful return from exile.

Once the best of friends, Henry had made Becket his Chancellor in 1155, elevating him to the position of Archbishop of Canterbury seven years later. However, the king and the archbishop later fell out. Leaving England for France in 1164, Becket returned home at the end of 1170. Days later he was dead. Perhaps the king complained about Becket, perhaps he did utter those famous words, 'Will no-one rid me of this turbulent priest?'. All that is certain is that four knights killed the archbishop on 29 December 1170. Becket's death deeply affected Henry II, who later did penance

at Canterbury Cathedral, the very place where the martyred Becket had been slain.

In the years after Becket's murder, Henry was often forced on to the back foot. During the mid-1170s there was a period of stability, but when his sons reached maturity, so territorial disputes began. The situation was further clouded by the deaths of Henry the Young King in 1183 and Geoffrey in 1186, while the old king suffered further setbacks when both Richard and John again took sides against their father.

Known as Curtmantle because of the distinctive, Continental-style cloak he liked to wear, Henry II is widely recognised as one of England's greatest monarchs. Yet like his grandfather before him and his son and successor, Richard I, he spent years as an absentee ruler. He is also best-remembered for the murder of Becket, but still the reputation of Henry II rises above such paradoxes. A dynamic ruler, able in mind and body, he was an energetic, powerful, sometimes volatile ruler. A successful warrior-king in his early years, his reign was also notable for the development of English common law, with many new processes being established.

Dying on 6 July 1189 at Chinon Castle in the heart of his Angevin territory, he was buried at Fontevraud Abbey and was succeeded by his son, Richard I.

))))➤ *John, Richard I, Stephen*

TOP RIGHT: Meeting between Philip II, Capetian king of France and Henry II

CENTRE RIGHT: Henry II as featured in a manuscript

HENRY III (1207-72)

King of England (1216–72); son of John. Henry III succeeded his father in 1216 and among English sovereigns only George III and Victoria have reigned longer than his 56 years. A boy at the time of his accession, his regents successfully expelled the French forces then occupying eastern England. Henry was unlucky in foreign affairs and at home Simon de Montfort led a rebellion in which Henry was captured. He was later freed and restored to the throne. On his death he was succeeded by his son, Edward I.

Born at Winchester on 1 October 1207, the eldest son of King John and his second wife, Isabella, Henry III succeeded his father when he was just nine years old. At the time of John's death in October 1216, much of eastern England was ruled over by Louis, the Dauphin of France. So, with London under French control, Henry III was crowned in a hurried ceremony held on 28 October 1216 at Gloucester Cathedral, rather than Westminster Abbey. Yet from such unpromising beginnings a reign unfolded that was notable for the absence of power struggles like those that had tainted life under John.

More remarkable still was the speed with which the king's regents, William the Marshal and Hubert de Burgh, successfully won back the territories snatched by Louis of France. Decisive victories in battles at Lincoln and off Dover effectively defeated the dauphin during 1217, a year that saw the unrest among the barons further diminished when Henry III signed an amended version of the famous Magna Carta. The original charter demanding concessions and changes in practice had been put before his father two years earlier.

LEFT: Henry and Philip of Spain embrace following the peace of Chateau Cambresis
RIGHT: Gold Penny showing Henry III
BOTTOM: The coronation of Henry III

Later, the young king enjoyed a second coronation. Staged on 17 May 1220 at Westminster Abbey, the choice of this great church was an apt one for a king who later would devote so much time, love and money to religious buildings such as Edward the Confessor's abbey church. Assuming full control over his kingdom seven years after he had been crowned for the second time, his early years as sole ruler were quiet enough, at least on the home front.

Henry III was the fourth king of the Plantagenet era and the dynasty's once-mighty empire had shrunk during the reign of King John. Henry's inheritance was small and getting smaller. When Henry III came of age the only French territory still held by the English Crown was the small province of Gascony. Yet, as England's dominions became ever fewer, so the influence of foreigners at the king's court grew, following the king's wedding in 1236. Marrying Eleanor of Provence, in time this marriage produced a large family including a son and heir, the future Edward I. In the short-term, though, English barons came to resent the growing number of Frenchmen taken into the monarch's inner circle.

The barons fired a shot across Henry's bows in 1234 when their anger forced him to dismiss the Bishop of Winchester, Peter des Roches, and his foreign aides, so staving off the threat of insurrection. However, friction remained as the king floundered. An unworldly, pious figure, many of his domestic policies antagonised, while a foreign policy that limped from one capitulation to another was epitomised in 1254 by the king's failed attempt to gain Sicily for his son, Edmund.

In 1258, as the patience of England's magnates continued to be tested, Henry III was reined in. First came the Provisions of Oxford in October 1258; they were followed exactly one year later by the Provisions of Westminster. The concessions the monarch made included an agreement to convene parliament at least three times a year. In addition, Henry agreed that future kings' councils would comprise an even split of his choices and magnates' men. For the next few years an uneasy truce was kept, but then, with the rise to prominence of the king's own brother-in-law, Simon de Montfort, came the descent into war.

The first exchanges took place early in 1264. However, the decisive battle was fought on 4 August 1265 at Evesham, where royalist troops, commanded by Prince Edward, defeated and killed de Montfort. They also freed the king, who had been held captive by his enemies since the Battle of Lewes some 14 months previously. With Henry III restored to the throne the last seven years of his reign proved uneventful.

A devoutly religious king, with a passion for architecture, Henry III was responsible for a spectacular burst of church building and rebuilding in an age that witnessed the birth of a new architectural style: Gothic. Art, too, attracted Henry's attention, while he also amassed a collection of exotic animals. Generally seen as a good man, but a poor king, who nonetheless wore England's crown for 56 years, he died on 16 November 1272 at Westminster. Buried in the abbey there, the great cathedral that Henry III himself had so lovingly rebuilt, he was succeeded by the eldest of his nine children, Edward I.

))) *Edward I, Edward the Confessor, John*

HENRY IV (1366–1413)

King of England (1399–1413); grandson of Edward III and the first Lancastrian king. Henry overthrew his cousin, Richard II, in 1399, but his short reign was marked by conflict and revolts. Among his main opponents were the Percy family, including Hotspur, and Owain Glyndwr. Embattled to the last he was succeeded by his eldest surviving son, Henry V.

The only child of John of Gaunt, son of Edward III and Blanche of Lancaster, Henry was born at Bolingbroke Castle, Lincolnshire, on 3 or 4 April 1366. A cousin of Richard II, in 1377 the 12-year-old Henry attended the coronation of the king he would later depose. Three years later Henry married Mary de Bohun. His first wife and the mother of his seven children, she died in childbirth on 4 July 1394. By that time, Henry Bolingbroke had already flexed his muscles as one of England's most powerful nobles by opposing Richard II, even fighting and defeating the king's men in battle in 1387.

In 30 January 1398 Bolingbroke was accused of committing treason by Thomas Mowbray, Earl of Norfolk. As tensions mounted, a duel between the

two nobles was arranged. However, before it could be staged, Richard II intervened to send both men into exile. Heading for France, Henry returned to England in July 1399 intent on taking back the estates of his late father, which the king had confiscated.

Once back on home soil he joined forces with the powerful Percy family and other northern barons. The rebels soon took control and although Henry Bolingbroke's claim to the throne was weak the Lancastrian armies were strong and by the end of 1399 Henry had become king. Striking while Richard II was away in Ireland attempting to crush a revolt there, shortly after his return in August 1399 he was forced to surrender. On 29 September, Bolingbroke was recognised by parliament as King Henry IV.

Henry was crowned at Westminster Abbey on 13 October 1399 while Richard II still languished in prison. The new king had no time to settle into his new role, however. Opposition arose in the shape of the Welsh prince, Owain Glyndwr, who began a hostile campaign in Wales in 1400 that continued until 1415.

Meanwhile, Hotspur, one of the Percy family, had switched allegiance and now opposed the king. He was routed at Shrewsbury on 23 July 1403 by an army commanded by the king and his son, Prince Hal. Yet despite such battlefield victories opposition continued to mount behind leaders such as the Earl of Northumberland and

ABOVE: Gold Noble showing Henry IV
LEFT: Cartoon version of Henry IV from Shakespeare's play
RIGHT: Henry IV is presented with a book by Occleve
BOTTOM RIGHT: Henry V crosses the Somme during the Battle of Agincourt

two influential men of York: the duke and the archbishop. There were plots, too, and France and Scotland were troublespots, while in 1411 even his son, Henry, Prince of Wales, was barred from the king's court.

Weighed down throughout his reign by an endless round of revolts and, it is claimed, wracked with guilt for the way in which he had come to be king, Henry spent his last years beleaguered and ill. He passed away on 20 March 1413 in the Jerusalem Chamber of Westminster Abbey. Henry IV was buried at Canterbury Cathedral.

)))▶ *Henry V, Owain Glyndwr, Richard II*

HENRY V (1387–1422)

King of England (1413–22); son of Henry IV. Henry V is remembered as the archetypal medieval warrior-king. Famously triumphant against the French at Agincourt in 1415, he was later recognised as heir to Charles VI, King of France. Marrying Catherine in 1420, Henry V died two years later, leaving only his infant son to take up the reins of power.

Born at Monmouth in September 1387, he was the second son of Henry Bolingbroke and his first wife, Mary de Bohun. Soon after his birth his father took to fighting the forces of Richard II at Radcot Bridge. Henry's mother died before he was seven years old; at the age of 12 his

father became king and he gained the title, Prince of Wales. It was in Wales that he learned the tactics of war before entering the fray at the Battle of Shrewsbury in 1403, a conflict in which he lined up against his former guardian, Harry Hotspur. Helping his father win that battle, after leading the struggle in Wales against Owain Glyndwr, Prince Hal became an increasingly influential figure at the royal court.

In fact, with Henry IV a sick and troubled man, the younger man asserted himself to such an extent that there was much talk of the king abdicating or being overthrown. Forced into the background for a spell, on 20 March 1413 the king died and Henry V ascended the throne. Crowned at the age of 25, Henry was already an accomplished man-of-war. His first test came in 1414, when a revolt by a religious sect known as the Lollards was put down. Then, in the following year, nobles supporting Edmund Mortimer, Earl of March, were stopped in their tracks as they pressed the earl's claims to be king. A short time later Henry V set sail for France.

Reaching the northern coast, the English king stood poised on the threshold of greatness as he prepared, with the support of Burgundy, to recapture the lands lost in France during the last years of the Angevin kings. First to fall was Harfleur, which had resisted stubbornly despite being besieged for five weeks. In contrast, the Battle of Agincourt was won by Henry V in the course of one momentous day. After capturing Harfleur, the English force had marched through north-western Normandy before finally arriving in late October at Agincourt, where they came face to face with a vast French army. Weary and with a far smaller army, on 25 October 1415 Henry won a famous victory, losing less than 500 men while cutting down some 7,000 enemy soldiers.

Retaining the initiative Henry V returned to France in 1417 to begin the recapture of Normandy. Then, in 1419, the English seized Rouen, the city where the heart of Richard I had been buried more than two centuries earlier. All that then remained was for a peace deal, the Treaty of Troyes, to be ratified. With this treaty ratified in 1420, the peace between England and France was sealed by the marriage of Henry to Catherine of Valois, daughter of the French king, Charles VI, who also confirmed Henry as his successor. Henry married Catherine at Troyes on 2 June 1420. Just 14 months later he was dead.

Struck down by dysentery in August 1422, he passed away at Vincennes in France. Buried at Westminster Abbey, Shakespeare's hero was survived by his young wife and succeeded by his baby son, Henry VI.

))➤ *Henry IV, Henry VI*

HENRY VI (1421–71)

King of England (1422–61, 1470–71); son of Henry V and the last Lancastrian king. Succeeding his father before he was one year old, within weeks he was also king of France. Crowned as French monarch in 1431, Henry had Normandy and Gascony claimed back from him by the

French heroine, Joan of Arc. Later defeated in the Wars of the Roses by the Yorkists, he was restored to the throne in 1470, but his 're-adeption' was brief. Murdered in 1471, shortly after his son was killed in battle, Henry VI was succeeded for the second time by Edward IV.

The only child of Henry V and Catherine of Valois, daughter of the French king, Charles VI, he was born at Windsor Castle on 6 December 1421. King of England at the age of eight months, by the time Henry was nine months old he was the king of France. Still in the cradle at the time of his father's early death, initially the young Henry VI was looked after by his mother with responsibility for government placed in the hands of two men: his uncles, Humphrey, Duke of Gloucester, who became regent in England, and John, Duke of Bedford, who took charge in France. There, Bedford's troops continued to make headway, achieving notable victories at Cravant in 1423 and at Verneuil in 1424, while later English successes led to the coronation of Henry as king of France. Taking place at Nôtre Dame, Paris, in December 1431, this service came two years after his English coronation at Westminster Abbey on 5 or 6 November 1429. Yet even as Henry was crowned in France the backlash against his rule there had already begun. Inspired by Joan of Arc and aided by the defection to the French cause of Burgundy, France had started to reclaim lost territory.

Assuming the reins of power in 1437, Henry's approach to kingship was in keeping with his character: personally generous; politically naïve. Often dismissed as a bad king, Henry VI was a kindly, deeply Christian man, who dressed plainly. He was interested in the mind as well as the spirit and during the 1440s he founded both Eton College and King's College, Cambridge. It was also in this period that the king wed his queen, the 15-year-old Margaret of Anjou, in April 1445. The couple's solitary child was born in 1453. Christened Edward, the boy's birth came at a

BOTTOM LEFT: Miniature from the Maresse code
ABOVE: John Lidgate, monk and author presenting book to Henry VI
BOTTOM RIGHT: Surrender of Harfleur to Henry VI in Hundred Years War

Queen Margaret. Taking the fight to Duke Richard, in 1459 her forces defeated the Yorkist army at Ludlow in Shropshire. The respite was brief. In 1460, Margaret's army was soundly beaten at the Battle of Northampton and a short time later Duke Richard was formally appointed as Henry VI's rightful heir. The queen then attacked again, winning at Wakefield on 30 December 1460, the battle claiming the life of Richard, Duke of York.

Still the war raged and in March 1461 the Duke of York's son was proclaimed king. Edward IV was crowned in London and the capital remained set against Margaret and her mostly northern troops. Less than four weeks after his accession, Edward then won a vital, vicious battle at Towton. Margaret and her young son fled into exile, Henry VI staying behind only to be taken prisoner in 1465. Henry VI was restored to the throne in October 1470, but all the power then lay with men such as the 'Kingmaker', Richard, Earl of Warwick. Cutting a sad figure Henry VI was doomed to reign but briefly second time around.

In 1471, Edward IV returned as king, sweeping aside the last Lancastrian opposition, including King Henry's son, Edward, who was killed at the Battle of Tewkesbury on 4 May. Then, on 21 May at the Tower of London, Henry VI died, aged 49. In all probability executed by the new Yorkist regime. In death, as in the last years of life, there seemed to be no sanctuary for Henry VI and so the remains of the late king were buried first at Chertsey Abbey, then at St George's, Windsor. Later still, the coffin may have been taken for reburial at Westminster Abbey.
))))➤ *Henry V, Edward IV*

time when Henry VI suffered from his first bout of insanity and coincided with the fall of Gascony, Normandy having been lost in 1450. So, by 1453, England's only French territory was Calais.

The fall in fortunes across the Channel was mirrored at home. In 1450, a popular revolt in Kent led by John Cade followed soon after the murder of one of the king's favourites, William, Duke of Suffolk, and it was in this year that Richard, Duke of York, abandoned his post as Lieutenant of Ireland. In England only the king owned more land than the Duke of York, the man who would soon become a key figure in the war that erupted between the houses of Lancaster and York. Initially, Richard was appointed Protector until Henry VI had recovered from a bout of insanity, but three months later, in May 1455, the Battle of St Albans was fought, so beginning the Wars of the Roses. With victory going to the Yorkists, the Duke of York started his second term as Protector.

Although the fortunes of the two rival houses then ebbed and flowed, one constant was the cameo role of Henry VI, with the leading actors in this brutal drama being the Duke of York and the king's tenacious wife,

Born at Pembroke Castle, Wales, on 27 or 28 January 1457, Henry VII was the only child of Edmund Tudor, Earl of Richmond, and Margaret Beaufort, daughter of the Duke of Somerset. A child of the Wars of the Roses, which he would later bring to an end, Henry's birth occurred three months after the death of his Lancastrian father. Spending his early years in Wales, Henry was 14 years old when his uncle, Jasper Tudor, was defeated at Mortimer Cross. Just months later Edward IV became king and his return to power in 1471 was the signal for young Henry Tudor, the new head of the house of Lancaster, to hurry into a long exile abroad.

Heading for France, for the next 14 years he lived in Brittany. Continuing to plot the downfall of the house of York, in December 1483 at Rennes Cathedral Henry pledged to marry Elizabeth, the eldest daughter of Edward IV, whose brother, Richard III, had become England's king a short time before. Then, in the summer of 1485 he sailed to Milford Haven in South Wales. From there he moved across Wales and east into England, gathering support as he went until he reached the small Leicestershire town of Market Bosworth. There fighting and defeating an army commanded by Richard III himself, on 22 August 1485 Richard's death in battle and Henry's victory saw him proclaimed King Henry VII.

Crowned at Westminster Abbey on 30 October 1485, he was back at the abbey less than three months later when he fulfilled his promise to marry Elizabeth of York. However, the marriage of two of the leading members of the Lancastrian and Yorkist factions could not prevent the revolts that were a feature of the first years of the new reign.

HENRY VII (1457–1509)

King of England (1485–1509). Henry VII was descended from ancient Welsh rulers and became the first Tudor king. He ascended the throne in 1485 after killing Richard III at the Battle of Bosworth Field. Later defeating the challenges of the imposters, Perkin Warbeck and Lambert Simnel, he revived the fortunes of the crown. Married to Elizabeth, daughter of Edward IV, their daughter, Margaret, married James IV of Scotland. The king's heir, Arthur, died young and so Henry VII was succeeded by his third-born son, Henry VIII.

TOP LEFT: Henry VII before the altar
RIGHT: Henry VII with Empeson and Dudley

A nephew of Richard III, the young Earl of Warwick had been imprisoned in the Tower of London after Bosworth Field, yet in 1487 the imposter, Lambert Simnel, pretended to be Warwick and was hailed as Edward VI. Defeat at the Battle of Stoke in 1487 ended Simnel's time in the spotlight, but his place as pretender to the throne was then filled by Perkin Warbeck. Impersonating the younger of the two 'Princes in the Tower', he was hailed as Richard IV. However, when Warbeck and the real Earl of Warwick were executed the likelihood of Henry VII being deposed began to fade.

At last able to concentrate fully on ruling over his kingdom, Henry's attempt at invading France ended in 1492 with the Tudor king winning a lucrative peace settlement via the Treaty of Etaples. Domestically, too, his policies proved profitable, the king accumulating great wealth and power. Transforming his financial fortunes, during his reign customs' taxation increased by 100 per cent and income from crown lands also doubled as a hefty debt became a vast surplus, while the workings of the Royal Council and its offshoots proved highly effective in governing a peaceful realm.

The father of seven children, in 1501 Henry saw his son and heir, Arthur, wed Catherine, the daughter of Ferdinand and Isabella of Aragon. Then, in 1503, his eldest daughter, Margaret, married James IV of Scotland. However, while the sudden death of Prince Arthur in 1502 was a personal tragedy and created a dynastic problem, there was a silver lining of sorts as Arthur's widow was married to the king's third child, by then King Henry VIII.

Outliving his wife, Elizabeth, who had died in 1503, Henry VII spent his last years quietly, this solemnity contrasting with his earlier days when he had enjoyed outdoor sports, music and a host of other pastimes. Passing away on 21 April 1509 at Richmond, where a grand palace had been built for him, Henry VII was buried at Westminster Abbey and was succeeded as king by his son, Henry VIII.

))》 *Henry VIII, Richard III*

HENRY VIII (1491–1547)

King of England (1509–47); son of Henry VII. The second Tudor king, Henry succeeded his father in 1509. He was a catalyst for the English Reformation: breaking with Rome, becoming head of the English Church and dissolving the monasteries. Wars were fought with Scotland and France, an Act of Union formally linked England and Wales and Henry VIII was acknowledged as king of Ireland. Married six times, three children succeeded him: Edward VI, Mary I and Elizabeth I.

The second son of Henry VII and the former Elizabeth of York, Henry was born at Greenwich Palace on 28 June 1491. At the time of his birth his father had been monarch for nearly six years and had already sired a son and heir. This child was Arthur, Prince of Wales. Later married to Catherine of Aragon, just five months after their wedding in April 1502 Arthur was dead. From that time on the life of Henry, Duke of York would never be the same again. His brother's death left him as heir to the throne and seven years later, the young prince became Henry VIII.

Succeeding his father on 21 April 1509, he was crowned at Westminster Abbey on 24 June – just 13 days after he had married Arthur's 23-year-old widow Catherine of Aragon. The first of the six wives of Henry VIII, she was five years older than her second husband. Destined to lead a sad and unfulfilled life, her marriage to Henry was dogged by miscarriages and infant deaths with only one child, the future Mary I, surviving. Cast aside by her second husband, their marriage was eventually dissolved in 1533.

Having convinced himself that his marriage to his brother's widow was contrary to Divine law, Henry eventually wed his second wife, Anne Boleyn. The younger sister of one of the king's former mistresses, she was a high-spirited woman who knew her own mind. Marrying the king in 1533, she gave birth to a daughter, later Elizabeth I, but was soon found guilty of adultery, divorced and then beheaded in May 1536 – four months after Catherine of Aragon had died from illness.

Jane Seymour was the king's third wife. This daughter of a Wiltshire knight became England's queen the day after the execution of Anne Boleyn. Queen Jane gave birth to a son, the future Edward VI, in 1537, but died just 12 days later. Marrying again in January 1540 Henry's fourth wife was Anne of Cleves. However, the king soon divorced the 'Flanders mare' and in July 1540 wed his fifth wife. Attractive, but flighty, Catherine Howard was destined to fall as the sovereign's second had fallen: found guilty of adultery, she was executed in February 1542.

Last of all came Catherine Parr. A widow twice over, this educated woman became wife number six in 1543. A caring stepmother to Henry's three children, she outlived her third husband, dying in 1548.

Notoriously fickle concerning his many wives, Henry VIII also favoured and then dispensed with three chief ministers. Sir Thomas More was canny enough to know that Henry VIII would readily sacrifice him, saying 'if my head should win him [Henry] a castle in France ... it should not fail to go'. Lord Chancellor for three years from 1529, More's head did 'go' when he was executed, having been found guilty of committing high treason. Earlier, Thomas Wolsey had filled the role of Lord Chancellor. A much-disliked figure, the powerful and immensely wealthy Cardinal Archbishop of York had tried to gain the pope's consent for an annulment of Henry's marriage to Catherine of Aragon. However, by 1529 Wolsey was a spent force. Cast aside, by 1530 he was dead.

Yet, just as the butcher's son, Wolsey, fell, so Thomas Cromwell rose. The king's chief minister from 1534, his reforming influence was well to the fore as the monasteries were dissolved. But then, in 1540, he was sacrificed and, like More before him, was sentenced to death and beheaded. Earlier, Acts that Cromwell had steered through parliament enshrined in law the English sovereign's position as Supreme Head of the Church of England, thereby sweeping away the country's long-standing loyalty to the pope. In an age of faith this was revolution indeed. Pope Leo X had awarded Henry VIII the title *Fidei Defensor* ('Defender of the Faith') in 1521, yet the break with Rome was all but sealed by 1536.

That same year the Tudor monarch had continued his attack on the English Church. A survey of the nation's religious houses had revealed many abuses and so a full-scale dissolution was ordered. Confiscating the estates and vast wealth of the monasteries, most of which had owed their ultimate allegiance to the pope, by 1539 Henry VIII had legally ransacked around 560 religious houses. Henry sold most of the lands he seized, but a few remained in royal hands, some of these existing today as London's major parks.

ABOVE: Henry VIII with Anne of Cleves

PL. CXXXVIII.

A larger-than-life monarch, who was sometimes carefree, sometimes cruel, Henry VIII reigned for almost 38 eventful, often turbulent years when he died at the age of 55. Dying on 28 January 1547 at Whitehall, he was buried at St George's Chapel, Windsor and was succeeded by his nine year-old son Edward VI.

⟫⟫ *Edward VI, Elizabeth I, Henry VII, Mary I*

Best known for his marriages, his ministers and the assault on the monasteries, as well as for the break with Rome and for his role in ushering in the English Reformation, Henry VIII had begun his reign in a very different vein. An ambitious, virile and wealthy ruler, in 1509 he had been eager to prove himself as a warrior-king winning glory and territory in foreign lands.

In league with Spain and Venice in 1512, he had waged war against France, with the king himself leading his forces in 1513. That same year the Earl of Surrey won a victory over the Scots at Flodden, killing the Scottish king, James V. However, this was a rare battlefield success for Henry. The wars with France were costly failures, while the war with Spain, declared in 1528, never started. Not returning to this trail until the last years of his life, Henry VIII then spent vast sums pursuing wars with Scotland and France.

In 1536 Henry had sent troops to the north of England where a rebellion known as the Pilgrimage of Grace was brought to a brutal end. Elsewhere in the British Isles, the Welsh and Irish were suppressed more by decree than by bloodshed. The Act of Union of 1536 had formally linked England and Wales, while Henry VIII was acknowledged as king of Ireland by the Irish parliament in 1541 and by the English parliament in 1542.

HYWEL AP EDWIN (d. 1044)

King of Deheubarth (1033–44); son of Edwin. After the death of Rhydderch ap Iestyn in 1033 Hywel reigned jointly with his brother, Maredudd. However, when Maredudd died in 1035 he was left to rule alone. Later repelling attacks by Viking raiders, in 1042 Hywel was defeated by the Gwynedd king, Gruffudd ap Llywelyn. In exile for the next two years, on his return Hywel was killed in a battle fought beside the Towi river by Gruffudd, who then fought Gruffudd ap Rhydderch for control of Deheubarth.

⟫⟫ *Gruffudd ap Llewelyn, Gruffudd ap Rhydderch*

FAR LEFT: Henry VIII with Cranmer and Cromwell
CENTRE LEFT: Henry VIII
BELOW RIGHT: Hywel Dda proclaims the laws of Wales to the Welsh parliament

HYWEL AP IEUAF (d. AD 985)

King of Gwynedd (AD 974–85); son of Ieuaf. Hywel twice defeated his uncle, Iago ap Idwal, in battle, on the second occasion (in AD 979) with Viking assistance. Capturing and overthrowing Iago in that conflict, in AD 980 he resisted a counterattack by Iago's son, Cystenin. Dying in AD 985, he was briefly succeeded by his brother, Meurig. The last of Ieuaf's sons, he died in AD 985.

)))➤ *House of Deheubarth, Iago ap Idwal*

HYWEL DDA (d. AD 950)

King of Deheubarth (*c.* AD 908–50); son of Cadell ap Rhodri and grandson of Rhodri Mawr. Hywel Dda enjoyed a long and successful reign that began *c.* AD 909, the year of his father's death. Hywel 'the Good' gained control of Gwynedd in AD 942, four years after he had made a pilgrimage to Rome. He was best-known for codifying his country's laws, for expanding his realm and for his pro-English outlooks.

With his power-base in Ceredigion (Cardigan), Hywel forged an enduring alliance with the great English sovereign, King Athelstan, while at home in Wales the man who came to be called the 'head and glory of the Britons' eventually gained control in Dyfed, Gwynedd and Powys. Blessed with the same energy and drive as Rhodri Mawr, like his grandfather he also realised the advantages to be gained from securing a good marriage. So it was that he married Elen, the daughter of Llywarch ap Hafaidd, King of Dyfed, this marriage alliance gaining the Deheubarth king control over much of South Wales, while the death of his cousin, Idwal ap Anarawd, in AD 942 left the way clear for Hywel to assert his authority in Gwynedd. The south-eastern territory of Morgannwg (Glamorgan) remained elusive, but still his territorial gains made him the dominant power in Wales.

The first Welsh king known to have issued his own coinage, Hywel Dda also set about establishing throughout his realm a uniform system of laws. This codification programme began in AD 930 at Whitland in South-West Wales. A major advance, the laws covering six main legal areas were so well framed that they endured more or less unchanged right up to the invasion by England's Edward I almost four centuries later. Shrewd, sometimes ruthless, Hywel Dda died in AD 950 after ruling over his kingdom for 41 years. He was succeeded in Gwynedd by his son, Owain ap Hywel.

)))➤ *House of Gwynned, Owain ap Hywel, Rhodri Mawr*

IAGO AP IDWAL (d. c. AD 979)

King of Gwynedd (AD 950–79); son of Idwal ap Anarawd. Iago was forced out of Gwynedd by Hywel Dda following his father's death in AD 942. After eight years in exile Iago and his brother, Ieuaf, seized power. Feuding then broke out and Iago imprisoned Ieuaf in AD 969. Defeated by Ieuaf's son, Hywel, in AD 974, five years later Iago was finally captured and deposed by him.

Driven into exile after his father's death by his second cousin, Hywel Dda, and his English allies, Hywel's death in AD 950 gave Iago and his brother, Ieuaf, the opportunity to reclaim Gwynedd, which they did by defeating Hywel's son and successor, Owain. However, in the years that followed Iago's accession, a family feud led to years of unrest. Iago defeated and imprisoned Ieuaf in AD 969 to establish an authority over his kingdom, that was recognised four years later when Iago was one of the select band of British rulers that paid homage to England's King Edgar at Chester. Also present at that great royal gathering was Ieuaf's son, Hywel.

The following year the two rivals would meet again with the nephew, Hywel, defeating his uncle, Iago. Five years later Hywel ap Ieuaf won again to bring to an end)))➤ the long and difficult reign of Iago ap Idwal.

Hywel Dda, Idwal ap Anarawd, Hywel ap Ieuaf

IDWAL AP ANARAWD (d. AD 942)

King of Gwynedd (AD 916–42); son of Anarawd ap Rhodri and grandson of Rhodri Mawr. Also known as Idwal Foel (Idwal the Bald), it is thought he succeeded his father following Anarawd's death in AD 916. Together with other contemporary Welsh kings such as Hywel Dda of Deheubarth he paid homage to Athelstan, regularly visiting the great king of all England at his court. He also supported Athelstan in the attack that he launched against the Scots' king, Constantine II, in AD 934. Eight years later, Idwal's death brought to power his sons, Iago and Ieuaf, however they were soon driven from Gwynedd by Idwal's cousin, Hywel Dda.

)))➤ *Anarawd ap Rhodri, Constantine II, House of Deheubarth, Athelstan*

INDULF (d. AD 962)

King of Scots (AD 954–62); son of Constantine II. Indulf succeeded his cousin, Malcolm I, in AD 954 thanks to the tanistry system, which saw monarchs elected from the male successors of Indulf's own father and those of Donald II.

Previously ruler of the sub-kingdom of Strathclyde, during his eight-year reign as king of the Scots their kingdom was enlarged. Parts of Lothian were annexed, while one of Indulf's last conquests was the city of Edinburgh. Killed in AD 962 by Vikings, he was succeeded by Dub, who had earlier replaced him in Strathclyde. However, Dub's reign was brief as he was killed, possibly by Indulf's son, Culen.

)))➤ *Constantine II, Culen, Malcolm I*

INTERREGNUM (1649–60)

When Charles I was beheaded on 30 January 1649, his dramatic death marked not only the end of the Stuart king's life, but also the end of the English Civil War. What came next was an extraordinary period in British history. The way to a brave, new, republican world was cleared by Pride's Purge: an interregnum lasting 12 years. Overseen by Colonel Thomas Pride in December 1648, his purge forcibly expelled all members of parliament then in favour of holding further talks with the defeated king, Charles I. Within weeks of this purge the king had been tried and executed and a republican parliament had assumed power. Known as the Rump Parliament, this body of MPs governed for four years (1649–53), a period in which parliamentary forces under the leadership of Oliver Cromwell were brutally successful in Ireland and in Scotland.

A leading Roundhead figure during the civil war, in 1649 Cromwell and his army showed no mercy in conquering Ireland, overwhelming Drogheda and Wexford and massacring many innocent people in the process. Next Cromwell defeated supporters of Charles II, the son of Charles I, first routing a Scottish force at Dunbar in September 1650, then overpowering the Royalist army at Worcester in September 1651.

Two years later Oliver Cromwell enjoyed still more success as he dissolved the Rump Parliament and replaced it with what was known as the Nominated Assembly or the Barebones Parliament. However, this was a short-lived body, its more extreme members bringing about a change of direction, which saw Cromwell appointed Lord Protector as part of the new-style administration outlined in a paper entitled the 'Institute of Government'.

The Protectorate formed in the last days of 1653 lasted for six years in all. A period of foreign war, the first Anglo-Dutch conflict (1652–54), ended with little gained by either side, so war was declared on Spain in 1655. That same year a Royalist group made a failed attempt to re-establish the monarchy, while two years later Cromwell rejected the proposal contained in the 'Humble Petition and Advice' for him to become king. Meanwhile, reflecting the military flavour of the times, the Major Generals exercised great power, these commanders effectively ruling as lords in the 11 zones into which England was then divided.

Then, on 3 September 1658, the Puritan soldier–statesman, Oliver Cromwell, died. He was

succeeded by his son, Richard Cromwell, who was Lord Protector for just eight months. Dissolving parliament in April 1659, the following month the younger Cromwell was deposed. The Rump Parliament and the revived Commonwealth then governed for a further 13 months until May 1660, when the king-in-exile, Charles II, returned to London to begin his reign in earnest.

)))》 *Charles I, Charles II*

JAMES I (SEE JAMES VI)

JAMES I (1394–1437)

King of Scots (1406–37); son of Robert III. James was in the Tower of London when he succeeded his father in 1406 and he spent the next 18 years in England before the payment of a king's ransom finally secured his release. Returning to Scotland, in 1425 he executed his cousin and former regent, the Duke of Albany. A committed reformer, James I introduced many new laws, but made powerful enemies during a reign that ended with his murder. He was succeeded by his son, James II.

The second son of Robert III and Queen Annabella, James I was still a child when his elder brother, David, died in 1402 making James heir to his father's throne. James was just 12 years old when he was seized by pirates as he made his way to France to escape assassination attempts in his native Scotland. Handed over to Henry IV, the English king promptly imprisoned his prize hostage, while news of his son's capture was said to have brought on the death of James's father later that year. A king in exile, James I would have to wait 18 long years before sitting on the throne. Scotland's interim rulers were the king's uncle, Robert, Duke of Albany, and from 1420, the Duke's son, Murdoch.

Four years later, though, James I returned to Scotland and asserted control by executing his cousin, Murdoch, and other members of the Scottish nobility. The same year James married Joan, a cousin of England's reigning monarch, Henry V, and a member of the influential Beaufort family. In 1430 Queen Joan gave birth to the royal couple's first child, James.

As king of the Scots, James I demonstrated his passion for law and order, introducing many new laws covering a wide area, from finances to fishing; in this way he effectively curbed the power of Scotland's lords. He also banned football games and restricted the hours in which alcohol could be consumed. However, with his rule characterised by a reforming zeal, James I made enemies among his subjects and the king had to combat rebellions in both the Highlands and the Lowlands. On 20 February 1437 a band of assassins gathered in Perth to stab the king to death in the presence of his queen. With James I dead the crown passed to his young son, James II.
)))➤ *James II, Robert III*

JAMES II (SEE JAMES VII)

JAMES II (1430–60)

King of Scotland (1437–60); son of James I. James succeeded his murdered father in 1437 at the age of six. King in his own right from 1449 he set about destroying the power of the

'Black' Douglas family. Said to have personally killed the young Earl of Douglas, the king died an equally violent death when a cannon exploded during a siege. James II was succeeded by his young son, James III.

The son of James I and Queen Joan, the younger James became king following the murder of his father while he was still a child. James II had to wait 12 years before winning the right to rule over his kingdom. Aided and abetted in his bid for power by the mighty Douglas family, in November 1440 the two young sons of the recently deceased 5th Earl of Douglas were murdered as they dined with the boy-king, James II. From that time James was on a war footing with the 'Black' Douglases, and in 1452 at Stirling Castle the 8th

FAR LEFT: Catherine Douglas tries to protect James I from the conspirators threatening his murder
BELOW: Edinburgh Castle
RIGHT: James II of Scotland

IACOBVS DEI GRATIA SCOTOR etc REX.
Engraved from a Scarce Print in the Possession of George Chalmers Esq.

Earl of Douglas was killed, allegedly by the sovereign himself.

By this time the minority of James II had come to an end and he was ruling in his own right. In 1449, the same year that his minority ended, he married the niece of the Duke of Burgundy, Mary of Guelders. Continuing to hound the Douglas family and its supporters and to move against other challengers such as John of the Isles, by the end of his reign James II was in full command of his kingdom.

Later switching his attentions to the border country, in 1460 the king laid siege to Roxburgh Castle. However, James II was killed when one of his own cannons exploded, his early death bringing to the throne yet another royal child, the late king's eight year-old son, James III.

James I, James III

JAMES III (1452–88)

King of Scotland (1460–88); son of James II. James III succeeded his father in 1460, while he was still a minor. Assuming power in 1469, he gained the Orkneys and Shetlands by marrying Margaret of Denmark the same year. His reign was often beset by internal strife, and he even imprisoned his own brothers in 1479. Captured by the English in Berwickshire in 1482, he was restored in 1483. Later challenged by Scottish rebels, James III was killed in battle at Sauchieburn and was succeeded by his son, James IV.

James was the son of James II and Queen Mary and for the first few years after he succeeded his mother acted as regent. She was replaced as regent shortly before her death in 1462 and a succession of regents governed Scotland until James III came of age in 1469. That same year his marriage to Margaret, the daughter of Christian I of Denmark and Norway, brought the Orkneys and the Shetland Islands under Scottish control.

Despite asserting his power throughout the 1470s, James III was persistently troubled by rebellious Scottish nobles. The 'Red' Douglas clan, spearheaded by the Earl of Angus, was one foe, while the faction led by the king's brothers, the Duke of Albany and the Earl of Mar, was especially troublesome. With matters coming to a head in 1479, James III imprisoned his brothers. However, while the earl died a suspicious death in custody, the duke escaped and headed for England. Returning three years later in the company of an English army, at Lauder to the north of Galashiels the king was seized and taken to Edinburgh, where he was imprisoned at the city's castle, while the English force captured Berwick. Restored to the throne in 1483, the monarch struggled to impose his authority, his confidence further dented by the death of his wife, Margaret, in 1486.

Two years later the king was forced to put down a revolt led by the leaders of the Campbell clan and the 'Red' Douglas family. However, forced to fight at Sauchieburn near Stirling on 11 June 1488, James III died during or shortly after the battle and was succeeded by his son, James IV.

))))➡ *James II, James IV*

JAMES IV (1473–1513)

King of Scotland (1488–1513); son of James III. James IV attained power in 1493. He married Margaret, daughter of the English Tudor king, Henry VII, despite his earlier support for the pretender, Perkin Warbeck. A dynamic, learned and popular Renaissance king, he was killed as the Scots were defeated at Flodden Field in 1513 by his brother-in-law, Henry VIII. He was succeeded by his son, James V.

Orphaned and crowned by the time he was 15 years old, James was the son of James III and Margaret of Denmark. Required to put down a rebellion in his first year as king, later he led successful military campaigns in the Highlands and islands before turning his attentions to the south. Offering his support to the Yorkist pretender Perkin Warbeck, with Warbeck's defeat James IV made his peace with Henry VII, the first Tudor king, who later gave his blessing for the wedding of his eldest daughter, Margaret, and the king of the Scots. A hugely important alliance for the long-term future of both Tudor and Stuart dynasties, in the short-term the marriage produced a son and heir, James.

9 September 1513 the Scots and the English clashed. Doing battle at Flodden Field, 16km (10 miles) southwest of Berwick, many Scottish lords, earls, chiefs and thousands of foot-soldiers were cut down. Also killed was James IV, his body taken to England by the victorious army of Henry VIII and the late king's brother-in-law was reputedly sent the bloodied tunic James had worn at Flodden.

Meanwhile, up in Scotland the crown sat uneasily on the head of yet another royal minor, the late king's baby son, James V.

)))➤ *Henry VII, James V*

FAR LEFT: James IV
LEFT: Henry VII
*   BELOW: Margaret Tudor, wife of James IV*

At home the king proved to be a well-liked figure, who promoted the arts and education and the introduction of the first Scottish printing presses. He also lavished vast sums of money on palaces and a huge warship known as the *Great Michael*. Yet for all the social, cultural and political advances, the king's early death and the accession of yet another minor threatened to undermine the good that James IV had achieved in his lifetime.

Renewing the Auld Alliance with France in 1512, the following year the Scots responded to England's attack on the French by sending the largest Scottish army ever assembled into battle. Marching south in 1513, James IV led his men into England. Crossing the River Tweed, on

JAMES V (1512–42)

King of Scotland (1513–42); son of James IV, nephew of Henry VIII and father of Mary, Queen of Scots. James V succeeded his father as a babe in arms in 1513. Regents then ruled until James V assumed power at the age of 16, thus ending the power struggles of his minority. Asserting control, he established his rule and enriched the Crown before waging war on England. Defeated at Solway Moss in 1542, James V died just a few weeks later and was succeeded by his new-born daughter, Mary, Queen of Scots.

James V was the son of James IV and Margaret, daughter of Henry VII. He was no more than a baby when he ascended Scotland's throne in September 1513. Initially his mother was nominated to act as regent, but after the queen married the Earl of Angus in 1514, she was replaced by John, Duke of Albany who maintained this position until 1524. When Albany went back to France control over the child-king and the country shifted to Angus.

Having spent his childhood years at Stirling Castle, James V escaped the clutches of the Earl of Angus. By this time the earl was separated from James's mother and in the summer of 1528 he was holding the king under lock and key. One day, however, James V managed to slip free and return to his childhood home at Stirling Castle to stake his claim to rule alone.

The king was just 16 years old when he first took the reins and began to rule in his own right, but it was not long before James V showed his determination to be a strong ruler. In revenge for the insult shown to his mother and for the way he had been treated as a child, held a prisoner in his own country, he sent the Earl of Angus scurrying into exile in England. When forced to deal with unrest in the north of his kingdom, he succeeded in putting down the uprisings there. He then turned his attention to other areas in which he felt the need to assert his authority. In 1532 he founded the central court, the College of Justice, while another major feature of his reign was the increasing wealth of the Crown, which was greatly enriched by taxing the Scottish Church.

During the period of the regency two main factions had arisen in Scotland: those who were pro-English, who later supported the Protestant Reformation, and those who were pro-France and therefore Catholic. There was no hope of reconciliation here: England and France had been enemies for centuries and Scotland had a long-term alliance with the country across the Channel. James knew where his loyalties lay and proved them by concluding a marriage alliance with France in 1537. James V then wed his first wife, Madeleine, the daughter of François I. However, when Madeleine died just a few months later, the king of the Scots swiftly took another French bride,

LEFT: James V of Scotland
RIGHT: Mary Queen of Scots

Mary of Guise-Lorraine. She bore him two sons, both of whom died in 1541. The following year she fell pregnant again.

Meanwhile, her husband was busy launching a fateful attack on England. Fighting a much larger English army, on 24 November 1542 the Scots were routed at the Battle of Solway Moss, near Gretna. The English won the day. Two weeks later James V died amid the splendour of his palace at Falkland. He was only 30 years old. Tragically, his death occurred just a few days after the birth of his daughter, the heir he had longed for to perpetuate his line. This was to be the ill-fated Mary, Queen of Scots.

)))➡ *James IV, Mary Queen of Scots*

JAMES VI (JAMES I OF ENGLAND) (1566–1625)

King of Scotland (1567–1625) and king of England and Ireland (1603–25). The son of Mary, Queen of Scots, James VI was eight months old when his father, Lord Darnley, was killed. Succeeding his deposed mother at the age of 13 months, he survived kidnap and assassination attempts, although his mother was executed in England in 1587. The first Stuart king of England and Ireland, the great-great-grandson of Henry VII united the thrones of Scotland and England on succeeding Elizabeth I in 1603. Later the Gunpowder Plot was uncovered (1605) and the King James Bible was published (1611). James was succeeded by his son, Charles I.

The sixth successive Stuart monarch to ascend the Scottish throne as a minor, he was the only child resulting from the short-lived marriage of Mary, Queen of Scots, and her second husband, Henry, Lord Darnley. Born at Edinburgh Castle on 19 June 1566 and baptised Charles James, long before his second birthday his father had been killed and his mother deposed and he had been crowned.

He was carried north to Stirling for his coronation on 29 July 1567 and for the first 14 years of James's reign as king of Scotland the Earl of Morton acted as regent. Despite the earl's protection the life of the young monarch was fraught with danger as was made all too clear in 1581: the regent's execution was followed in 1582 by the Raid of Ruthven, which saw a Protestant group kidnap the king. Soon escaping from captivity, James Stuart took up the reins of power at the age of 17. In 1587 he learned of the beheading of his mother, Mary, Queen of Scots, following years in exile in England, while in 1600 a plot to kill him was uncovered.

Meanwhile, as the king's kidnapping had shown, religious issues continued to inflame a land increasingly dominated by Protestantism. A Protestant himself, James VI was a sovereign who believed in the divinity of kings and was reluctant to see the Crown lose its control over Church affairs. Yet despite this reluctance the Presbyterian form of Church government was legalised in 1592, although James VI did succeed in heading off moves to dispense with bishops, who were traditionally appointed by the crown.

In the last hours of her life the English queen, Elizabeth I, named James VI of Scotland as her successor and on her death on 24 March 1603, Scotland's Stuart king ascended the English throne. It is somewhat ironic that James succeeded the woman who had been instrumental in his mother's execution. His claim to the English crown stemmed from the marriage of his great-grandmother, Margaret. A daughter of Henry VII, she had married James IV of Scotland exactly 100 years before. Uniting the crowns of England and Scotland, on 25 July 1603 the king of the Scots was crowned King James I of England and Ireland at Westminster Abbey.

Crowned with him that day was his wife, Anne. The daughter of Frederick II of Denmark and Norway, she had married James in 1589 and was, by the time of her coronation in England, the mother of six of the eight children she was to produce. The eldest child was Henry, a boy of whom much was expected, but the 18-year-old prince died in 1612 to leave his brother, Charles, as son and heir. Of the other children, only Elizabeth reached maturity, the second-born child later marrying Frederick V, Elector Palatine of the Rhine and King of Bohemia. An important marriage for the future of the British monarchy, Elizabeth's daughter would become the mother of the future George I.

Once called 'the wisest fool in Christendom' by the French king, Henri IV, James was an intellectual who wrote on subjects as diverse as tobacco and kingship, but he was rarely a popular monarch. Frequently ruling without recourse to parliament, his tendency to promote male favourites also rankled. Beginning his reign in England by ending the long-running war with Spain, at home all was not well and the continuing conflict over religion threatened to come to a head as Puritans pressed for the total abolition of Catholic rituals in church services.

On 5 November 1605 the notorious Gunpowder Plot was foiled. Guy Fawkes has become the best-known conspirator and under him a band of Catholic extremists had planned to kill James while he attended the state opening of parliament, by exploding 30 barrels of gunpowder secreted in the cellars of the parliament building. Although the Gunpowder Plot proved to be

ABOVE: Royal heraldry of James I

the last serious attempt at insurrection during his reign, religious discord remained, even though, like Elizabeth I before him, the king generally adopted a conciliatory position between the ideological extremes. This policy took solid form when the Authorized Version of the Bible was published in 1611, but was not forced upon worshippers. Also known as the King James Bible, this edition was the work of 47 scholars, who were divided into six groups to translate different sections of the Bible. Their translations were then assessed by a 12-man commission, before finally a bishop and a doctor of theology edited the final text.

Outliving his queen, who had passed away in 1619, James I died on 27 March 1625 at Theobalds Park in Hertfordshire. He was buried at Westminster Abbey, where the following February his son was crowned Charles I.

▶ *Charles I, Elizabeth I, Mary Queen of Scots*

JAMES VII (JAMES II OF ENGLAND) (1633–1701)

King of Great Britain (1685–88); son of Charles I and brother of Charles II. Succeeding Charles II in 1685, as a Catholic king in a Protestant land he fought a losing battle to keep his crown. Defeated by the Glorious Revolution of 1688, he fled the country and was succeeded by his son-in-law, William III, and his daughter, Mary II. Also the father of Queen Anne, after his defeat at the Battle of the Boyne in 1690 he lived out the rest of his life in France.

Born at St James's Palace, London on 14 October 1633, he was the fourth child born to Charles I and Queen Henrietta Maria. James enjoyed only a few settled years of childhood, then in 1642 the English Civil War broke out. Created Duke of York the following year, the next phase of the young prince's life was dominated by war as his father's Royalist forces fought the Parliamentarians in a series of battles. In 1646 Charles I was forced to abandon his Oxford headquarters and James was taken prisoner.

An invaluable hostage, in 1648 the future king escaped from Parliament's grasp and was spirited out of the country disguised as a girl. Next heading for Holland, which was home to his elder sister Mary, later he was joined there by his elder brother Charles. This period of exile then lasted until the Restoration was confirmed by the coronation of James's brother as King Charles II.

In the interim James had fought for the French army, and then its Spanish counterpart, before taking his place at the court of Charles II. Appointed Lord High Admiral, with the outbreak of the second Anglo-Dutch War he led the English navy to a victory at Lowestoft in June 1665, but he was also in charge during the third war with Holland when the Dutch fleet foiled his attempts to win the Battle of Solebay.

However, more than a decade earlier, two aspects of the future king's private life had been the talk of society. One topic was his concealed marriage, the second was James's interest in Roman Catholicism. A public wedding was then arranged for 3 September 1660, James's marriage to Anne Hyde later producing eight children, the two surviving beyond infancy becoming the Stuart queens, Mary II and Anne. Then, after the death of his first wife in March 1671, James married Mary of Modena, the daughter of an Italian duke, who became the mother of six children, including a boy, also James, whose birth would hasten the overthrow of his father.

He resigned as Lord High Admiral in 1673, when that year's Test Act required all men in high office to take Communion, thereby excluding Catholics such as James. Five years later he was in the news again as the Popish Plot unfolded, the alleged plotters intending to assassinate Charles II and replace him with his Catholic brother, James. Back in office in 1680, when he was made Lord High Commissioner for Scotland, he held this post for two years, ending his brother's reign with a second stint as Lord High Admiral.

Succeeding Charles II on 6 February 1685, on 23 April he was crowned king at Westminster Abbey. Monarch for less than four years, as James VII of Scotland and Britain's James II he ruffled feathers with his often dismissive attitude and his commitment to the Catholic faith. He was also the subject of two attempted overthrows just months after his coronation. The Marquees of Argyll led a force against him in Scotland, while in southern England the Duke of Monmouth commanded another band of rebels.

Yet both these insurrections were crushed, with Monmouth and his men defeated at the Battle of Sedgemoor in July 1685. Retribution was swift, too, as the Bloody Assizes of the notorious Judge Jeffreys saw to it that no fewer than 230 of the English rebels, including Monmouth, were condemned to death, while others were flogged or deported.

A brief lull then followed before further tensions provoked James to dismiss parliament on 20 November 1685. Then came two Declarations of Independence, which relaxed restrictions placed on Catholics and other religious Nonconformists. However, these attempts to force through change were destined to founder during 1688.

The first significant event was the birth that summer of a son and heir to James II, especially as there were allegations that the baby had not been born to Queen Mary, but had been smuggled into her bedchamber. With these rumours still circulating, just three weeks after the birth of Prince James came the acquittal of seven bishops, who had been put on trial by the king charged with seditious libel. Then, with acrimony in the air, an invitation was sent out to William of Orange pleading with him to replace James II.

The monarch's son-in-law, through marriage to the king's eldest daughter, Mary Stuart, he took up the invitation, landing on English soil on 5 November 1688. Next marching from Devon towards London, the size of his army and the volume of support for William saw

the Glorious Revolution succeed with ease as James fled. Caught while making his escape, he was soon allowed to slip away to France, where he arrived on Christmas Day 1688.

In January 1689 England's parliament formally declared that James II had abdicated, a short time later proclaiming the accession of William and Mary. Meanwhile James plotted his return to power. Still recognised as king in Ireland, on 1 July 1690 he led an army into action at the Battle of the Boyne, but was defeated there by William's troops.

Retiring to France to lick his wounds at his palace at St Germain-en-Laye, near Paris, he was living there in June 1692 when his wife gave birth to his fourteenth child, Louise, and he was there when he heard of the death of his daughter, Mary II, in December 1694. Then, on 6 September 1701, the ex-king died at his Parisian home. Buried at the Church of the English Benedictines in Paris, later his remains were reburied at St Germain-en-Laye. Just 13 years old at the time of his father's death, his son James, the Jacobites' Old Pretender, later carried on the fight to restore the old king's descendants to the British throne.

LEFT: The flight of James II after the Battle of the Boyne
TOP: The Duke of Monmouth pleads for his life before James II

))))➤ *Charles I, Charles II, William III*

but Henry the Young King was crowned as his father's successor during the lifetime of Henry II, while older brothers Richard and Geoffrey were both ahead of John in the Angevin pecking order. Despite his low standing, he was a favourite son of the king and his increasingly estranged queen, yet for all the affection shown to John by his father territory was at a premium and so young John earned the nickname Lackland.

Another problem for the king and for his successor, Richard I, was John's ambition, his notorious schemings making him a liability. Nevertheless, his actions, however deceitful or selfish, were usually forgiven by his family. An early example of his failings came to the fore in 1185, when the 17-year-old John was sent to Ireland. Made Lord of Ireland in 1177, 8 years later his expedition was a failure, the prince alienating Irish leaders and failing to rein in landowners such as Hugh de Lacy.

John's star would soon rise again, however, as in 1186 his brother, Geoffrey, died in a tournament. Then, in 1189, Henry II passed away and John's elder brother was crowned as Richard I. John himself was presented with large swathes of land, but with Richard away on crusade it was not long before he moved to seize power. Chasing William de Longchamp from London in 1191, with the appointed justiciar (chief justice) out of the way, and with his brother fighting in the Holy Land, John was able to assert his control.

JOHN (1167–1216)

King of England (1199–1216); son of Henry II; nicknamed 'Lackland' and 'Softsword'. John succeeded his brother, Richard I ('the Lionheart'), in 1199. He seized power during Richard's reign. Punished for this coup, during his own reign he lost Anjou and Normandy and incensed England's barons, clergymen and others. Forced to set his seal on the Magna Carta in 1215, he was driven from London by the French dauphin, Louis, in 1216. Dying that same year, John was succeeded by his son, Henry III.

Born at Beaumont Palace in Oxfordshire on 24 December 1167, John was the eighth and youngest child born to Henry II and his wife, Eleanor, Duchess of Aquitaine. The first-born son, William, died young,

However, when a large ransom was paid for the release of the imprisoned King Richard, the king returned to England early in 1194 to find that his young brother had assumed power and had given away part of Normandy in exchange for military aid. John was punished by having his castles and land seized, but would have to wait only five more years before becoming king.

The death of Richard I on 6 April 1199 saw John ascend the English throne without objection and the story was the same in Normandy, while in Aquitaine the new king's mother, Eleanor, ruled on her son's behalf. Only in Anjou, Maine and Touraine was there serious opposition to John's accession, the nobles there choosing as their ruler the 11-year-old Arthur of Brittany. The son of John's late brother, Geoffrey, young Arthur had been the natural heir in England, but Richard had opted for John. However, in 1200 Arthur was denied a second time by his uncle, John.

Eleven years earlier, in August 1189, John had married the Countess of Gloucester, Isabella. A forbidden marriage, at least in the eyes of the Church, John's father had given his blessing. The relationship lasted 10 years, but was annulled in 1200 on the grounds that, as husband and wife were second cousins, the couple were too closely related to be legally married. So, with this annulment freshly announced, King John married a second bride: Isabella of Angoulâme. However, in marrying this 12-year-old girl, England's monarch further upset the French king, who was already irate at the way John had brushed aside (and possibly killed) Arthur of Brittany. As a result, Philip II offered his support to Hugh X of Lusignan, the duke who had previously been betrothed to Isabella of Angoulâme.

Fighting then broke out in 1203. Initially the English king held his own, but in 1204 Château-Gaillard and Rouen fell and Anjou and Normandy were taken by French forces. Forced to return to England, John made his presence felt by inflicting massive taxation on a population already suffering the effects of rampant inflation. The clergy, too, was soon at odds with John, his objection to Stephen Langton's appointment as Archbishop of Canterbury sparking a crisis that led directly to the king's excommunication. However, by 1212 the threat of attack by France loomed large and so

TOP LEFT: King John stag hunting
LEFT: King John confirming the Magna Carta

John sought papal protection, effectively regaining the support of Pope Innocent III in May 1213 by making England a pawn of the Vatican.

Before bowing down to the pope and returning to war with France, King John had marched into Wales to invade the kingdom of Llywelyn ap Iorwerth. The Gwynedd ruler, Llywelyn had married John's illegitimate daughter, Joan, in 1205 and had then been able to count on his father-in-law's backing as he expanded his Welsh empire. But then, in 1211, the tables were turned as England's monarch attacked, forcing Llywelyn into submission.

Back in France in 1214, once there John was defeated at the Battle of Bouvines. Also troubled at home at this time, in May 1215 rebels stormed London. Then, as the net closed in on the increasingly despised king, on 15 June 1215 his enemies backed him into a corner, forcing him to put his seal on the Magna Carta at Runnymede, near Windsor.

The Magna Carta, or Great Charter, was a long list by England's leading barons and churchmen, which itemised 63 complaints and intended reforms. King John's opponents insisted that citizens found guilty of committing offences should be punished according to the law of the land, while there were also clauses covering principles of government and restrictions on royal powers, including taxation, and other restrictions relating to the freedom of the Church and to foreign policy. Yet even after John had reluctantly agreed to address the grievances listed in the Magna Carta, still the pressure continued to mount against him as the Dauphin Louis, the son of Philip II of France, sided with the rebels, marching into London in May 1216. Forced to take flight, just five months later King John was dead. Dying at Newark Castle in Nottinghamshire on 18 October 1216, 'Bad' King John was buried at Worcester Cathedral.

His eldest son and his successor was Henry III, while one daughter, Eleanor, later married Simon de Montfort and a second, Joan, wed Alexander II of Scotland.

)))▶ *Henry II, Henry III*

KENNETH I MAC ALPIN (d. c. AD 858)

King of the Scots (AD 840–58); on of Alpin. Also known as Cinaed mac Alpín, in AD 843–47 the ruler of the Scots of Dalriada defeated the Picts and formed the new nation of Alba. At a time of persistent Viking raids, little is known about his life or reign, but his descendants flourished. Succeeded by his brother, Donald I, later kings included Kenneth's sons, Constantine I and Aed.

He was an all-conquering king, who ruled over Dalriada from AD 841 and united the Scots and the Picts. With Pictish ancestry of his own, King Kenneth I took seven years to bring the Picts' land under his control within a united kingdom known as Alba or Scotia.

Leading Alba in its fight against Viking assaults, Kenneth moved the centre of his operations from the west to new fortresses at Forteviot, Dunkeld and Scone where, legend has it, Kenneth I mac Alpin set the sacred coronation stone in AD 850. Moved from Dunstaffnage Castle to Scone, there the stone remained until, more than three centuries later, it was removed by England's warrior-king, Edward I, and taken south to Westminster Abbey.

The father of Constantine I and King Aed, Kenneth I died at Forteviot and was succeeded by his brother, Donald I.

》》》 *Aed, Constantine II, Donald II*

KENNETH II (d. AD 995)

King of the Scots (AD 971–95); son of Malcolm I. Also known as Cinaed II, he succeeded Culen who was murdered in AD 971. Ceded Lothian by Edgar of England, his reign was marked by the royal in-fighting that probably cost Kenneth II his life. The father of Malcolm II, he was succeeded by Constantine III.

Becoming king following the death of Culen, in AD 973 he bowed down before Edgar at Chester, his reward for recognising the English king as overlord being the valuable territory of Lothian. Such a deal with a southern sovereign cut little ice closer to home, however, as his 24-year reign was scarred by the fight to choose the successor to Kenneth II, whose life came to a brutal, if mysterious end in AD 995.

Possibly killed on the orders of his successor, Constantine III, one tale tells of how the king was killed as an act of revenge by the mother of a son that Kenneth II had killed. This noblewoman named Finvela was said to have lured Kenneth to her home by telling him that

LEFT: Edward I steals the stone from scone
TOP RIGHT: Mural from Portrait Gallery of Scotland showing Scottish kings and queens, including Kenneth MacAlpin

she would there unveil a band of men who had betrayed their monarch.

However, after a drunken feast, Finvela led the king to a room containing a statue. On this statue was placed a golden apple, which Finvela offered up as a token of peace. Accepting this gift, as Kenneth II plucked the apple from the statue he unwittingly triggered his own death, for the apple had been connected to a series of hidden crossbows, the bolts they fired killing the unlucky king.

))))▶ *Constantine III, Culen, Malcolm I*

KENNETH III (d. 1005)

King of the Scots (AD 997–1005). In the violent world of eleventh-century politics he who lived by the sword often died by the sword. Thus, Kenneth III, who was implicated in the death of his predecessor, Constantine III, was himself killed by an enemy force led by Kenneth's own successor, Malcolm II. Ruling from AD 997 to 1005, Kenneth, the grandson of Malcolm I and the son of King Dub, died in battle alongside his son, Giric.

))))▶ *Constantine III, Malcolm II*

LANCASTER, HOUSE OF

The House of Lancaster was, strictly speaking, a branch of the Plantagenet line. The Wars of the Roses between the houses of Lancaster and York have featured so large in the history of England, however, that the two have been accorded their own dynastic status. The House of Lancaster originated in 1267 when the younger son of Henry III, Edmund, was created Earl of Lancaster. The earldom was turned into a duchy for Henry of Grosmont and in this form it passed to John of Gaunt through his marriage to Grosmont's daughter, Blanche. The first Lancastrian king, Henry IV, was the son of John of Gaunt. When the Plantagenet king, Richard II, seized Lancastrian estates, Henry Bolingbroke fought back and put forward his own claim to the throne.

He evetually overthrew Richard and settled down as king. As a usurper, Henry experienced many difficulties at the beginning of his reign from those who supported Richard, but Henry succeeded in holding on to his title.

It was his son, Henry V, who has become the most celebrated Lancastrian king. The epitome of everything a medieval warrior-king should be, Henry had shown his mettle as a prince early on and the country rejoiced on his accession. His successes in France only served to enhance

THE HOUSE OF LANCASTER

1399–1413	Henry IV
1413–22	Henry V
1422–61, 1470–71	Henry VI

his reputation. Had he not died so young, the history of the English monarchy might have been very different, but he left a nine-month-old child as king in 1422 and this child, Henry VI, was to lose everything his father and grandfather had fought so hard for. The line ended with his overthrow by the Yorkist Edward IV.

LLYWELYN AP GRUFFUDD (c. 1228–82)

King of Gwynedd (1247–82); the first leader to be styled Prince of Wales; son of Gruffudd ap Llywelyn. Also known as Llywelyn the Last, in Gwynedd he succeeded Dafydd ap Llywelyn in 1246. Winning a power struggle in Gwynedd, he was often at war with England. Regaining lost lands from 1256 and recognised as Prince of Wales in 1257, two decades later he was defeated by Edward I. Fighting back, he was killed in action in 1282 and was succeeded by his brother, Dafydd.

The grandson of Llywelyn ap Iorwerth and son of Gruffudd ap Llywelyn, his father had died while making his escape from the Tower of London in 1244. However, Llywelyn did not have long to wait to scale the heights of power in Wales because on 25 February 1246 his uncle and enemy, Dafydd ap Llywelyn, died, the death of the Gwynedd king opening the door to Llywelyn and his brothers.

However, an even more powerful opponent than Dafydd lived on in the form of Henry III and in 1247 the English king forced Llywelyn to sign the Treaty of

TOP LEFT: Henry, Duke of Lancaster, in black at left of throne, recognised as King in 1399
ABOVE: Llwelyn is defeated and beheaded
RIGHT: Head of Llewelyn ap Gruffydd is paraded through streets

Woodstock. Conceding land and control, the fightback began in 1255. First winning a struggle with his brothers, Owain and Dafydd, in 1256 he set out to take back the lands seized earlier by the English by winning battles and forging alliances with other Welsh rulers and with Simon de Montfort, the leader of the English rebellion against Henry III.

Then in September 1267 came the climax of Llywelyn's campaign of attacks when the Treaty of . Montgomery saw him recognised by the English Crown as the Prince of Wales. This recognition was only granted in exchange for a huge monetary payment and so it was not long before Llywelyn was fighting to win more territory. But then in 1272 Edward I became the new king of England, his accession marking the beginning of the end for Llywelyn the Last.

Deserted again by his brother, Dafydd, in 1277, Llywely – and his defiantly independent stance tired Edward who took arms against him. Soon defeating him, in October 1277, Llywelyn was faced with the option of

signing the Treaty of Aberconwy or watching helplesly as his people starved. He signed the treaty. Then confined to one part of his former kingdom, he married Simon de Montfort's widow, Eleanor, before being reunited with his brother, Dafydd.

However, Llywelyn's comeback bid was soon ended as in December 1282 he was killed in a skirmish at Cilmeri, near Builth Wells, and was succeeded by Dafydd.

➠ *Dafydd ap Llwyelyn, Gruffudd ap Llywelyn*

LLYWELYN AP IORWERTH (c. 1173–1240)

King of Gwynedd (1200-40); son of Iorwerth Drwyndwn and grandson of Owain Gwynedd. Also known as Llywelyn the Great, he succeeded Dafydd ap Owain. Later extending his kingdom, he was attacked and defeated by his father-in-law, King John, but recovered to regain Gwynedd. Recognised as the leading Welsh ruler in 1218, Llywelyn retired to a monastery in 1238 and was succeeded by his son, Dafydd ap Llywelyn.

Growing up in the Powys homeland of his mother, Llywelyn first served notice of his ambitions when he took on and defeated the Gwynedd ruler, Dafydd ap Owain, at the Battle of Aberconwy in 1194. However, he did not find it easy to build on this victory and so it was not until the beginning of the thirteenth century that he secured control over all Gwynedd.

Ever conscious of the powerful presence of England, Llywelyn paid homage to King John in 1203, the year that he pledged to marry John's illegitimate daughter, Joan. With English support, the next few years saw Llywelyn push south from his base in North-West Wales, gradually overwhelming Powys, where Gwynwynwyn and later his son, Gruffudd, led the resistance to the attacks from the north.

The increasing power of the Gwynedd king did not go unchecked, though. Reacting to Llywelyn's southern conquests, King John marched against his son-in-law, invading in 1211, England's king further humiliating Llywelyn by taking hostages as well as land. Hit hard by this defeat, Llywelyn ap Iorwerth recovered so quickly that by 1213 Gwynedd was again under his rule.

LEFT: Welsh hero, Iorwerth is murdered
RIGHT: Macbeth instructing the murderers

Later, as this revival in fortunes gathered pace, he conquered South-West Wales and captured the border town of Shrewsbury, while the Magna Carta of 1215 included a commitment by John to hand back the Welsh lands he had overrun and retained. Then, as English minds concentrated on civil war, Llywelyn made further gains. With South Wales already his, he banished the Powys ruler, Gwynwynwyn, and gained further recognition of his status as the most powerful Welsh king at the Treaty of Worcester of 1218.

Reigning over his kingdom another two decades, Llywelyn established an English-style administration, while at the same time encouraging Welsh bards and monasteries. Unsuccessfully attacked by Henry III in 1228 and again in 1231, the ruler who gloried in the titles of Prince of Aberffraw and Lord of Snowdon retired to the Cistercian monastery at Aberconwy in 1238. He was succeeded in Gwynedd by his son, Dafydd ap Llywelyn.

))))▶ *Dafydd ap Llywelyn*

LLYWELYN AP SEISYLL (d. 1023)

King of Deheubarth and Gwynedd (1005–23). Following years of unrest in which battles had been fought and kings deposed, he became ruler in Deheubarth following the death of his father-in-law Maredudd ap Owain, in AD 999. Then seizing Gwynedd in 1016, he retained possession of it until his violent removal in 1023. Possibly killed and buried near Pentrefoelas in North Wales, Llywelyn was succeeded by his son, Gruffudd ap Llywelyn.

))))▶ *Gruffud ap Llywelyn, Maredudd ap Owain*

LULACH (d. 1058)

King of Scotland (1057–58); stepson of Macbeth and the son of Macbeth's wife, Gruoch, by her first marriage to Gillacomean. Also known as Gille Comgáin, he was a cousin of Macbeth and, until his death in 1032, the Mormaer (or Earl) of Moray. Twenty-five years later his son, Lulach, was proclaimed king of the Scots at Scone following Macbeth's murder, but his reign was ended almost before it had begun. Ambushed in 1058 at Essie in the Strathbogie region to the north-west of Aberdeen, the young king was killed by his successor, Malcolm III.

))))▶ *Macbeth, Malcolm III*

Duncan's father, Abbot Crinan. There were more challenges to face, however, not least those launched by Duncan's sons, the future kings, Malcolm III and Donald III. Nevertheless Macbeth still felt confident enough to make a pilgrimage to Rome. But then at Dunsinane in 1054 his forces, bolstered by Norman recruits, were routed by the combined English, Scandinavian and Scottish armies led by the Northumbrian Earl Siward. Suffering such a crushing defeat deep in the heart of his kingdom, Macbeth could only look on in dismay as the eldest son of Duncan I, Siward's nephew, Malcolm, was installed as ruler in Lothian and Strathclyde.

The net was closing in on the king and in 1057 Malcolm launched the fateful strike that claimed his life at Lumphanan to the west of Aberdeen. Avenging Duncan's death, Malcolm III Canmore did not become king until 1058 when Macbeth's stepson and successor, Lulach, was killed.

⏵ *Lulach, Malcolm III*

MACBETH (1005–57)

King of Scotland (1040–57). Immortalised by William Shakespeare in his play of the same name, Macbeth killed and then succeeded Duncan I. Married to Gruoch, a granddaughter of Kenneth III, Macbeth became king in 1040. His reign lasted 17 years before revenge for his father's death was exacted by Duncan's son, who then killed Macbeth's stepson, Lulach, to succeed as Malcolm III.

The son of Findlaech of Moray in North-East Scotland, Macbeth's mother was a sister of Malcolm II. Coming to power in Moray in 1032, his marriage to Gruoch further strengthened his hand, as she was the granddaughter of Malcolm II. Soon caught up in a struggle for power with the new king, Duncan I, the Mormaer (or king) of Moray eventually killed his enemy when Duncan led a raiding party into Macbeth's home territory in 1040.

But Macbeth was unable to rest on his laurels and during a battle fought in 1045 King Macbeth killed

MAC CARTHAIG, CORMAC (d. 1138)

King of Munster (*c.* 1122–38). Reigning from about 1122, Cormac mac Carthaig took on the might of the Connacht king, Toirrdelbach Ua Conchobair, and the Uí Briain clan. He was deposed and sent into exile in 1127. Although he was later restored, relations with rival kings such as Diarmait Mac Murchadha remained tense. Cormac's chapel at Cashel in County Tipperary was consecrated in 1134, four years before Cormac Mac Carthaig was killed.

⏵ *Diarmait Mac Murchada, House of Uí Briain, Toirrdelbach Ua Choncobair*

MAC LOCHLAINN, MUIRCHERTACH (d. 1166)

King of Cenél'nEógain; high king of all Ireland (1156–66). Ruling in Cenél nEógain from 1145, four years later he moved south from his kingdom in modern-day Donegal to invade Dublin. Then winning the support of the Leinster king, Diarmait Mac Murchadha, in 1156 he succeeded Toirrdelbach Ua Conchobair as high king. Subduing the threat posed by Toirrdelbach's son, Ruaidrí, in 1161, after he blinded the King of Ulaid (in the north of Ireland) an invasion force poured into Muirchertach's kingdom and killed him.

))))▶ *Diarmait Mac Murchada, Toirrdelbach Ua Conchobair*

MAC MÁEL NA MBO, DIARMAIT (d. 1072)

King of Leinster. Rising to prominence in 1046, he fought for the right to become king following the death of the Leinster ruler. A warrior-king, he continued to fight in neighbouring provinces. Defeating the Vikings of Dublin by 1054, he took control of that kingdom, placing his son, Murchad, in command there. Later forming alliances with the kings of Connacht and Munster, in the latter province he helped Toirrdelbach Ua Briain to become ruler in 1063. Said to have offered sanctuary to the sons of Harold II following the Battle of Hastings in 1066, King Diarmait was himself killed in battle six years later.

MAC MURCHADA, HOUSE OF

Reigning in the eastern province of Leinster, the Mac Murchada (or MacMurrough) stronghold was Ferns, County, Wexford, and the surrounding area. It was there in the south of Leinster that the Uí Chennselaig lived. Periodically this tribe had provided Leinster with kings, but it was only with the emergence of Diarmait mac Máel na mBó in the eleventh century that the Uí Chennselaig took centre-stage again in Leinster.

Ninety years after this great ruler died, Diarmait Mac Murchadha (or Dermot MacMurrough) rose to power. Like his famous predecessor he, too, was a member of the Uí Chennselaig clan, which had retained power throughout Leinster since the death of

Diarmait mac Máel na mBó. Becoming king of Leinster in 1132 Diarmait Mac Murchadha was a Christian, who founded religious houses such as the Augustinian abbey at Ferns (where he died in 1171), but he was also an ambitious, sometimes ruthless king who abducted the wife of the king of Bréifne and raped the abbess of a Kildare nunnery.

King until 1166, shortly after his great rival Muirchertach Mac Lochlainn became high king, the king of Bréifne took revenge on the man who had stolen his wife by driving Diarmait from Ferns and into exile. Eventually reclaiming his kingdom in 1170 with the help of his future son-in-law, Strongbow, he then died the following year.

Much later another Mac Murchada became king of Leinster. Ruling there from 1375, Art Mac Murchadha became a staunch opponent of Richard II Aggrieved at having his wife's inheritance seized in 1391, three years later the English king responded by sailing to Ireland to force Art to back down. However, the Leinster ruler soon bounced back and by 1399 he was proclaiming himself to be the king of all Ireland.

THE HOUSE OF MAC MURCHADA

d. 1171	Diarmait Mac Murchada
d. *c.* 1416	Art Mac Murchadha

MAC MURCHADHA, ART (d. c. 1416)

King of Leinster (1370s–1416); also known as Art MacMurrough. He ruled in eastern Ireland from the 1370s until his death. An enemy of Richard II, after Art's marriage to the heiress, Elizabeth Calf, the English king attacked in 1394. Conceding defeat, the Leinsterman refused to give up his lands and so retained his independence despite a fresh English attack in 1399.

))))▶ *Richard II*

MAC MURCHADHA, DIARMAIT (d. 1171)

King of Leinster (1132–66, 1170–71); also known as Dermot MacMurrough. He reigned from 1132 to 1166 and 1170 to 1171. Abducting Devorguilla in 1152, he was overthrown and banished in 1166, but returned to power in 1170 with the help of Strongbow and the support of Henry II. The founder of many religious houses, he has often been represented as a pro-English king.

Fighting his way to the kingship of Leinster by 1132, 12 years later the 'high king' Toirrdelbach Ua Conchobair divided up an area of land in Meath between Diarmait and the Bréifne king, Tigernán. In 1144 Diarmait abducted his rival's wife, Devorguilla). He continued to rule over Leinster for another two decades.

Diarmait was a devoutly Christian king, who worked to reform the Irish Church and founded many religious houses. Secure in his kingdom until 1166, it was in that year that King Diarmait's world and his reputation were changed by a series of setbacks. The first of these was the death of the 'high king' Muirchertach Mac Lochlainn, the second was the selection of Ruaidrí Ua Conchobair

instead of Diarmait as his successor. Immediately going on the warpath Ruaidrí took Dublin, while Tigernán forced Diarmait to leave Ferns (in County Wexford), the place the Leinster king had made his capital.

Leaving Ireland, he sailed to England, where he was soon given the permission of Henry II to raise an army to help him recover his kingdom. Partially successful in 1167, he returned three years later with a larger force, which included in its ranks Diarmait's future son-in-law and successor, Richard de Clare (alias Strongbow). Winning Waterford in August 1170, in September Dublin was recaptured. King of Leinster once more, the second reign of Diarmait Mac Murchadha lasted only a few months as he died early in 1171.

))))▶ *Henry II, Toirrdelbach Ua Conchobair*

MADOG AP MAREDUDD (d. 1160)

King of Powys (1132–60). Madog was the last ruler of the whole of Powys. At the beginning of his reign he held a position of great authority, but this declined throughout his time as king of Powys. Aiming to retain good relations with Henry I and King Stephen of England and he worked hard to gain equally good relations with his neighbours in Wales. He married the daughter of Gruffudd ap Cynan and for a while harmony was established between Powys and Gwynedd. Later, though, Madog was forced to fight it out with Gruffudd's successor, Owain, in 1149. This was the start of the decline of his power: Owain won the day and by the end of the year much of Powys was in his hands. It was not until 1157 that Henry II of England rewarded Madog's former loyalty by restoring him to power in Powys. The remainder of Madog's reign was relatively peaceful and he was much mourned on his death.

)))»» *Henry I, Henry II, Stephen*

TOP LEFT: Art Mac Murchada, Irish King of Leinster
ABOVE: Henry II agrees to help Diarmait Mac Murchada
LEFT: Kilkenny Castle built by 'Strongbow' in 1172

MÁEL SECHNAILL I (d. AD 862)

King of Tara (AD 846–62). One of the southern Uí Neill family centred on the ancient site of Tara in County Meath, Máel Sechnaill came to power in AD 846. He was later acknowledged as Ireland's 'high king' and during his reign he fought off challenges from Vikings and native kings and extended the borders of his kingdom.

)))»» *House of O'Neill*

MÁEL SECHNAILL II (d. 1022)

King of Tara (AD 980–1022); also known as Malachy and Máel Sechnaill II mac Domnaill. Máel Sechnaill II enjoyed a long reign and for much of it his destiny was interlinked with that of the great Brian Bóruma.

The two had been allies since AD 997 and five years later Máel Sechnaill II and other Irish kings were forced to accept Brian Bóruma as 'high king'. However, after the latter's defeat at the Battle of Clontarf in 1014, Máel Sechnaill II assumed his long-time rival's role as high king of all Ireland.

)))»» *Brian Bóruma*

MALCOLM I (d. AD 954)

King of Scotland (AD 942–54); son of Donald II; also known as Mael Coluim I. Malcolm succeeded his cousin, Constantine II, and two years later he concluded a deal with Edmund of England, in which they agreed that Malcolm I would retain sovereignty over Strathclyde and Cumbria, lands that Edmund had previously invaded.

Forced like his predecessors to tackle the threat of Viking attacks, Malcolm's main foe was Eric Bloodaxe. However, the king of the Scots was killed not by Norsemen, but by the natives of Moray, a region he had earlier captured. Although he was the father of King Dub and Kenneth II, he was succeeded on his death by his cousin, Indulf.

)))»» *Constantine II, Donald II*

MALCOLM II (c. AD 954–1034)

King of Scotland (1005–34); son of Kenneth II; also known as Mael Coluim II. In 1005 Malcolm killed Kenneth III and seized his throne. It did not take him long to negotiate a marriage alliance with the Viking, Sigurd of Orkney. Later he routed the Northumbrians at the Battle of Carham and gained control of Lothian, then Strathclyde. Defeated by Cnut towards the end of his reign, Malcolm II died in 1034 and was succeeded by his grandson, Duncan I.

Malcolm became king of the Scots a decade after the death of his father, Kenneth II, and ruled for 29 years. Three years after his ascension, Malcolm's daughter married the Norse Earl of Orkney, Sigurd the Stout. With Sigurd's realm encompassing Caithness, Sutherland and the Western Isles, this marriage effectively extended the influence of the Scots, particularly in the Western Isles, where the Norse inhabitants had remained largely outside the control of either Scottish or Scandinavian kings for more than 100 years.

In 1018 Malcolm II seized Lothian and Strathclyde by routing the army led by his long-standing enemy, Earl Uhtred. The Northumbrian had put together a fighting force of English and Viking warriors, but at the Battle of Carham, by the banks of the River Tweed, Malcolm and his ally, Owen the Bald of Strathclyde, won the day. Later King Owen's death enabled the Scots' monarch to establish his rule in Strathclyde, while the Northumbrian land of Lothian also came under his complete control.

Hailed by his fellow Scots as the 'honour of all the west of Europe', it was only in his last years that Malcolm II suffer a major setback, when an attack by Cnut in 1027 forced the king of the Scots to recognise Cnut as his overlord. He died seven years later from injuries sustained in battle. Malcolm II was succeeded by Duncan I, the son of his daughter, Bethoc.

➤ **Cnut, Duncan I, Kenneth I, Kenneth II**

MALCOLM III (c. 1031–93)

Kings of Scots (1058–93); son of Duncan I; also known as Mael Coluim III Cenn Mór (or Bighead). Malcolm III had been king of Strathclyde before he murdered his father's archenemy, Macbeth, and Macbeth's stepson, Lulach, to claim the throne in 1058. His second wife, Margaret, was English, but Malcolm III frequently attacked northern England until humbled by William I the Conqueror in 1072. Also defeated by William II Rufus in 1092, the king of the Scots was killed in an ambush the following year and was succeeded by his brother, Donald III.

The long reign of Malcolm Cenn Mór, or Canmore followed the assassination of two key rivals. The first was the famous Scottish king, Macbeth, who had killed Malcolm's father, Duncan I. Macbeth's murder in 1057 and the killing the following year of the pretender to his throne, Lulach, paved the way for Malcolm III to seize power. Formerly a king of Strathclyde, Malcolm's 36 years as Scotland's sovereign were dominated by wars with the old enemy south of Hadrian's Wall, while at home Scotland mirrored the Norman castle-building programme by constructing a number of motte-and-bailey castles.

By 1069 Malcolm III was firmly established as Scotland's king. In that year he married the Wessex princess, Margaret, his second wife. Margaret was a granddaughter of Edmund Ironside and a sister of England's would-be-king, Edgar the Atheling. A learned and devoutly Christian woman, Scotland's queen set about reforming the Scottish Church at the same time as her husband was fighting to win land in northern England. She was sanctified in 1250.

Attacking Northumbria in 1070, Malcolm braced himself for the retaliatory attack he knew would come. Pushing north, the soldiers of William I swept aside all opposition, eventually forcing the humiliated Scottish king to concede defeat to the Normans. Bowing down before William at Abernethy, near Perth in 1072, the king of the Scots then

TOP LEFT: Malcolm II
ABOVE: Malcolm III
RIGHT: Malcolm is hunting when a serf complains that his daughter has been raped

looked on helplessly as England's king rode south with two prize hostages: Malcolm's son, Duncan, and his brother-in-law, Edgar the Atheling.

Malcolm, however, refused to give up the struggle and launched assaults on Northumbria in 1079 and again in 1090. This last attack provoked England's new king, William II, and he marched into Scottish territory during 1092. Malcolm then launched yet another attack the following year, but was killed in an ambush by Arkil Morel, the nephew of Robert Mowbray, Earl of Northumberland. Also killed was Edward, the king's eldest son, while Queen Margaret died a short time later, reputedly of a broken heart. A great, long-reigning monarch, Malcolm III was succeeded by his brother, Donald III.

)))➤ *Duncan I, Donald III, Lulach, Macbeth*

MALCOLM IV (1141–65)

King of Scots (1153–65); grandson of David I; also known as Mael Coluim IV and nicknamed Malcolm the Maiden. Malcolm succeeded his grandfather in 1153 at the age of 11. Four years later he ceded control of Cumbria and Northumbria to Henry II and in return the English monarch made Malcolm Earl of Huntingdon. Beset by unrest at home, the pious Malcolm was succeeded by his brother, William I 'the Lion'.

Malcolm was the son of Henry, Earl of Northumbria, who was David's acknowledged heir from 1144. Malcolm rose to become king of the Scots after the deaths in quick succession first of his father in 1152 and then of his grandfather just a year later. The accession of a minor caused a flurry of activity in Scotland. The Norwegian king attacked Aberdeen and there were other attacks and uprisings in other parts of the kingdom.

Order was eventually restored, but in 1157 England's new king, Henry II, ordered Malcolm IV to return lands in Cumbria and Northumbria to him. As part of the deal,

Henry made Malcolm the Earl of Huntingdon. A devout Christian who died unmarried, Malcolm the Maiden reigned for 12 years before his death brought to the throne his brother, William

))))▶ *Henry II, William I, David I*

MAREDUDD AP BLEDDYN (d. 1132)

King of Powys (1116–32). Maredudd followed his brothers into the rulership of Powys and proved himself less worthy than they had been. He had been held prisoner by the English for five years, but escaped in 1108. When Henry I launched his invasion of Wales in 1114, Maredudd paid homage to the English king and in return was allowed to rule the area as overlord. Later invasions by Henry, however, resulted in Maredudd's flight to Gwynedd to seek sanctuary. The Gwynedd king, Gruffudd ap Cynan would not risk annoying the English king by taking Maredudd in, however, and was forced to sue for peace to his own detriment. Maredudd died in 1132, having lived well into his sixties. He was succeeded by his son, Madog.

))))▶ *Madog ap Maredudd, Henry I, Gruffudd ap Cynan*

MAREDUDD AP OWAIN (d. AD 999)

King of Deheubarth and Gwynedd (AD 986–99); son of Owain ap Hywel and grandson of Hywel Dda. Maredudd ruled jointly in Deheubarth with his father until Owain's death in AD 986. After taking sole command he attacked Gwynedd, killing Cadwallon ap Ieuaf and banishing Cadwallon's heir, Idwal. From that time on Maredudd reigned supreme in both Deheubarth and Gwynedd despite regular Viking attacks. The grandfather of Gruffudd ap Llywelyn, Maredudd was succeeded by his son-in-law, Llywelyn ap Seisyll.

))))▶ *Gruffudd ap Llywelyn, Llwelyn ap Seisyll*

LEFT: Kilmartin stones that date back to the time of Malcolm the Maiden BELOW: LEFT: Mural from the National Portrait Gallery of Scotland with kings and queens of Scotland, including Maclom IV.

MARGARET (1283–90)

Queen of Scotland (1286–90); granddaughter of Alexander III; known as 'the Maid of Norway'. Margaret succeeded her grandfather as Scottish monarch in 1286. She became engaged to Edward, the eldest son of Edward I, as part of the Treaty of Birgham of 1290, but died later that same year.

The daughter of Eric, King of Norway, and Margaret, daughter of Alexander III, Margaret was still a baby when she was acknowledged as heir to the Scottish throne after a series of deaths in the royal family put her first in line. The first wife of Alexander III, his two sons and then Margaret's mother had all died before the king himself passed away.

She was still an infant at the time of her grandfather's death in March 1286, but the Maid of Norway was soon the subject of a marriage deal proposed by England's sovereign, Edward, suggesting that little Margaret be married to his own young son, the future Edward II. The proposal was ratified by the signing of the Treaty of Birgham in 1290.

Sadly, though, Scotland's queen-in-waiting did not live long enough to marry her English prince. Sailing from her Norwegian home to Scotland the seven-year-old Margaret got no further than the Orkneys before she died. The death of the young girl caused Scotland to be thrown into a state of turmoil and it was not until 1291 that Margaret's successor, John Balliol, was appointed by Edward I, the man who, had she lived long enough, would have become her father-in-law.

))))▶ *John Balliol, Edward I, Edward II, Alexander III, Alexander II*

MARY I (1516–58)

Queen of England (1553–58); daughter of Henry VIII; known as 'Bloody Mary'. England's first female sovereign, since the Empress Matilda, succeeded her half-brother, Edward VI, in 1553, after deposing the Nine-Day Queen, Lady Jane Grey. She ruled alongside her husband, Philip II of Spain, whom she adored. Her reign was traumatic: Thomas Wyatt led a revolt, protestants were burnt at the stake and England fought France with the result that Calais was lost. The Catholic Mary died childless and was succeeded by her Protestant half-sister, Elizabeth I.

Born at Greenwich Palace in London on 18 February 1516, Mary was the daughter of Henry VIII and his first wife, Catherine of Aragon. Her childhood was happy enough, but even then the storm clouds were gathering. Rarely healthy, Mary's lot was made worse when her father made an outcast of her mother. The king was desperate for a son and heir, yet Mary proved to be the only child of Henry's marriage to Catherine.

As Henry VIII set about annulling his marriage, his daughter was separated from her mother and sent away to Ludlow Castle in Shropshire. Mary had been made 'Princess of Wales'

in 1525, but the age of 17 she was rendered illegitimate when her parents' marriage was formally annulled. In 1533 Mary's half-sister, Elizabeth, was born. In 1537, the king's legitimate family was completed with the birth of a son, Edward, by his third wife, Jane Seymour.

Ten years later, on 20 February 1547, the bastardised daughter of Henry VIII looked on from the sidelines as her half-brother was crowned Edward VI. A Catholic in an increasingly Protestant land, her woes were multiplied when

Lady Jane Grey was hailed as Edward's successor when the young king died on 6 July 1553.

Mary was in East Anglia when 'Queen Jane' was proclaimed on 10 July. Nine days later Mary rode to London to seize the Crown so recently worn by her late half-brother. Gaining control with little difficulty, the leader of the coup, John Dudley, Duke of Northumberland, and others were rounded up and summarily executed and Lady Jane Grey was imprisoned. Mary ascended the throne on 19 July and was crowned 10 weeks later, on 1 October 1553, at Westminster Abbey.

The new queen was 37 years old by this time and still a single woman. Although she had often been put forward as a pawn in the political game of marriage none of the plans had come to fruition. No sooner had she become queen, however, than she was betrothed to the Spanish king, Philip II, a widower and a devout Catholic. A special occasion for the queen, the royal wedding of 25 July 1554 inflamed religious tensions and provoked hostility among English nationals, who disliked the idea of their monarch being married to a foreign prince. Opposition was so intense that four rebellions were planned in 1554, although only the one fronted by Sir Thomas Wyatt posed a serious danger to Mary before it was put down. However, before long the queen's marriage was over in all but name as Philip II abandoned his English wife and returned to the Low Countries.

Despite the difficulties she faced at the start of her reign, Mary I wasted no time in undoing the Protestant legislation that had been put in place during the previous two reigns. She soon returned England to the papal fold, overturning the anti-Catholic laws introduced by her father and half-brother. In addition three former statutes relating to heresy were reintroduced, while in 1556 the papal legate, Cardinal Reginald Pole, became the new Archbishop of Canterbury.

By the time Pole was appointed, the latest religious upheaval to afflict England had already claimed the lives of many protestants. The first 'heretics' had been burned to death at Smithfield in London in February 1555, but many more would die in the months that followed these. The leading bishops, Hugh Latimer and Nicholas Ridley, died at the stake in 1555, while a later victim was Thomas Cranmer, the former Archbishop of Canterbury, who had introduced the revolutionary English Prayer Book in 1552 and oversaw the annulment of the marriage of Mary's parents.

As the purge of leading Protestants continued, so Mary's enemies waged a propaganda war against the queen and Archbishop Pole. Then, Mary herself went on the warpath. Forming a military alliance with her husband, in 1557 she declared war on the French monarch, Henri II. The first French campaigns went well enough, but then Calais was lost. A major port, Calais was the last remaining outpost of England's once-mighty empire in France. It, too, was recaptured by the French in January 1558 and 10 months later Mary I was dead.

The queen died at St James's Palace, London, on 17 November 1558. The first female sovereign to rule in England was buried at Westminster Abbey and was succeeded by the second queen to reign alone: her half-sister, Elizabeth I.

))) ➤ *Edward VI, Elizabeth I, Henry VIII, Lady Jane Grey*

RIGHT: Mary Tudor

MARY II (1662–94)

Queen of England (1689–94); daughter of James II and wife of William III of Orange. Mary II succeeded her deposed father in 1689. Reigning jointly with William III, she was queen when James II was defeated at the Battle of the Boyne (1690) and when troops committed the Glencoe Massacre (1692). She predeceased her husband and he ruled alone until his death in 1702. Mary's sister, Anne, then came to the throne.

Born at St James's Palace in London on 30 April 1662, Mary was the eldest daughter of the future James II (VII of Scotland) and his first wife, Anne Hyde. Mary was one of eight children born to the couple. She grew up at a time when the monarchy had only just been restored and Mary's birth was overshadowed by another happy royal event: the marriage of Charles II and Catherine of Braganza.

Their wedding took place just three weeks after the birth of the king's niece, and soon hopes of an heir were high, with rumours abounding early in 1663 that the new queen was pregnant. However, the rumours then and later proved false and Catherine remained childless throughout nearly 23 years of marriage to Charles II. As the years passed, the likelihood increased of the monarch's brother, Mary's father, James, becoming the next Stuart sovereign, a concern to Protestants, given the strength of James's Catholic faith.

In the meantime Mary's own circumstances changed dramatically over a six-year period. Suffering the loss of her mother when she was still only 10 years old, two years later her father remarried. At the age of 15, Mary herself was married. She took as her husband her much older cousin, William of Orange. At the time the marriage was arranged Mary had been dismayed at the thought of marrying the son of her aunt, Mary, but the wedding duly took place in London in November 1677.

After the wedding Mary made her home in the Netherlands, but then, in April 1685, Mary's father was crowned king. Both the new monarch's daughters were staunch Protestants, yet James was a Roman Catholic, his faith and his personality immediately setting him on a collision course with parliament. Consequently, in his short reign, problem followed problem until the day when the king's second wife gave birth to a son. Also called James, his birth jeopardised the chances of Mary's succession as well as threatening to transform the royal House of Stuart into a Catholic dynasty. Such a prospect galvanised Whigs and Tories alike and so Mary's husband, William of Orange, was invited to sail to England to depose and succeed Mary's father, James II.

James landed with a large army in November 1688, but within a month he had fled. As the old king headed for exile in France, William III and Mary II were proclaimed king and queen. Named as joint sovereigns on 13 February 1689, they were crowned together at

LEFT: A waxwork Queen Mary II
TOP RIGHT: William III and Mary listen to the Bill of Rights

Westminster Abbey on 11 April. Although they agreed to rule together from the start, in reality William ruled alone, with Mary deputising for the king during his period's abroad.

Mary was queen for just five years, but during her reign English forces were active in Ireland, France and Scotland. Immediately faced with the threat posed by James II and his French allies, William and Mary declared war on France in May 1689. However, there were also foes to be fought in Scotland. Officially recognised as king and queen of the Scots in April 1689, William and Mary continued to be opposed by Jacobites such as John 'Bonnie Dundee' Graham. A loyal supporter of James VII and II, Graham was killed in action in July 1689 as the fighting men of the Scottish Highlands fought royal forces in Perthshire. The year 1689 also saw James besiege Londonderry, but in July 1690 he was decisively beaten in Ireland when losing the Battle of the Boyne.

However, while the old king sailed back to France, the Highlands of Scotland continued to resist the call to recognise William and Mary as monarchs in Scotland.

Ordered to do so by New Year's Day 1692, most clans met the deadline. Even the MacDonald clan eventually toed the official line, but then on 13 February 1692, soldiers from the Earl of Argyll's Regiment of Foot perpetrated the Glencoe Massacre, the object of which was to kill every MacDonald under the age of 70.

Meanwhile, in England, Mary's reign saw important pieces of legislation emerge. The Toleration Act of 1689 gave citizens greater religious freedom, while the same year's Mutiny Bill banned the reigning monarch from maintaining a standing army without parliamentary consent. Then came an Act committing the monarch to calling parliament at least every three years, while at the same time limiting the life of a parliament to three years. Known as the Triennial Act, this became law in 1694, a year that ended with Mary's death.

Dying at Kensington Palace, London, on 28 December 1694, she was buried at Westminster Abbey. Her widowed husband then ruled alone, until his death in 1702 brought to the throne Mary's sister, Anne.

))⧐ *Anne, James II, William III*

MARY, QUEEN OF SCOTS (1542–87)

Queen of Scotland (1542–67) and briefly queen of France; daughter of James V. Mary succeeded her father when she was just a few days old; she was to reign for 25 years. In Scotland she was a central figure in the murders of her secretary, David Rizzio, and her husband, Lord Darnley. The mother of James VI (later James I of England), she was succeeded by him when forced to abdicate in 1567. In England for the next 20 years, in 1587 she was linked to the Babington Plot designed to assassinate her cousin, Elizabeth I, and was executed.

Mary was the daughter of James V of Scotland and his second wife, Mary of Guise. The younger Mary was just six days old when her father died in December 1542, his death following hard on the heels of the Scots' crushing defeat at the Battle of Solway Moss. Left to grow up without a father, in 1543 it was decided that the infant Mary would marry the young son of Henry VIII, the future King Edward VI. In the meantime England continued to attack its northern neighbour. During Edward VI's reign, France's king declared war on England after landing 6,000 soldiers in Scotland having first evacuated Mary. In the jostling for power that followed, the young Scottish queen was betrothed to the French dauphin, François, although the wedding was not scheduled to take place until 1558, by which time the bride-to-be would have reached the age of 16.

If Mary's childhood was eventful, then the decade that followed was truly action-packed, colourful incident following colourful incident. In 1558 Mary's own marriage to the dauphin was closely followed by the death of the English queen, Mary I. With her namesake's passing an opportunity arose for the Scottish monarch to press her claim to be the second successive queen of England. Sure to attract support from France as well as from Catholics at home and abroad, Mary was also the great-granddaughter of Henry VII. However, passed over in favour of her cousin, Elizabeth, the potential for seizing the English crown by force was soon bolstered when Mary's husband, François, became king of France in July 1559. But in 1560 the tables were turned.

Mary was briefly queen of France while her mother Mary of Guise acted as regent in Scotland. By the end of 1560 her mother and her husband were both dead. Earlier that same year a prolonged siege of Leith, near Edinburgh, had led to English success and the Treaty of Edinburgh, which acknowledged Elizabeth as the rightful English monarch, while a short time later the Scottish parliament renounced the pope's authority in Scotland. A bad year for Mary came to a sorry end when her husband, François II, was taken ill and in December 1560 died.

She returned to Scotland in 1561, at a time when the country was changing fast under the increasing influence of the Calvinist strain of Protestantism preached by zealots such as John Knox. The queen was a continuing target for Knox's attacks. At the same time, Mary herself remained a thorn in the side of her cousin, Elizabeth I of England.

In July 1565 Mary married another cousin, Henry Stuart, Lord Darnley. Darnley and Mary shared the same grandmother, Margaret Tudor. However, such close family ties were no guarantee of a lasting marriage as the queen of Scots soon discovered. She was pregnant by March 1566 and that month the queen's secretary, David Rizzio, was stabbed to death by the jealous Darnley and his accomplices. Three months later, on 19 June 1566, Mary gave birth to her son and heir, James. Darnley himself was murdered in February 1567, strangled at Kirk-o'-Field outside Edinburgh. His death was followed two months later by Mary's third marriage, to James Hepburn, 4th Earl of Bothwell.

The dramas still came thick and fast as, with Hepburn (and possibly Mary) implicated in Darnley's downfall, Mary was seized by a band of Scottish nobles, who imprisoned her at Loch Leven Castle. Soon her reign as queen of Scots would be over and so, too, her relationship with Bothwell. Forced to abdicate on 24 July 1567, Mary was succeeded by her one-year-old son, who was crowned James VI of Scotland.

Returned to prison on the banks of Loch Leven, the former queen of Scots escaped to mount one last attack in the hopes of reclaiming her crown. Defeated, however, she headed for England, where she threw herself on the mercy of Elizabeth I. The English queen permitted her to stay in England, but the price Mary had to pay was a lifelong sentence of house arrest.

Frequently linked to pro-Catholic plots against the Protestant Elizabeth, she was moved from country house

to country house. But then, with the uncovering of the Babington Plot in 1586, the Stuart queen was arrested, found guilty of involvement in the plot to murder Elizabeth I and then beheaded at Fotheringhay Castle in Northamptonshire. Buried without ceremony at Peterborough Cathedral, after her son, James, became England's king her remains were reburied at Westminster Abbey in 1611.

⫸ *James V, James VI, Elizabeth I*

MATHGAMAIN (d. AD 976)

King of the Dál Cais (AD 964–76); son of Cennétig mac Lorcán. Building on the success of his father, who he succeeded in AD 964, Mathgamain consolidated his dynasty at the expense of the fading Eóganacht confederation. Fighting many battles in Munster and beyond, he was killed in AD 976 and succeeded by his younger brother, the famed Brian Bóruma.

⫸ *Brian Bóruma, Cennétig mad Lorcán*

NÉILL, BRIAN (d. 1260)

King of Cenél nEógain (1238–60). Brian Néill was later proclaimed high king of all Ireland. He became ruler of the northern kingdom from 1238 and three years later he asserted his authority by attacking and defeating the Mac Lochlainn clan. Continuing to fight for supremacy in the north, the chief of the Uí Néills forged various alliances with native Irish leaders, which culminated in 1258 in his claim to be high king of Ireland. However, two years later Brian Néill was killed in the Battle of Down.

)))▶ *House of O'Neill*

NÉILL, DOMHNALL (d. 1325)

King of Cenél nEógain; also known as Donal O'Neill. This son of Brian Néill had three spells as king.

First claiming power in 1283 following the death of his father's successor, Buidhe Néill, his initial reign lasted three years. King again in 1291, after 1296 he reigned unopposed until losing territory to the 'Red Earl', the powerful Richard de Burgh. Then linking up with Edward Bruce in 1315, he supported the brother of Robert the Bruce in his bid to become king in Ireland. However, after the death of Edward at the Battle of Faughart in 1318 retribution soon followed and Domhnall was deposed. Recovering some territory in the years that followed, he died in 1325.

)))▶ *Edward Bruce*

NIALL GLUNDUB (d. AD 919)

King of Cenél nEógain; king of Tara and later high king of all Ireland. A son of Aed Findliath Mac Néill, the king of the northern Uí Néill clan, Niall Glundub ('Niall Black-knee') became king of Tara in eastern Ireland in AD 916. Reigning in both kingdoms at a time of regular Viking raids, the Norsemen landed at Waterford in AD 914 and attacked Munster in AD 915. Back in increasing numbers in AD 917, two years later Niall Glundub was killed

in battle when attacking the Vikings of Dublin, his name living on in the O'Neill surname.

)))▶ *House of O'Neill*

NORMANDY, HOUSE OF

The dynasty of the Conqueror and the Conquest, the *Domesday Book* and domination, the Norman era lasted less than 100 years, yet such was the influence of the invaders and settlers from Normandy that life in all four corners of the British Isles was radically and for ever changed.

Reigning in England from 1066 to 1154, the House of Normandy originated not in northern France, but in Scandinavia. For it was from there that Rollo the Ganger sailed to pillage and plunder. The son of Rognvald of Moer and nephew of Sigurd the Mighty, Rollo, or Rolf, conquered Normandy. Later gaining acceptance by the French king, Charles the Simple, the Viking duchy of Normandy continued to maintain strong links with Danish rulers during the tenth and eleventh centuries and so the grandfather of William the Conqueror, Richard II of Normandy, married Svein Forkbeard's sister, Astrid.

However, the Norman dynasty also forged marriage alliances with other royal houses, for example, the marriage of William the Conqueror to Matilda, the daughter of the Count of Flanders. There was also a strong English connection and it was this link that ultimately led to the Norman Conquest of England. For when Emma, the daughter of Richard I of Normandy, married first

THE HOUSE OF NORMANDY

1066–87	William I the Conqueror
1087–1100	William II Rufus
1100–35	Henry I
1135–54	Stephen

Ethelred II the Unready and then Cnut, the fortunes of England and Normandy became inextricably linked. And so it was that the mother of Edward the Confessor and the sister of William the Conqueror's grandfather gave Duke William a good claim to be Edward's successor.

Norman sources suggest that the duke was promised England's crown by both Edward and his eventual successor, Earl Harold of Wessex, but when the Confessor died and was succeeded by Harold II, the Duke of Normandy was forced to claim the crown by force. Landing on England's south coast in September 1066, William won the Battle of Hastings in October and was crowned king on Christmas Day that year.

Within two years of his coronation the Norman Conquest was so well-advanced that William could afford to return to his duchy on the other side of the English Channel leaving his half-brother, Odo of Bayeux, to oversee his affairs in England. Meanwhile the Norman revolution continued. Castles and cathedrals were built and Norman customs were introduced. English clergymen were replaced by Normans and Norman nobles were granted land seized from the Anglo-Saxon nobility.

In fact William I effected such an overhaul of English society that, in the course of just two decades, it had been substantially and irrevocably altered, the nature of this change shown clearly by the Domesday Book. The Great Inquest or survey of English life was compiled 1086–87, and was intended to discover the ownership of land and livestock and was collated in two volumes known as the Great and Little Domesday Books.

The tough and uncompromising warrior-king like William I the Conqueror, was succeeded by William II as the English king. He saw off the challenge from barons loyal to his brother, Robert, and defeated Gwynedd and

the Scots, but fell out with St Anselm, the man he had appointed as Archbishop of Canterbury. William II Rufus was succeeded by his English-born brother, Henry I, who was another strong ruler. Also opposed by his brother, Duke Robert, he overcame this threat by capturing and imprisoning him and by taking possession of the duchy of Normandy. Known as Beauclerc, he continued the process of imposing the Crown's control.

However, like William II Rufus, Henry I did not leave a son to succeed him and so when King Stephen came to

TOP RIGHT: O'Brien's Castle, County Galway,
TOP LEFT: Chepstow Castle
LEFT: A Norman hunting scene

the throne civil war broke out with the king fighting to stave off the challenge of Henry's daughter, the Empress Matilda. Undefeated by the empress in war, he 'lost' the peace by agreeing to let Matilda's son, Henry of Anjou, succeed him. And so with Stephen's death in 1154, the House of Normandy gave way to the House of Anjou, Henry II becoming England's first Angevin or Plantagenet king.

▶▶▶ *Henry I, William I, William II*

EVENTS OF THE NORMAN ERA

1066 The Battle of Hastings is fought in the same year that a comet appears in the sky; this comes to be known as Halley's Comet

1075 The Turks capture Jerusalem

1078 Work begins on the White Tower of the Tower of London. The building is completed in 1300

1086 Compilation of the *Domesday Book* begins

1094 The famed Spanish knight, El Cid, defeats the Moors occupying Valencia; St Mark's in Venice is completed more than a century after work had begun on the great church

1099 The first Christian crusade captures Jerusalem

1120 Prince William, the heir to the English throne, dies in the wreck of the *White Ship*

1123 St Bartholomew's Hospital is founded in London

1148 The second Christian crusade fails to take the ancient city of Damascus

1154 Geofffrey of Monmouth dies. The author of the *Historia Regum Britanniae*, his account of ancient English kings introduced the legend of King Arthur

O'CONNOR, HOUSE OF

Sharing the same name as the County Offaly clan, which was well to the fore in central Ireland during the fifteenth century, the O'Connors of Connacht were the descendants of Conchobar (or Connor). A ruler of the Uí Briain Aí, a line said to have descended from the fifth-century king, Brión (Brian), Conchobar's small kingdom covered part of modern-day County Roscommon.

Retaining this Roscommon heartland, later leaders extended the borders to the north and south-west.

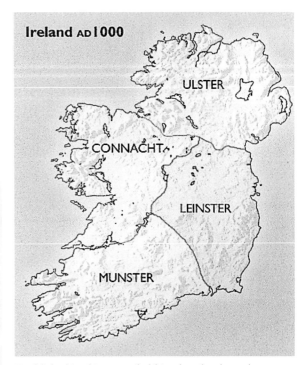

Established in this expanded kingdom by the early eleventh century, one of the first kings of note was Gaí Bernaig (or Aedh). He was one of a number of Irish kings who joined forces to fight Brian Bóruma's son, Donnchad, before being killed in 1067 by his northern rival, Art Uí Ruairc (O'Rourke). Later, Gaí Bernaig's son Ruaidrí na Soide Buide, briefly succeeded in becoming the king of all Connacht, but after he was blinded in 1092 by the Uí Fhlaithbertaig (O'Flaherty) tribe, the dynasty's fortunes faded.

However, power returned in spectacular fashion with the rise of Toirrdelbach Ua Conchobair. Also known as Turlough O'Connor, he was chosen as king of Connacht in 1106. Retaining this title for the next 50 years, by 1138 he had conquered Munster and other provinces and was duly recognised as Ireland's high king.

After Toirrdelbach's death in 1156, his Connacht crown passed to his son, Ruaidrí Ua Conchobair (Rory O'Connor). Like his father, he also rose through the ranks of Irish rulers to succeed Muirchertach Mac Lochlainn as Ireland's last-ever high king. Next defeating the king of Leinster, Diarmait MacMurrough, in 1171 Henry II campaigned in Ireland. Successful in forcing into submission other Irish kings, in

LEFT: Ireland at the time of the Viking battles

1175 Henry persuaded Ruaidrí to acknowledge him as his overlord.

Deposed a short time later, no O'Connor king after Ruaidrí Ua Conchobair would ever again hold so much power. His brother or half-brother, Cathal Crobderg, was recognised as Connacht's king by King John in 1204, but in the last years of his reign he had to fight hard against the powerful Anglo-Irish landowners, Richard de Burgh and Hugh de Lacy. Cathal was succeeded by his son, Fedlimid, who was reduced to the role of tenant-king after 1235, the year in which de Burgh won full possession of Connacht.

)))**➤** *Toirrdelbach Ua Conchobair, Muichertach Mac Lochlainn*

THE HOUSE OF O'CONNOR

d. 1067	ed in Gaí Bernaig
d. 1118	Ruaidrí na Soide Buide
d. 1156	Toirrdelbach (Mór) Ua Conchobair
d. 1198	Ruaidrí Ua Conchobair
d. 1224	Cathal Crobderg Ua Conchobair
d. 1228	ed Ua Conchobair
d. 1265	Fedlimid Ua Conchobair

O'NEILL, HOUSE OF

A dominant force in the north of Ireland for four centuries, the Uí Néill dynasty took its name from Niall Noígallach. A semi-legendary figure, who flourished in the fifth century, Niall of the Nine Hostages lived and died as a celebrated raider of various British locations.

A possible descendant of Niall was the fifth-century figure, Lóegaire mac Néill, who may have been king of Ireland during St Patrick's time. Thereafter, various Uí Néill rulers expanded the clan's realms, one branch extending south to become an independent dynasty. The northern Uí Néills also gained a separate identity as the O'Neill family claimed its line of descent from the mighty high king of Ireland, Niall Glúndub. Forced to take up arms against Viking raiders, he died in battle at Dublin in AD 919.

Following his demise, the northern Uí Néills were never quite the same force until the emergence of Áed Méith and then Áed's nephew, Brian O'Neill. Like his great ancestor,

Niall Glúndub, he became Ireland's high king, Brian claiming this title in 1258, some 20 years after he had become head of the Cenél nEógain clan, but just two years before his death at the Battle of Down.

His successor was Áed Buidhe O'Neill, but in 1283 Brian's son, Domhnall, became king after fending off a challenge from Áed Buidhe's brother. Deposed just three years later, Domhnall enjoyed a brief return to the seat of power in 1291 before fully regaining control in 1296. Then reigning until his death in 1325, Domhnall O'Neill sided with Edward Bruce in 1315, supporting the Scot in his vain bid to overturn English power in Ireland and so become the country's king.

The last true chief of the family was Hugh O'Neill (1550–1616). The Earl of Tyrone, he led a brief Catholic revolt against the English before heading into exile as part of the Flight of the Earls. Taking place in 1607, traditionally the exodus of Hugh O'Neill, Rory O'Donnell (the Earl of Tyrconnel) and Cúchonnacht Maguire (the Lord of Fermanagh) has been viewed as a critical event in Ireland's history: after the earls fled, their estates were seized and the so-called 'plantation' in Ireland of non-Catholics began in earnest.

)))**➤** *Niall Glúndub*

OWAIN AP GWYNEDD (c. 1100–70)

King of Gwynedd (1137–70); son of Gruffudd ap Cynan; also known as Owain ap Gruffudd. Owain succeeded his father with the aid of his brother in 1137. He went on the warpath in Wales in his early years when he was untroubled by English opposition. During this campaign Owain captured Carmarthen, Mold and the kingdom of Powys. But after 20 years as ruler of Gwynedd, he was attacked and defeated by England's new king, Henry II. Beaten again by Henry in 1163, from then on Owain of Gwynedd continued to side with the English monarch against the Deheubarth king, Rhys ap Gruffudd.

In 1165 he then switched tack to join forces with Rhys and the Powys king, Owain Cyfeiliog. The successful campaign to drive Henry II out of Wales lasted until 1167. Three years later Owain of Gwynedd died. Possibly buried at Bangor, North Wales, he was succeeded by his son, Dafydd ap Owain.

)))**➤** *Dafydd ap Owain, Henry II, Gruffudd ap Cynan*

OWAIN AP HYWEL (d. AD 988)

King of Deheubarth (AD 950–88); son of Hywel Dda. Owain succeeded his famous father in AD 950. Despite carrying out several invasion attempts in Gwynedd in the first part of his reign, it was only after his younger son, Maredudd, assumed control in his father's later years that Gwynedd was annexed by Deheubarth. Owain's eldest son, Einion, had been killed in AD 984, so Owain ap Hywel was succeeded by Maredudd.

))))➤ *Hywel Dda, Maredudd ap Owain*

OWAIN GLYNDWR (c. 1355–c. 1416)

Self-styled Prince of Wales (1400–16); also known as Owen Glendower. He has maintained his status in the popular imagination but not in academic circles which refute his claims of majesty. He was descended from the royal families of Powys and Deheubarth and was an ancestor of Henry VII. Forming alliances with French collaborators and English barons such as Mortimer, Northumberland and his son, Hotspur, he seized towns and land. Later pegged back as the future Henry V asserted his dominance, Owain Glyndwr evaded capture to ensure his status as a great Welsh rebel hero.

Possibly born at Little Treffgarne near Haverfordwest, Owain Glyndwr was a Welshman of royal blood, a man who in his younger days had fought for the English king, Richard II. In 1400, however, his life was transformed. Holding a grudge against Henry IV for not ruling in his favour in a dispute over land, Glyndwr was declared the Prince of Wales on 16 September 1400 and led attacks against several English towns in North-East Wales.

After that little more was heard of the rebel until 1402 when his first major victory was made sweeter still by the capture of Sir Edmund Mortimer, who was a potential challenger to Henry IV. Then, in 1403 near Shrewsbury, the Welsh-born son of the English king, Prince Henry, restored the balance by killing Glyndwr's ally, the feared warrior Hotspur. However, this was a minor setback as strong new alliances were sealed, with France providing military support, while in 1405 he joined forces with Mortimer and Henry Percy, the Earl of Northumberland and father of Hotspur.

Known as the Tripartite Indenture, this deal committed the three leaders to dividing England and Wales into three parts should they succeed in overthrowing Henry IV. Ultimately, such a victory was to elude Owain Glyndwr and his allies, but for a time at least, the Welsh leader scored several notable successes and held parliaments at Dolgellau, Harlech and Machynlleth.

From 1406, however, English forces fought back to telling effect and Glyndwr was forced to retreat. Aberystwyth and Owain Glyndwr's capital, Harlech, were recaptured, while the remarkable rebel was made to live the life of an outlaw for the rest of his days.

))))➤ *Henry IV, Henry V*

CENTRE AND BOTTOM LEFT: Owain Glyndŵr
ABOVE: War between Philip II and Henry II

PLANTAGENET, HOUSE OF

The Plantagenets were England's ruling dynasty for more than 300 years; there were 14 kings in all spread across the different houses of Anjou (or Angevin), Plantagenet, Lancaster and York. Henry II, the first king of this dynasty, began his reign in 1154, while the last Plantagenet, the Yorkist monarch, Richard III, was killed in battle in 1485.

The name Plantagenet dates back to the time of Geoffrey of Anjou. The father of Henry II, this Angevin count was renowned for fastening to his helmet a sprig of broom. The Latin name for this plant is Planta genista, while the French word for it is *genàt*: hence Plantagenet.

When Henry II became England's king he also ruled over a vast French empire, the reclaiming of which would become a priority for many of his successors. His son, Richard I the Lionheart, died trying to recover lands lost by his brother, John, while King John himself not only lost most of England's French possessions, but he was also forced to take flight when the French dauphin, Louis, invaded London. In the reign of Edward III the Hundred Years War with France began, the English winning and then losing vast expanses of French territory. Later Henry V would emulate his greatest achievements paving the way for his son and successor to be crowned king of France in 1431. Then the backlash began and by 1453 England was left clinging to its one possession: Calais.

The Plantagenet kings were also frequently engaged in fighting the Scots. Edward I was so successful north of the border that he earned the nickname the 'Hammer of the Scots', but Edward II was routed by Robert I the Bruce at Bannockburn in 1314. Edward I also campaigned in Wales, where he succeeded in establishing English control, chiefly by conquest and castle-building. King John also invaded Wales, but as Lord of Ireland he was far less successful than his father, Henry II, whose invasion force of 1171 began England's conquest of Ireland.

Civil war was an occupational hazard for medieval kings, while deposed kings and new ruling houses were another feature of the Plantagenet era. The first Angevin king, Henry II, came to power following years of civil strife and later had to contend with overly ambitious sons. Nevertheless the rebellion of 1173–74, which came soon after the martyrdom of Thomas Becket, did not mushroom into full-blown war. Then in the period overlapping the reigns of his son, John, and his grandson, Henry III, civil war was compounded by the presence in England of the French dauphin, Louis. Later still Henry III was challenged by his brother-in-law, Simon de Montfort, and then captured in 1264, before emerging triumphant in 1265.

Edward II was not so lucky. War broke out in 1323 with the king opposed by his queen, Isabelle, but after initially repelling his enemies, in 1327 he was caught, imprisoned, dethroned and done to death. Richard II was another monarch to antagonise England's barons and in 1399 this antagonism cost him his crown and probably his life, too. Deposed by his own cousin, he died in prison soon afterwards, while the

THE HOUSE OF PLANTAGENET

Henry II	(1154–89)
Richard I	(1189–99)
John	(1199–1216)
Henry III	(1216–72)
Edward I	(1272–1307)
Edward II	(1307–27)
Edward III	(1327–77)
Richard II	(1377–1400)

(see also House of Lancaster and House of York)

accession of Henry IV completed the rise to power of the house of Lancaster.

Remaining the royal house as Henry V and his son, Henry VI, were crowned, first blood in the Wars of the Roses was drawn by the house of York. Fighting the king's forces from 1455, Edward IV became the first Yorkist king six years later when he deposed Henry VI. The last Lancastrian ruler was briefly reinstated but, deposed a second time, in 1471 he was executed.

Edward IV established his dynasty on solid foundations, but when he died in 1483 the walls of the house of York came tumbling down. Firstly his son and heir, Edward V, became one of the Princes in the Tower as Richard, Duke of York (a brother of Edward IV), made his successful bid to become king. However, the reign of Richard III was as troubled as it was short. Finally and fatally attacked by the new Lancastrian leader, Henry Tudor, at Bosworth Field in 1485, the last Plantagenet king also earned the dubious distinction of being the last English king to die in battle.

Away from the battlefields, there were many advances in English common law during the years of the Plantagenet kings.

Black Death. The former was the name accorded the king's warrior-son, Edward, whose deeds in battle during the Hundred Years War were highly acclaimed. The latter was the name given to the plague epidemic that swept across England from 1348 killing over a million.

Like famine, the 'great mortality' of plague was a recurring pestilence in the fourteenth century, but other aspects of life in England continued to evolve. English replaced French as the official language, while a one-time civil servant, Geoffrey Chaucer was still writing *The Canterbury Tales*, one of the great masterpieces of English literature at the time of his death in 1400. In the century that followed, William Caxton made his mark by introducing the first printing press to England, while in architecture there were changes as English Gothic was replaced from the 1350s by the Perpendicular style.

)))▶ **House of Lancaster, House of York**

EVENTS OF THE PLANTAGENET ERA

1170   Murder of the Archbishop of Canterbury, Thomas Becket

1189   The third Christian crusade begins

1215   King John sets his seal on the Magna Carta (Great Charter)

1254   The Venetian explorer, Marco Polo, is born

1258   Baghdad razed to the ground by Mongol hordes

1260s   Kublai Khan, the son of Genghis Khan, rules in China

1267   Henry III acknowledges Llywelyn ap Gruffudd as Prince of Wales

1284   Wales finally conquered by England's king, Edward I

1348   The Black Death reaches England. Spreading from southern ports it kills around one third of the population

1360s   Tamurlane begins his conquest of Asia. In China the Ming Dynasty is established

1362   English becomes the official language of England's parliament and courts

1377   After 68 years in exile in Avignon, the papacy returns to Rome

John was confronted with the Magna Carta in 1215, this great charter holding the king to account for what his opponents saw as his abuses of power. In contrast, the rash of law-making in the reign of Edward I led to his admirers referring to the king as the 'English Justinian' (a reference to the sixth-century emperor of Constantinople who was famed for codifying Roman law).

The grandson of Edward I and his namesake, Edward III, emulated his grandfather's achievements in war, if not in the administration of his realm. However, he ruled for 50 years, his reign best-remembered for the outbreak of the Hundred Years War, but also for the Black Prince and the

LEFT: Geoffrey Plantagenet, founder of House of Plantagenet
ABOVE: Lincoln Cathedral displaying Plantagenet figures

RAGNALL I (d. AD 921)

King of York (AD 910–21). Ragnall was one of the many Vikings expelled from Dublin in AD 902 and immediately after this event he took to making border raids on Strathclyde and Scotland. In AD 910 he seized the kingdom of York and began extending its boundaries. In around AD 914 he declared himself king of Strathclyde, an area that he had continued to bombard with attack since his time in York. He came into conflict with Ethelflaed, the Lady of the Mercians, in AD 917, but her death the following year proved fortuitous for Ragnall. Constantine II of Scotland then joined the fray, assembling a small army to march against Ragnall, but the Dane was successful once again.

On his return to York he discovered that various factions had arisen and there was opposition to his place as ruler. Undeterred he reasserted his authority in this Danish kingdom. His luck eventually ran out in around AD 920 and he was forced to submit to Edward the Elder. He died in AD 921.

))))➤ *Ethelflaed, Edward the Elder, Constantine II*

RHODRI AP OWAIN (d. 1195)

King of Gwynedd (1170–90); son of Owain ap Gwynedd. Rhodri joined his brother, Dafydd, in their attack on the elder sons of Owain, Gwynedd to throw them out of the territories they had inherited and claim them for themselves. Although their mission was successful, Dafydd turned on his borther and imprisoned him in 1174. Rhodri escaped the following year and sought his revenge, driving Dafydd into the east and seizing most of the kingdom of Gwynedd. He ruled until 1190 when his nephews conspired against him and drove him into exile. Rhodri is buried at Holyhead.

))))➤ *Owain ap Gwynedd, Dafydd ap Owain*

RHODRI MAWR (d. AD 878)

King of Gwynedd (AD 844–77); son of Merfyn Frych. Rhodri was the first Welsh king to earn the mantle 'Mawr' (meaning 'Great'). At the height of his powers he ruled over every part of Wales except the far south-eastern and south-western corners. The slayer of the famous Viking leader, Gorm, two decades later Rhodri was forced to flee by a Danish militia. Sailing to Ireland

in AD 877, the following year he returned to Wales, but was killed in battle. Succeeded by his son, Anarawd ap Rhodri, a second son, Cadell ap Rhodri ruled over the new kingdom of Deheubarth.

Born Rhodri ap Merfyn, when his father, King Merfyn, died in AD 844 after 19 years as ruler in North Wales, the new sovereign inherited a sizeable kingdom: Gwynedd from his father and Powys from his mother. Eight years later Rhodri sent shock waves reverberating throughout northern Europe by killing the feared Gorm and defeating his Viking force at Anglesey. Then in AD 872 the Welsh king further reinforced his hold on power by marrying Angharad, the sister of the Ceredigion (Cardigan) king, Gwygon ap Meurig.

Said to have built a castle at the great Deheubarth capital of Dinefwr in AD 876, Rhodri was forced into exile during AD 877 by invading Vikings. Soon mounting a challenge to take back his Gwynedd kingdom, in AD 878 he died in battle at Prestatyn. Possibly killed when fighting an alliance of Norsemen and Mercians led by Ceowulf, for much of his reign Rhodri Mawr had been the most powerful of all Welsh kings.

Succeeded in Gwynedd by his son, Anarawd ap Rhodri, after Rhodri's death no native-born ruler would ever again rule over such a large realm, the kingdom the monarch passed on then being divided into two regions: Gwynedd (north) and Deheubarth (south). A younger son, Cadell ap Rhodri, reigned in the former, while Rhodri Mawr's grandson was the famed Deheubarth king, Hywel Dda.

))))➤ *Hywel Dda, Anarawd ap Rhodri*

RHYDDERCH AP IESTYN (d. 1033)

King of Deheubarth (1023–33). Hailing from South Wales, Rhydderch seized power after the death of Llywelyn ap Seisyll in 1023 and then ruled over Deheubarth for the next 10 years. Succeeded by the brothers, Hywel and Maredudd ap Edwin, 14 years after his death, Rhydderch's son, Gruffudd ap Rhydderch, became Deheubarth's king.

⟫⟫ *Gruffudd ap Rhydderch, Hywel ap Edwin, Maredudd ap Edwin*

RHYS AP GRUFFUDD (c. 1130–97)

King of Deheubarth (1155–97); son of Gruffudd ap Rhys; known as 'the Lord Rhys'. Just a child when his father died, he became the last true ruler of Deheubarth when taking control of the kingdom from his half-brothers, Anarawd and Cadell. A warrior-king, when young he waged war on Henry II, but eventually agreed a peace that lasted until 1189.

The son of Gruffudd ap Rhys and his wife Gwenllian, he first made his mark in 1157, helping Welsh kings to begin the fightback against Henry II of England. He brought to this long campaign the experience of war he had gained when fighting with his half-brothers, Anarawd and Cadell, against the Clares of Ceredigion (Cardigan) and the Cliffords of Llandovery. Battling with the Clares and Cliffords again in 1159, four years later the struggle against the English enemy took a turn for the worse when Henry II defeated Rhys and forced him to surrender his hold on Ceredigion and to forsake the title of king.

Then dubbed the Lord Rhys, the Deheubarth leader was down, but not out and he

LEFT: Anglesey

retook Ceredigion in 1164. Next assuming power in Cyfeiliog, in 1171 Rhys made his peace with Henry II.

Allowed to retain his lands in South Wales, Rhys was also given the rôle of justiciar (or chief justice) in his native territory. From that time on Rhys ruled in peace over his domain until 1189. With his capital at Dinefwr, near Carmarthen, he introduced Plantagenet ways and built castles, while also establishing the Welsh tradition of eisteddfods, where poets met and recited verse.

Despite family in-fighting Rhys ap Gruffudd retained his hold on power until his death. However, with the end of his long life, so the kingdom he ruled over disintegrated. Survived by his sons, Gruffudd ap Rhys, Maelgwyn and Rhys Gryg, after his death the fortunes of the kingdom of Deheubarth went into a slow, but terminal decline.

RHYS AP OWAIN (d. 1078)

King of Deheubarth (1072–78); brother of Maredudd ap Owain. Rhys proved to be an ineffectual ruler, unable to defend his kingdom from the marauding Normans in their attacks in 1073 and 1074. He is remembered as the man who arranged the murder of the Gwynedd king, Bleddyn ap Cynfan, although he gained nothing from this death.

⫸ *Maredudd ap Owain*

RHYS AP TEWDWR (d. 1093)

King of Deheubarth (1078–93), a descendant of Hywel Dda, also known as Rhys the Great. Once in exile in Brittany, Rhys ap Tewdwr fought with Gruffudd ap Cynan and his cousin, Rhys ap Maredudd, when winning the Battle of Mynydd Carn, which was fought near Tenby in South-West Wales in 1081. However Rhys ap Maredudd was killed during the heat of battle and so Rhys ap Tewdwr succeeded him in Deheubarth, while Gruffudd took control in Gwynedd.

Forced to submit to William the Conqueror, after England's king had marched into his kingdom in 1082, Rhys ruled for six more years before being chased out of Deheubarth by raiders from neighbouring Powys. Sailing to Ireland, he remained there until returning to Deheubarth in 1091 with a Viking army and taking back his kingdom. Two years later, however, Rhys ap Tewdwr was killed.

⫸ *Hywel Dda, William I, Gruffudd ap Cynan, Rhys ap Maredudd*

RICHARD I (1157–99)

King of England (1189–99); son of Henry II. Best-known as Richard the Lionheart (or Côeur de Lion), he succeeded his father in 1189. Richard has become a famed warrior-king who fought on crusades. He was later imprisoned in Austria. After his release he regained lands lost in France, but was wounded there and died of gangrene. He was survived by his wife, Berengaria, but was succeeded by his brother, John.

Born at Beaumont Palace, Oxfordshire, on 8 September 1157, he was one of the eight children of Henry II and Queen Eleanor. Richard was the fourth-born child and so, until he was 15 years old, he was only second in line to the English throne. Before 1172 he was Duke of Aquitaine, the French region where his mother had grown up. Then, in the space of six eventful years, the course of the young duke's life was changed by two deaths in the royal family.

First to die was Henry the Young King, Richard's elder brother. His death on 11 June 1183 was followed by the death of Henry II on 6 July 1189. Previously hostile to his father, later he had made up with the old king and so, after returning from two years on crusade, Richard's coronation service occurred at Westminster Abbey on 3 September 1189, just a short time after his investiture as Duke of Normandy.

Typically, his stay in England was a short one. Soon returning to Normandy, he spent the next winter there before once again taking the Cross. Leaving for the Holy Land in July 1190, his journey to the Middle East took Richard I via Cyprus, where he met up again with Berengaria, the daughter of King Sancho VI of Navarre. Friends since childhood, Richard and Berengaria were married in Limassol and then travelled together throughout Richard's time on Crusade.

Taking the Palestinian city of Acre in 1191, Richard the Lionheart went on to defeat the feared Saracen leader, Saladin, at Arsuf, near Jaffa, but fell short of capturing Jerusalem. With a truce agreed in September 1192, the English king and his queen then left the Holy Land. Berengaria headed for Italy, but Richard ventured across Europe only to fall foul of his enemy, Duke Leopold of Austria. Imprisoned by the duke in December 1192, Richard spent the next 13 months in a castle beside the River Danube.

While there, legend has it, he was visited by Blondel de Nesle. A French poet, Blondel is said to have sat beneath one of the castle's windows and sung a song that he and Richard had composed together years before. Pausing halfway through his recital, the song was taken up and completed by a voice sounding out from behind the solid stone walls.

Finally released from his faraway prison in February 1194, after a huge ransom of 100,000 marks had been paid, Richard I returned to the kingdom that he had left in the hands of William Longchamp. Appointed chancellor in 1189, Longchamp's main antagonist was the king's notorious younger brother, John, who forced Longchamp from office in 1191. However, on the king's return John was punished for seizing power in his absence and for giving up control of territories in France. Attempting to regain these lost lands, in May 1194 Richard I left England for the last time with government in his English kingdom given over to

Hubert Walter, the Archbishop of Canterbury who made his mark as a capable administrator, initially as justiciar or chief justice.

Meanwhile, on the other side of the English Channel, the warrior-king largely succeeded in recovering French territories, while at the same time building castles such as the great stronghold known as Château-Gaillard. Continuing to carry the fight to his former friend and ally, the French king, Philip II, he was wounded by a crossbow bolt during a siege at Châlus. The injury was not life threatening, but gangrene set in and on 6 April 1199 the great soldier died and was laid to rest at Fontevraud, although his heart was buried separately at Rouen. Survived by Berengaria, who is unique in being the only queen of England never to visit the country, Richard I was succeeded by his younger brother, John.

)))⯈ *Henry II, John, House of Plantagenet*

BOTTOM LEFT: Powys Castle
LEFT: Richard I in prison in Vienna 1192
TOP RIGHT: Richard I and Saladin
RIGHT: The coronation of Richard I

RICHARD II (1367–1400)

King of England (1377–99); son of Edward the Black Prince and grandson of Edward III. Richard succeeded his grandfather in 1377. The Peasants' Revolt occurred in 1381, while the 'Merciless Parliament' of 1388 gave a foretaste of the rebellion that would bring down an unpopular king a decade later. Led by his cousin, Henry Bolingbroke, in 1399 this rebellion deposed Richard II, who died in prison a short time later. He was succeeded by Bolingbroke who was crowned Henry IV.

The second son of Edward the Black Prince and Joan of Kent, he was born at Bordeaux on 6 January 1367. At that time the likelihood of his becoming king of England was remote. However, during the first 10 years of his life, the deaths of three Plantagenet males, all named Edward, propelled him into the spotlight. Richard's seven-year-old brother Edward of Angoulàme, died in 1372. Then, in June 1376, the 'Black Prince' was struck down by a fatal illness that was probably dysentery, while one year later, on 22 June 1377, Richard's grandfather, Edward III, passed away.

King at the age of 10, Richard II thus became the first minor to become king of England since Henry III had ascended the throne in 1216. Crowned at Westminster Abbey on 16 July 1377, the young monarch was then steered through the first decade of his reign by his mother and tutor,

and by his uncle, John of Gaunt. In time, men such as Robert de Vere, Sir Michael de la Pole and the Earl of Arundel also exerted their influence at the royal court until Richard II came of age.

By then, though, the king had already made a favourable impression during the first major crisis of his reign. Known as the Peasants' Revolt, this occurred when crowds of peasants from Essex and Kent marched on London. Fronted by Wat Tyler and John Ball, the chief cause of the revolt was the introduction of a new poll tax. To be paid by all adults at the steep rate of a shilling (modern equivalent £50) per person, this amount was three times higher than any previous poll tax.

On reaching London, the marchers laid waste to parts of the city, before coming face to face with the 14-year-old monarch. Richard II gave Wat Tyler an audience, but when scuffles broke out Tyler was killed. Then, as the mood became increasingly ugly, the young king rode out before the angry peasants defying them to take arms against him. But the mob had no grievance with the king, their slogan being 'With King Richard and the true-hearted commons', and so the Peasants' Revolt was brought to a peaceful conclusion.

With this uprising at an end, Richard II did not have long to wait for the next crisis to arrive. Increasingly at odds with leading members of the nobility, he clashed with restless barons including his own uncle, the Duke of Gloucester. Themselves jostling for power and angered by the influence of the king's inner circle of ministers, the

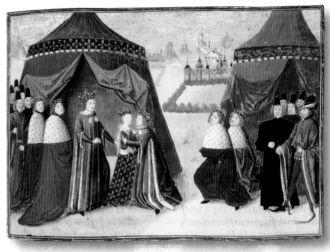

barons eventually brought about the impeachment of
men such as de Vere and de la Pole, the 'Merciless
Parliament' of 1388 further clipping the wings of the
young king's men.

The next nine years saw calm return. A time of mixed
emotions for Richard, it was during this period that he
mourned the loss of his first wife. Marrying Anne of
Bohemia, the daughter of the Holy Roman Emperor
Charles IV, early in 1382, the royal couple enjoyed a
happy, though childless marriage. But then Anne fell ill
and died of the plague in 1394. So overcome was the king
by his wife's death that he ordered the demolition of the
palace at Sheen in which his beloved queen had died.
Despite his attachment to his first wife, two years after
her passing the king remarried. A daughter of the French
king, Charles VI, Isabella was a child-bride, who was still
eight days short of her seventh birthday when she was
married to Richard II at Calais on 1 November 1396.

However, this marriage was destined to end just three
years later with the death of the king. The chief architect
of Richard's fall was his cousin, Henry Bolingbroke. The
son of John of Gaunt, he led the rebellion against the
king while Richard II was back in Ireland, where he had
enjoyed success earlier in his reign. Taking advantage of
the king's absence, his enemies launched their attempted
coup. Carrying all before them, even the king's famed
Cheshire archers backed off and so, when the king
returned to England, he paid the price for the harsh line
that he had adopted in previous years. Backed into a
corner from which there would be no escape, the
sovereign conceded defeat in Conwy in North Wales
and was formally deposed on 29 September 1399

After the accession of Bolingbroke as Henry IV, the
former king remained a prisoner at Pontefract Castle,
where he died on, or a short time after, his 33rd
birthday on 6 January 1400. Some suggested the king
had a died a natural death, others claimed he had been
murdered on Bolingbroke's orders, while a third rumour
spread the fiction that the last monarch from the house of
Anjou had escaped and would one day return to reclaim
his crown.

TOP LEFT: Richard II placed under guard by the Earl of Northumberland
LEFT: Richard II meets his new bride, Anne of Bohemia

But Richard II was dead. For many years his corpse
was kept at the royal palace of King's Langley in
Hertfordshire until 1411. Then, at last, the body was
buried at Westminster Abbey, where it had been taken on
the orders of Henry V, the son of the man who had
succeeded Richard II some years earlier.

))⯈ *Edward III, Henry IV*

RICHARD III (1452–85)

King of England (1483–85); brother of Edward IV; nicknamed Richard Crookback. Richard was the last king of the long Plantagenet line and of the house of York. Fighting alongside his Yorkist brother in the Wars of the Roses, after the death of Edward IV he succeeded his nephew, Edward V, one of the 'Princes in the Tower'. Implicated in their deaths, he himself was killed at the Battle of Bosworth Field by the victorious Lancastrians and was succeeded by the first Tudor king, Henry VII.

The eleventh child and eighth son of Richard, Duke of York, and his wife, Cicely, he was born at Fotheringhay Castle in Northamptonshire on 2 October 1452. Just three years old when the Wars of the Roses broke out between the houses of Lancaster and York, his father was a leading light of the Yorkist cause and had twice been Protector of the Realm before his death in 1460.

After Richard's elder brother had snatched the crown to become Edward IV, he distinguished himself as a military man and as the governor of territories in Wales and the north of England. Accompanying Edward IV into exile in 1470 following the restoration of Henry VI, when the Yorkists staged their successful fightback in 1471 Richard was in the forefront in the victorious battles at Barnet, Hertfordshire, and at Tewkesbury, Gloucestershire.

Honoured with the title, Duke of Gloucester, in 1461, some 22 years later Richard assumed the role of Protector shortly after the death of Edward IV on 9 April 1483. The uncle of his brother's appointed successor, Edward V, in under three months a whirlwind series of events saw Richard, Duke of Gloucester, crowned Richard III. The heir to the throne was the former sovereign's 12-year-old son, but the unfortunate boy was to be king for less than three months.

Riding to London with Edward V in his clutches, opponents were rounded up and executed, the younger brother of Edward V, the nine-year-old Richard, was taken from his refuge at Westminster Abbey and then the marriage of Edward IV to Queen Elizabeth was declared illegal. Proclaimed king on 26 June 1483, just

the short period from 1483 on was a traumatic one with the deaths of his son and heir, Edward, in 1484 and his wife, Anne, the younger daughter of Warwick the Kingmaker, whom Richard had married in 1472.

The third and last Yorkist sovereign, Richard III has long been denounced as the personification of evil, a misshapen man who killed his own nephews to attain power. What really happened to the 'Princes in the Tower' will probably never be known, but what is certain is that the death of their uncle in 1485 marked the end of the line for the Plantagenet dynasty established by Henry II in 1154.

Killed on 2 August 1485 at the Battle of Bosworth Field by Henry Tudor's troops, his Lancastrian conqueror won the battle and was crowned Henry VII. Meanwhile, the body of Richard III was buried at Greyfriars Abbey, Leicester, but was later dug up and thrown into the River Soar.

))➤ *Edward IV, Edward V, Henry VII*

10 days later the coup of Richard III was complete when he was crowned at Westminster Abbey.

King for little more than two years, at Bosworth Field in Leicestershire he became the last English monarch to die in battle. So ended a brief reign that had begun with his nephews, Edward V and Richard, imprisoned in the Tower of London. From such unpromising beginnings his reign staggered from one problem or calamity to another and always there was the threat of insurrection. The dark shadow of the Lancastrian leader, Henry Tudor, loomed large, while the Duke of Buckingham paid with his life for plotting against Richard III. On a personal level, too,

LEFT: Two portraits of King Richard III, from the play by William Shakespeare
RIGHT: Richard III and Queen Anne

ROBERT I (THE BRUCE) (1274–1329)

King of Scotland (1306–29); elder brother of
Edward Bruce. One of the greatest names in
Scottish history, legend has it that this triumphant king of
the Scots was inspired to fight on against the might of
England by the persistence of a spider weaving its web.
Crowned Robert I in 1306, but later forced to flee as
Edward I invaded. Rallying in 1307, the Scots won back
lost lands before gaining their greatest victory at
Bannockburn in 1314. Asserting Scotland's independ-
ence, Robert the Bruce died in 1329 and was succeeded
by his young son, David II.

Born at Turnberry in West Scotland, he was the eldest
son of Robert Bruce, Lord of Annandale, and Marjorie,
Countess of Carrick. Becoming Earl of Carrick, when he
was 18 years old he married his first wife, Isabel. After her
death, he remarried, his second wife being Elizabeth de

TOP: Before Bannockburn Robert the Bruce kills Sir Henry de Bohun
RIGHT: Robert the Bruce monument, Stirling

Burgh, the daughter of the Earl of Ulster. For many years
a loyal supporter of England's king, waging war with
Edward I against John Balliol, Robert the Bruce's loyalty
had seen his family granted many privileges. However, in
1297, two years after recognising Edward as Scotland's
king, Robert the Bruce allied himself with William
Wallace, the celebrated freedom fighter who was leading
the struggle for Scottish independence.

Briefly back in the English fold (1301–02), following
Wallace's execution in 1305 he declared himself Scotland's
king and was crowned Robert I at Scone on Palm Sunday
1306. Angering England's king, his accession was doubly
audacious because, just a short time before, he had been
excommunicated by Scotland's Church for killing a rival
noble in a Dumfries kirk. So, disowned by the Church
and set on a collision course with Edward I, Robert I was

then assailed by a large army led by Aymer de Valence. This intimidating force, which had marched to Methven, to the west of Perth, promptly annihilated the Scots' forces. Further defeats followed, causing Robert the Bruce to take to his heels. For months he roamed from place to place, as Edward's henchmen rounded up and killed his supporters, including three of Robert's brothers. A testing time for the toppled king, it was during this period that he laid low on Rathlin, the island where, it is said, he was inspired to begin his fightback by a persistent spider, which he watched weave and re-weave its web.

Returning to the fray in 1307, that year Robert I started a sequence of victories, while in June that year the ailing Edward I led a vast army on the long trek northwards, only to die en route. Continuing to make gains, he won at Inverary in 1308, subjugating the rest of northern Scotland by 1309. He won the support of the Scottish Church in 1310, while cross-border raids ravaged towns in North-East England in 1311. A good situation improved still further on 24 June 1314 when the king of the Scots annihilated the English enemy at Bannockburn near Stirling. A historic victory, after Bannockburn Edward II struggled in vain to retain even a foothold in Scotland. Robert captured Berwick in 1318. Then, in 1320, the Declaration of Arbroath was signed by prominent Scottish bishops and leading lords. This declaration called for recognition of Robert's kingship and for Scotland's independence, but was ignored south of the border, hostilities continuing unchecked, despite a truce agreed in 1323. Then, in 1327, with English barons turning on Edward II, the Scottish sovereign launched a major offensive in northern England, which led to the treaties of Edinburgh and Northampton. Acknowledging Robert the Bruce to be Scotland's rightful king, England also recognised Scotland's independence. However, native delight at these gains was soon tempered by the passing of the Scottish king. Possibly struck down by leprosy, the 53-year-old Robert the Bruce died at Cardross on 7 July 1329. His body was buried at Dunfermline, but not his heart, which was removed so that Sir James Douglas could carry it with him on crusade and bury it in the Holy Land. However, Douglas was killed while campaigning in Spain in 1330 and so the heart was returned to Scotland to be reunited with the rest of Robert the Bruce's mortal remains.

))))➤ *House of Bruce, Edward Bruce, Edward I, Edward II*

ROBERT II (1316–90)

King of Scotland (1371–90); grandson of Robert the Bruce. Scotland's first Stewart (later Stuart) monarch is also known as Robert the Steward. Succeeding his uncle, David II, in 1371, after serving two spells as David's deputy, he reigned for 19 years. S een as an ineffective king, he passed power to his son, John, in 1384. Dying six years later, Robert II was succeeded by this same son, who was crowned as Robert III.

The son of Walter, the Great or High Steward of Scotland and Marjorie, daughter of Robert I the Bruce, he was just a baby when he became heir presumptive to his grandfather's throne. Passed over when King Robert's second wife gave birth to the future David II, during the reign of his young uncle Robert the Steward married Elizabeth Muir and raised a family. The couple's eldest son would later become Robert III, while their daughter, Jean, wed Sir John Lyon, the Thane of Glamis in eastern Scotland and an ancestor of Queen Elizabeth the Queen Mother.

First pushed into the spotlight when he was appointed regent at the age of 17, he stepped aside in 1338 having paved the way for King David's return to power in 1341. However, he was reinstated for a second term in 1346 following his uncle's capture at the Battle of Neville's Cross. With David II in the custody of Edward III, Robert deputised until 1357, when the king was released under the terms of the Treaty of Berwick.

Eventually gaining power in his own right after David's death in 1371, his reign was marked by unrest and infighting among the Scottish nobility, by a succession of border raids and by a depressed economy. Unable or unwilling to tackle the problems facing his kingdom, Robert II stood aside in 1384 giving day-to-day control to his eldest son, John. Then, in 1388, power effectively passed to the king's second son, Robert, Duke of Albany and Earl of Fife. However, Robert II was nevertheless succeeded two years later by John, who chose to be crowned as Robert III.

||||➤ *Edward Balliol, Robert III, Robert the Bruce*

ROBERT III (c. 1336-1406)

King of Scotland (1390–1406); son of Robert II. Robert was handed power in 1384 while his father was still king. The following year he was seriously injured when kicked by a horse. Well enough to succeed Robert II in 1390, he ruled for nine years. His son, David, then became regent until his death in 1402 to be succeeded by the king's brother, Robert, Duke of Albany. The monarch's son and successor, the future James I, was kidnapped, then imprisoned by England's Henry IV in 1406. Weeks later Robert III died.

Given the name John at birth, he succeeded his father in 1390, six years after he had been placed in day-to-day charge of the Crown's affairs. Badly injured when kicked by a horse in 1385, his continuing ill health did not prevent him from being crowned as Robert III. However, just as his younger brother, Robert, Duke of Albany, had been the power behind the throne in the last years of their father's reign, so the duke wielded considerable influence in the first years of the new reign.

In 1399 Robert III stepped aside to be replaced by his eldest son, David, Duke of Rothesay. Regent for just three years, in 1402 David died in suspicious circumstances. The Duke of Albany was implicated, but not charged, and so regained the hold on power he had so briefly lost. Four years later, as fears about the safety of his young son, James, continued to mount, Robert III sent the boy into exile. However, when the ship carrying James to France was intercepted by English pirates, the heir to Robert's throne was kidnapped. Later passed into the hands of England's monarch, Henry IV, James soon became a king in exile, while Robert III died within a month of his son's capture.

||||➤ *James I, Robert II, Henry IV*

LEFT: At Bannockburn, Robert the Bruce kills Sir Henry de Bohun
ABOVE: Robert II

SAXE-COBURG-GOTHA, HOUSE OF

Often seen as the last of the Hanoverian monarchs, Edward VII was actually Britain's first and only Saxe-Coburg-Gotha sovereign. Sometimes described as the House of Wettin, this royal house took its unwieldy title from the German duchy of the same name.

Edward VII was descended from this line on his father's side, Prince Albert having been the son of Duke Ernest I of Saxe-Coburg and Gotha. A long-lived dynasty with the branches of its family tree growing from tenth-century roots, during the last years of the nineteenth

ABOVE: His Royal Highness, the Duke of Saxe-Coburg-Gotha
LEFT: Maria Clementina Carolina of Orleans, Princess of Saxe-Coburg-Gotha
FAR RIGHT: Edward VII

century Edward VII's younger brother, Alfred, was duke until his death in 1900.

King for just nine years, Edward VII began his reign following the death of his mother, Queen Victoria, in 1901. Like her he gave his name to the period in which he reigned, the Edwardian age coming to be viewed by many as a golden late-summer before the storms of World War I killed millions and destroyed the old order.

However, the monarch himself played little part in shaping Britain's destiny in the first decade of the twentieth century. A time when Britain was busy forming alliances with Japan, France and Russia, at home the Labour Party was born and the Liberals were reborn, returning to power after 10 years in opposition.

After the death of Edward VII in 1910, the royal family retained the name of Saxe-Coburg-Gotha until 1917. Then, with World War I still raging, Edward's son and successor, George V, renamed his dynasty the House of Windsor.

EVENTS OF THE SAXE-COBURG-GOTHA ERA

1901 The Trans-Siberian Railway is opened; William McKinley becomes the third US president to be assassinated. He is succeeded by his fellow Republican, Theodore Roosevelt; Queen Victoria dies

1902 The Boer War comes to an end

1903 At Kitty Hawk, North Carolina, the brothers, Wilbur and Orville Wright, complete the very first flight in a heavier-than-air machine

1904 Entente Cordiale reached by Britain and France recognising British interests in Egypt; the composer, Antonin Dvorák, dies

1905 The *duma*, Russia's first parliament, is established

1906 San Francisco is destroyed by an earthquake; the Labour Party is formed in Britain

1907 Rasputin becomes an influential figure at the Russian court

1909 Old-age pensions are introduced in Britain; Henry Ford's Model T car is launched

1910 The literary giant, Count Leo Tolstoy, dies in his native Russia

SIGTRYGR CAECH (d. AD 927)

King of York (AD 921–27); brother of Ragnall. Sigtrygr was one of the Vikings expelled from Dublin in AD 902 and joined Ragnall on his raids in Strathclyde and Scotland. He regained control of Dublin in AD 917 and ruled there until AD 921. With the death of Ragnall in that year, Sigtrygr decided to make a claim to his brother's kingdom of York. While Ragnall had acknowledged Edward the Elder as his overlord, Sigtrygr maintained his own kingship, but on the death of Edward and the succession of Athelstan he realised the support of Mercia for the Wessex king could pose problems and signed a treaty with him in AD 926. By the terms of this treaty the Dane converted to Christianity and married Athelstan's sister, Edith. It was not long before Sigtrygr reneged on his agreement, though. He did not live to face the consequences of this betrayal, dying in AD 927.

))))➤ *Athelstan, Edward the Elder, Ragnall II*

STEPHEN (c. 1096–1154)

 King of England (1135–54); nephew of Henry I. The last Norman king, Stephen of Blois succeeded his uncle in 1135. Opposed by Empress Matilda, the daughter of Henry I, for the last 14 years of his reign there was civil war. Captured and imprisoned by his enemies in 1141, Stephen was later released. Normandy was lost in 1144, but the war continued in England. The father of three sons, Stephen outlived them all and was succeeded by the empress's son, Henry II.

Born in 1096 or 1097, he was the youngest son of Adela, a sister of Henry I, while Stephen's father was Stephen, the Count of Blois and Chartres. However, when he died in 1102, the younger Stephen was raised by his mother. In time, though, the boy's future became more and more linked to the fate of Henry I, his uncle presenting Stephen with so much land that he became the second mightiest landowner in the kingdom. A powerful figure, he also profited from his marriage to Matilda, the only daughter of the Count of Boulogne.

Marrying in 1125, for the next 10 years Stephen remained loyal to Henry I, despite the king's problems regarding who would succeed him. Until 1120 the succession issue was settled, but then on 25 November that year Henry's son and heir was killed when the *White Ship* ran aground. The king's only son, even a second marriage could not produce a new male heir and so Henry I chose his daughter, Matilda, as his successor. Nominated by her father nine years before his death, the Empress Matilda, as she came to be known, would strive long and hard to claim her inheritance. However, when the old king died on 1 December 1135, it was Stephen who seized the crown.

Initially content to lodge a peaceful objection to Stephen's accession, the Empress Matilda continued to enjoy considerable support for her claim, even if her case was weakened because she was a woman and because her husband, Geoffrey, Count of Anjou, was not well-liked. In addition, the empress was viewed by many as a foreigner, even though King Stephen had not been born or brought up in England. Yet, while his claim was weaker, Stephen's strike had been swift and assured. He had hurried from Boulogne to be first to state his case in London, but he also enjoyed the support of people in high places, not least his brother, Henry, Bishop of Winchester.

Crowned king on 26 December 1135, his St Stephen's Day coronation was staged at Westminster Abbey less than four weeks after Henry's death, his right to rule validated by Pope Innocent II. Also recognised as Duke of Normandy at this time, the first two years of King Stephen's reign passed very quietly, but then the peace was shattered as the monarch was attacked.

By the autumn of 1139 the early exchanges in the north and west of the kingdom and in Normandy had given way to a full-scale civil war in England, large numbers of men rallying around the flag of the Empress Matilda. Then

came the first decisive battle when the enemy forces clashed at Lincoln in February 1141 and Matilda's army succeeded in capturing the king. Imprisoned in Bristol, Stephen was forced to look on helplessly as the empress, who had been hailed as the 'Lady of the English', planned her coronation. However, there were to be several more twists in the tale.

One important development occurred when Stephen was realeased in return for the Empress Matilda's half-brother, Robert of Gloucester. Free again, in 1142 the king laid siege to Oxford Castle with the empress trapped inside. However, a great opportunity was lost as she slipped away unnoticed, Matilda fleeing the castle dressed from head-to-toe in white so that she could blend in with the snowy landscape. Still the fighting continued in England, while across the English Channel the king suffered a serious defeat as Geoffrey of Anjou invaded

ABOVE AND LEFT: King Stephen

Normandy in 1144. After this setback King Stephen stayed in England for the next 10 years, a decade dogged by the continuing civil war.

Stephen was a handsome, well-liked man, who was also a fierce, yet chivalrous warrior, but traditionally his kingship has been seen as weak. His wife Queen Matilda, on the other hand, is usually portrayed as a strong and bold woman, whose stand against her namesake, the Empress Matilda, proved crucial in recapturing London in 1141. The mother of Stephen's son and heir, Eustace, and four other children, the queen died in 1152. The following year the death of Eustace further devastated the king and in November 1153 the Treaty of Westminster stated that Stephen would rule for the rest of his days, while acknowledging that his successor would be the son of the Empress Matilda. Henry of Anjou did not have long to wait: less than a year later the king was dead.

Passing away at Dover Castle on 25 October 1154, Stephen was buried at Faversham Abbey near Canterbury and was succeeded by Henry of Anjou who was duly crowned Henry II.

STEWART, HOUSE OF

Scotland's royal house for almost 350 years, the first monarch from this dynasty was crowned Robert II in 1371. Becoming king of the Scots in succession to David II, he was the grandson of Robert I the Bruce and the son of Walter fitzAlan, who was the sixth high steward of Scotland. From this hereditary title was derived the family name of Stewart. Later still, the name changed to Stuart from the French-style 'Steuart', which was appropriate as the fitzAlan family had its roots in Brittany.

Nicknamed Old Blearie, because of his bloodshot eyes, Robert II Stewart reigned for 19 years, having previously served two terms as regent in the reign of his predecessor. An old man when he finally stepped aside, Robert's eventual successor was his son, John, who adopted the title Robert III. Lame after being kicked by a horse in 1385, he was king of the Scots for just nine years. Then, like his father before him, he stood down. Handing power to his son, David, after David's death in suspicious circumstances, the king's brother, the Duke of Albany, ruled. However, when Robert III died in 1406 he was succeeded by his son, James I.

At the time of his accession young James was a prisoner in the Tower of London. Kept in England for the next 18 years, when he returned to Scotland he set about establishing his control in a kingdom that had been ruled over in his absence by the Duke of Albany and his son, Murdoch.

James I was a reforming ruler, a monarch who introduced many new laws. He also made enemies in the north and in the south of his realm and in 1437 he was assassinated. This murder signalled the beginning of a remarkable sequence, for when James I was succeeded by his son, James II became the first of six successive monarchs to ascend the throne as a minor.

Six years old when he became king, James II did not assume full control over his kingdom until he reached maturity. Early in his reign he was supported by the

Douglas family, but later the king cut down to size the Douglases and other powerful opponents. Killed when a cannon exploded, James II was succeeded by his young son, James III. Like his grandfather and his father before him, he had to fight hard to establish his kingship in the face of strong opposition from Scottish nobles. He was even forced to imprison his own brothers, while James III himself was briefly taken captive in 1482. Restored the following year, when he was killed by rebels in 1488 he became the third Scottish king in a row to die an early and violent death.

Once again a young prince ascended the Scottish throne, but James IV, like his predecessors, lived long enough to rule without regents. A popular, educated king with a worldly approach to government, it was James IV who linked the Scottish royal house with the

ABOVE: Mary Queen of Scots
LEFT: Mural from the National Portrait gallery of Scotland with the Stewart kings and queens

THE HOUSE OF STEWART

1371–90	Robert II Stewart
1390–1406	Robert III
1406–37	James I
1437–60	James II
1460–88	James III
1488–1513	James IV
1513–42	James V
1542–67	Mary I, Queen of Scots
1567–1625	James VI*

* From 1603 James VI of Scotland reigned in England as James I, the list of his Stuart successors appearing at end of following entry

ruling family in England by marrying Margaret Tudor, a daughter of Henry VII. Killed at Flodden Field when fighting the forces of his brother-in-law, Henry VIII, James's death led to the coronation of his baby son, James V.

Able to seize control only after he had escaped the clutches of his mother's second husband, the Earl of Angus, James V was forced to tackle many of the same problems that had confronted his Stuart predecessors, putting down various uprisings and fighting the English. However, shortly after the Scots were routed at Solway Moss in 1542 James V died, the crown then passing to his infant daughter, Mary, Queen of Scots.

One of the most famous Scottish monarchs, she spent very little of her adult life in Scotland. Briefly queen of France, after the death of her husband, François I, she returned home in 1561. The next four years passed off without incident, but Mary's life was turned upside down following her marriage to her cousin, Henry Stuart. Better known as Lord Darnley, in 1566 he killed his wife's secretary, yet within a year he, too, had been murdered.

By then the mother of a young son, James, Mary soon married for the third time, but five months after Darnley's death she was forced to abdicate and was imprisoned. Escaping from custody, Mary, Queen of Scots, made one last attempt at reclaiming her crown before heading south to England, remaining there in the kingdom of her cousin, Elizabeth I, for the rest of her life. In Scotland her place as monarch was taken by her baby son, who was crowned James VI in 1567.

Somehow reaching adulthood with his crown intact, James VI ruled over Scotland until his death in 1625. Often a moderating influence in matters of religion, the king still clashed with Presbyterians and others, but such tussles as there were between the Scottish king and his subjects became long-distance affairs after 1603, as in that year the king of the Scots united the Scottish and English crowns for the first time. Known as James I in England, after his coronation at Westminster Abbey the Stuart king returned just once to the land of his birth, where matters of faith and rebellious clans were dominant features of Scotland's political landscape during the last years of James VI.

STUART, HOUSE OF

The ruling house for most of the seventeenth century, the first Stuart monarch to reign on both sides of Hadrian's Wall was the son of Mary, Queen of Scots. James VI of Scotland, in England in 1603 he succeeded Elizabeth I and was crowned James I.

This historic union of the crowns of two countries that had frequently been sworn enemies came about when England's last Tudor sovereign died without producing an heir. Because of this James VI of Scotland, who was the great-great-grandson of Henry VII, ascended the English throne having sat on the Scottish throne for 35 years.

He had endured an eventful reign in Scotland and his time in England began in a similar vein with the uncovering in 1605 of the Gunpowder Plot. Allegedly a Catholic plot to blow up parliament, the Protestant James was well-used to ruling over a land where religious tensions ran high, and he would experience more of the same during his reign in England with Protestant settlers being 'planted' in Ireland and the Pilgrim Fathers setting sail for a new life in New England. James's reign also witnessed the publication of the Authorized Version of the Bible.

EVENTS OF THE STUART ERA

1603 The population of England and Wales was about 4 million. There were about 1 million people living in Ireland and approximately 800,000 resident in Scotland

1605 The Gunpowder Plot is foiled and Guido (Guy) Fawkes, one of the plotters, is tortured, then hanged, drawn and quartered

1611 The Authorized Version of the Bible (also known as the King James Bible) is published in England

1616 Shakespeare and Cervantes, the author of *Don Quixote*, both die in this year

1620 The Pilgrim Fathers set sail for America aboard the *Mayflower*

1624 Cardinal Richelieu is appointed chief minister by the French king, Louis XIII

1628 William Harvey publishes his treatise on the circulation of blood

1642 The great English scientist, Sir Isaac Newton, is born

1644 In China the Ch'ing or Manchu dynasty replaces the Ming dynasty

1660 Samuel Pepys begins his famous diary chronicling life in London

1664 English forces oust the Dutch from New York

1665 The Great Plague of London claims many lives

1666 The Great Fire of London rages

1669 Rembrandt, the great Dutch artist, dies

1674 John Milton, the author of *Paradise Lost*, dies

1675 The Royal Observatory at Greenwich in London is founded

1687 Nell Gwynne, the orange-seller turned actress and mistress of Charles II, dies

1694 The Bank of England is established

1697 The painter and satirical cartoonist, William Hogarth, is born

1701 The population of England and Wales tops the 5 million mark. Approximately 2 million people live in Ireland with 1 million resident in Scotland

1711 Wren's rebuilt St Paul's Cathedral is completed

FAR LEFT: William III with Anne, her husband, George, and son, William
LEFT: Charles I on scaffold in Whitehall

In the reign of Charles I tensions between Protestants and Nonconformists continued, but a still greater problem proved to be the friction between the king and parliament. This friction ultimately resulted in a civil war pitting Royalists (or Cavaliers) against Parliamentarians (or Roundheads). Lasting seven years this conflict ended dramatically in 1649 with the execution of Charles I and the creation of a republic that remained in place until 1660.

During this 11-year Interregnum the king-in-waiting was the exiled Charles II. The son of Charles I, he was finally restored in 1660. The reign that followed was one of contrasts. The king fathered no legitimate children, but sired a number of illegitimate sons and daughters and, while he was acknowledged as a charming personality with 'the common touch', Charles II often clashed with parliament. In addition the Restoration period was dogged by religious differences. Various Acts relating to faith and public life were passed, the Test Act of 1673 barring Catholics and other Nonconformists from holding political office.

Despite this ban, Charles was succeeded by his Catholic brother, James II, who was known as James VII in Scotland. King for less than four years, his short reign began with rebellions, but with these soon crushed James sought to lift many of the restrictions then placed on Nonconformists. However, when he introduced two Declarations of Indulgence in 1687 and 1688, he found himself set on a path that led directly to his own deposition.

The fate of the doomed king was sealed when his wife, Mary, gave birth to a son, James, in the summer of 1688. Six months later James was a king without a crown, his successors his own daughter, Mary, and her husband, William of Orange. Years earlier William had fought on the Netherlands side in the Third Anglo-Dutch War, but in 1689 he was crowned jointly with his wife.

The first couple to reign in the British Isles since Mary I and Philip II of Spain had ruled over England for a short time during the 1550s, William III (but William II in Scotland) and Mary II were joint monarchs until the latter's death in 1694. William then ruled alone for the last eight years of his life, one of the more significant pieces of legislation passed during his short reign being the Act of Settlement of 1701, which determined that the head of the House of Hanover would be crowned if Queen Anne should die without a natural heir.

William was succeeded in 1702 by his sister-in-law. Anne was the younger sister of Mary II, her 12 years as monarch dominated by the War of Spanish Succession and the victories at Blenheim and Ramillies, while at home the two main political parties to emerge were the Whigs and the Tories. Anne's reign also witnessed the passing of the Act of Union in 1707. Formally uniting the kingdoms of England and Scotland, this Act led to the dissolution of the Scottish parliament. Seven years later Queen Anne died and was succeeded by the first Hanoverian sovereign: George I.

THE HOUSE OF STUART

1567–1625	James VI*
1603–25	James I*
1625–49	Charles I
1649–60	Interregnum
1660–85	Charles II
1685–88	James II and VII
1689–1702	William III and Mary II**
1702–14	Anne

* From 1603 the crowns of Scotland and England were joined, James VI of Scotland becoming James I of England in that year. Succeeding Stuart kings are listed with their Scottish and English titles where the two are different.

** After James VII and II went into exile there was a brief interregnum before William II and III and Mary II were formally proclaimed as the new king and queen.

SVEIN FORKBEARD (d. 1014)

King of England (1013–14); first Danish king of England. The son of Harald III Bluetooth, he had succeeded his father as king of Denmark by AD 988. Later launching a series of attacks on England, he deposed Ethelred II the Unready in 1013. However, after reigning less than two months he died, his death leading to the return of King Ethelred II. Twice married, Svein Forkbeard's second son by his first marriage was Cnut.

The son of Denmark's sovereign, Harald III Bluetooth, he had replaced his father as king by AD 988. Soon establishing a reputation in northern Europe as an aggressive warrior-king, he was a leading light in a massive attack launched on England in AD 994. Allied with the Norwegian, Olaf Tryggvason, that year the two Scandinavian leaders had sailed across the North Sea at the head of a fleet of 94 Viking longships. However, despite the size of their invasion force, they did not conquer the English kingdom of Ethelred II the Unready, settling instead for peace and a payment of £16,000.

Lesser raids followed, but it was not until the early years of the eleventh century that they approached the size and intensity of the attack of AD 994. Then, in 1003, Svein Forkbeard masterminded a successful campaign, which was probably launched in retaliation for an atrocity carried out in England the previous year. Known as the St Brice's Day Massacre, this slaughter of Danes living in England claimed many lives, including, it is said, Svein's sister, Gunhild.

Gunhild was also the name of his first wife. A fiery Polish woman, she became the mother of two sons, the eldest, Harald, succeeding his father as king of Denmark, the youngest, Cnut, succeeding Edmund II Ironside as England's ruler. Svein's second wife, Sigrid the Haughty, gave birth to a daughter, whose second husband was Duke Richard II of Normandy, the grandfather of William I the Conqueror.

Cnut eventually joined his father in fighting against Ethelred II, but he was still a young boy when Svein Forkbeard sacked and set fire to Norwich in 1004. Gradually securing more and more English land with each passing year, in 1013 the Danes invaded. Beginning their invasion in August 1013, they moved from Sandwich in Kent to Gainsborough in Lincolnshire.

TOP RIGHT: Viking longship

There, gaining the support of Northumbria, the Five Boroughs of the Midlands and other surrounding regions, Svein's forces moved south, and Oxford and Winchester surrendered without a fight. Then London was attacked.

Besieged in AD 994, two decades later London was defended by Thorkell the Tall, the same Dane who had launched a second attack on London just four years before. In 1013, as in 1009, the city stood firm and so the Danes headed west to overrun Wallingford in Oxfordshire and Bath. Then, with the eventual fall of London, Ethelred II fled.

Acknowledged as England's new king in December 1013, Svein Forkbeard reigned just a few weeks. Dying on 3 February 1014 at his English base of Gainsborough, he was buried in Roskilde Cathedral in his native Denmark. England's first Danish king, he was succeeded by the man he had deposed, Ethelred II the Unready, but was survived by his son Cnut, who later succeeded Ethelred's own son, Edmund II Ironside.

▶ *Cnut, Edmund II*

TRAHEARN (d. 1081)

 King of Gwynedd (1063–81); son of King Caradog of Arwystli. Trahearn seized power following the murder of Gruffudd ap Llywelyn in 1063. Ruling over his kingdom for 18 years, in 1078 he extended its borders by defeating the Deheubarth king, Ryhs ap Owain. However, three years later Gruffudd ap Cynan and his Deheubarth ally, Rhys ap Tewdwr (a cousin of Rhys ap Owain) killed Trahearn when winning the Battle of Myndydd Carn.

TUDOR, HOUSE OF

With deep-rooted Welsh origins this great English dynasty saw one of its monarchs take the title King of Ireland before making way for the Scottish royal house of Stuart. Ruling in England from 1485 to 1603 the Tudors reigned at a time when the Renaissance and the Reformation were in full flow and explorers were discovering the New World.

The first Tudor sovereign was Henry VII. Born in Wales, Henry Tudor (or Harri Tewdwr) was related to Welsh rebels such as Owain Glyndwr and great Welsh

THE HOUSE OF TUDOR

1485–1509	Henry VII
1509–47	Henry VIII
1547–53	Edward VI
1553–58	Mary I
1558–1603	Elizabeth I

rulers such as Rhodri Mawr, while some family trees have even linked him to the legendary King Coel (whose name lives on in the nursery rhyme).

Henry VII's years in exile ended in 1485 with victory at Bosworth Field. Killing Richard III there, the Lancastrian leader was then crowned as the first Tudor monarch, his coronation effectively ending the Wars of the Roses. His marriage to Elizabeth, the daughter of Edward IV, symbolised the coming together of the two rival houses, while a symbol introduced at this time was the Tudor Rose, which combined the white Yorkist rose and the red Lancastrian rose to form a new design.

On the throne for nearly quarter of a century, Henry VII established the House of Tudor on firm foundations, foundations that survived the shaking they were given

during the reign of Henry VIII. Probably the best-known of all English kings, the son of Henry VII married six wives, fathered three future monarchs, broke with Rome, dissolved the monasteries and was a catalyst for the English Reformation. He became the Defender of the Faith, Head of the English Church and King of Ireland and he waged war on France and Scotland, while the chief ministers of his reign, More, Wolsey and Cromwell, were each named Thomas.

Reigning 38 years, Henry VIII was succeeded by his young son, Edward VI. A minor at the time of his

But the reign of Good Queen Bess or Gloriana was not all sailing, plain or otherwise. She was excommunicated by the pope and so was vulnerable to Catholic plots, while Mary, Queen of Scots, posed a real or imagined threat. In exile in England for 20 years, eventually Mary, Elizabeth's, cousin was linked to the Babington Plot and was executed in 1587. Elizabeth I, though, lived on until 1603, when she, the last Tudor monarch died and was succeeded by the son of Mary, Queen of Scots, the Stuart king, James VI of Scotland, who was crowned James I of England.

EVENTS OF THE TUDOR ERA

1492	Christopher Columbus reached the West Indies
1494	Agreeing to divide the 'New World' between them Spain and Portugal signed the Treaty of Tordesillas
1513	Machiavelli writes *The Prince*
1517	Martin Luther nailed his controversial theses to the door of the church of Wittenberg
1519	Ferdinand Magellan sets out to circumnavigate the globe
1521	Cortes the Conquistador conquers Mexico
1522	Cardinal Wolsey founded Ipswich School and Cardinal College, now known as Christchurch College
1532	Francisco Pizarro conquers Peru
1533	Ivan the Terrible becomes Tsar of Russia
1543	Copernicus, the founding father of astronomy, dies
1564	The playwright and poet, William Shakespeare, is born; the painter and sculptor, Michelangelo, dies
1577	Sir Francis Drake begins his three-year-long round-the-world voyage
1582	The Gregorian or New Style Calendar is introduced. Ten days, the 5–14 October were lost that year and leap years were established by inserting a leap day after 28 February every four years, apart from years divisible by 100 but not 400.
1600	The English East India Company is formed

accession, he was still only 15 years old when he died. However, although there was a brief succession struggle, Lady Jane Grey was Queen Jane for just nine days before the eldest daughter of Henry VIII took her place on England's throne. A Catholic queen, Mary I came to be known as 'Bloody Mary' as her short reign saw nearly 300 Protestants burned at the stake as heretics. Briefly reigning with her Spanish husband, Philip II, she overturned Protestant laws, re-aligned England with the pope in Rome and lost Calais, the last fragment of a once-mighty English empire in France.

England's queen for just five years Mary was succeeded by the youngest daughter of Henry VIII: Elizabeth I. Sovereign for 44 years and 69 years old at her death no English monarch before her had ever lived to so great an age. Queen during an era of exploration and colonisation, Sir Walter Raleigh named the American state of Virginia after the Virgin Queen, while Sir Francis Drake became the first English mariner to circumnavigate the globe. Drake, of course, was also the man who singed the king of Spain's beard and helped to defeat the Spanish Armada.

LEFT: Henry VIII, Edward VI and Elizabeth I
ABOVE: Wallpaper with pattern of Tudor roses and portcullis

UA BRIAIN, TOIRRDELBACH (d. 1086)

King of Munster (1063–86); grandson of Brian Bóruma and a son of Teige. Also referred to as Turlough O'Brien, he was king from about 1063. Later seizing Leinster and Dublin, at his death he was the most powerful ruler in Ireland. He was succeeded by his son, Muirchertach Ua Briain.

Toirrdelbach was already a seasoned campaigner when he succeeded his uncle, Donnchad, in 1063. Having won power in Munster, with the aid of his cousin, Diarmait Mac Máel Na Mbo, when the Leinster king died in 1072 Toirrdelbach then pressed his claim to be called high king of Ireland by asserting his control in southern Ireland. Taking Leinster, he overran Dublin and appointed as ruler his son and eventual successor, Muirchertach Ua Briain, but found Connacht and Meath tougher nuts to crack.

⫸ *Muirchertach Ua Briain*

UA CONCHOBAIR, CATHAL (d. 1224)

King of Connacht (1198–1224). Also known as Cathal O'Connor and nicknamed 'Crobderg' ('The Red-Handed'), he was the son of Toirrdelbach Ua Conchobair. Becoming king after the death of his brother Ruaidrí, he fought off challenges to hold power in Connacht until his death.

Possibly an illegitimate son of the great high king, Toirrdelbach Ua Conchobair, he struggled with his elder brother (or half-brother), Ruaidrí, for control in Connacht from 1189. He had to wait his turn, though, as the ruling king stood down in favour of his son, Conchobar. Finally becoming the Connacht ruler after Ruaidrí's, death in 1198, during his reign he smoothed the way for the accession of his son by recognising King John's position as Irish overlord, but he resisted attacks by Richard de Burgh, the nephew of Henry III's regent. Cathal also fought the rebel, Hugh de Lacy, Earl of Ulster, in 1220 and again in the year of his death.

UA BRIAIN, MUIRCHERTACH (d. 1119)

King of Munster and Dublin (1075–1119); son of Toirrdelbach Ua Briain. Also referred to as Muirchertach O'Brien, he ruled in Dublin from 1075 and in Munster from 1086 following the death of his father. Controlling Connacht, Leinster and Meath by 1096, he was unable to conquer the north, but remained the most powerful ruler in Ireland. A Christian king and religious reformer, who passed the ancient Celtic site of Cashel to the Irish Church in 1101, he fell seriously ill in 1114, dying of his illness five years later.

⫸ *Toirrdelbach Ua Briain*

UA CONCHOBAIR, RUAIDRÍ (d. 1198)

King of Connacht (1156–85); the last high king of all Ireland and son of Toirrdelbach Ua Conchobair. Also known as Rory O'Connor, he succeeded his father in 1156. Ten years later, he became high king following the death of Muirchertach Mac Lochlainn. Driving out

Diarmait MacMurrough, the Leinster king returned with Strongbow and other English forces. He acknowledged Henry II as overlord in 1175, but relinquished power in 1183 and was deposed in 1185 or 1186.

The heir of Toirrdelbach Ua Conchobair following the death of his brother, Conchobar, Ruaidrí became king following his father's death in 1156. Little is known about the first decade of the new ruler's reign, but by 1166 he was powerful enough to take over as high king of Ireland when Muirchertach Mac Lochlainn was killed in battle. Soon moving to defeat the threat of Leinster's king, Diarmait MacMurrough, when the exiled Diarmait tried to recover his lost kingdom he was beaten back.

Continuing to take the fight to Ruaidrí, the exiled Diarmait was supported by Henry II, who then campaigned in Ireland from September 1171. With nothing settled by fighting, in 1175 England's sovereign and the ruler of Connacht signed the Treaty of Windsor, which allowed Ruaidrí to rule in Connacht and keep his position as high king. For his part Ruaidrí recognised Henry as overlord and agreed to pay him a percentage of his income. However, as Henry had previously beaten the Irish Church and most of Ruaidrí's fellow Irish kings into submission, the appointment of his son, John, as Lord of Ireland marked the beginning of centuries of English rule in Ireland.

Retiring to a monastery in 1183, Ruaidrí attempted a comeback a short time later, but was permanently deposed in 1185 or 1186. Dying at an Augustinian abbey at Cong in County Mayo, Ruaidrí Ua Conchobair was buried alongside his father at Clonmacnois in Offaly.

)))**▶** *Toirrdelbach Ua Conchobair*

UA CONCHOBAIR, TOIRRDELBACH (c. 1088–1156)

King of Connacht (1106–56); high king of Ireland. Also known as Turlough O'Connor, he became king in 1106. Seizing Munster and other provinces, from 1138 he claimed the title of high king. Later challenged by Muirchertach Mac Lochlainn, he ruled over Connacht for 50 years and was succeeded by his son, Ruaidrí.

Supported by his uncle, Muirchertach Ua Briain, in 1106 he was elected king of the O'Connor province of Connacht in western Ireland. Continuing to broaden his horizons, Toirrdelbach became ever more powerful. Then, when Muirchertach Ua Briain died in 1119, the Connacht king took advantage of the power vacuum created by his death. He gained more territory during the next 12 years, but was then pegged back.

On the offensive again from 1138, it was at this time that Toirrdelbach assumed the role of high king. Challenged in his declining years by the Cenél nEógain ruler, Muirchertach Mac Lochlainn. A warrior-king on land and sea, who famously built castles and bridges, he died at the age of 68 and was buried at the holy site of Clonmacnois in County Offaly. Toirrdelbach Ua Conchobair was succeeded by his son Ruaidrí.

FAR LEFT: The Irish Saint Columba arrives in Inverness to convert the Picts
LEFT: Henry II presents papal bull to Irish clergy

VICTORIA (1819–1901)

Queen of England (1837–1901); granddaughter of George III and niece of George IV and William IV, she succeeded the latter in 1837. The last Hanoverian monarch and Empress of India from 1876, she reigned longer than any other British sovereign. Queen for 63 years she gave her name to an era, her reign dominated by the rise of the British Empire, the Industrial Revolution and by men such as Dickens and Darwin and women such as Florence Nightingale and the female writer known as George Eliot. Disraeli and Gladstone were eminent prime ministers and the Crimean and Boer wars were fought. Victoria was succeeded by her son, Edward VII.

Alexandrina Victoria was the only child of Edward, Duke of Kent and Victoria of Saxe-Coburg. Born at Kensington Palace on 24 May 1819, she was only a few months old when her father died in 1820. That same year also saw the passing of her grandfather George III and the accession of Victoria's uncle, George IV.

Ten years later another uncle, William IV, ascended the throne. Already 64 years old he had fathered four children in the first years of his marriage, but none had survived. So it was that he was eventually succeeded by his 18-year-old niece, Victoria. Ascending the throne on 20 June 1837, Victoria was not crowned until the following summer, her coronation at Westminster Abbey taking place on 28 June 1838. Unmarried at that time, a short time later she would marry the love of her life, Prince Albert.

Victoria and Albert had met at Windsor in 1836, but when their paths crossed three years later they fell in love and before long the 20-year-olds were engaged to be married. The younger son of the Duke and Duchess of Saxe-Coburg and Gotha, Albert was a first cousin of Victoria as his father and her mother were brother and sister. Married in London on 10 February 1840, before her marriage the young Queen Victoria had been heavily dependent on the advice and support of her prime minister, Lord Melbourne, and her trusted uncle, Prince Leopold of Belgium. Yet, while their influence remained strong, increasingly her husband, Prince Albert, became her main adviser.

Inevitably, some politicians questioned the role of the newly arrived German prince, but it was not too long

ABOVE: Victoria and family at Osborne House

before he was accepted as a force for good and, in June 1857, he was given the title of Prince Consort. By then the father of five girls and four boys, his death in December 1861 so depressed Queen Victoria that for years she lived a semi-reclusive existence.

Blaming the high-spirited exploits of her son, Albert, for the death of her husband, Albert, the queen did not remarry. However, two very different men did enter her life. The Indian Abdul Karim, known as 'The Munshi', was one, while the second was John Brown. Starting out as a ghillie on the royal estate at Balmoral in Scotland, later the Scot came to be a trusted confidant. Less popular with the queen were some of the prime ministers she had to deal with during her 63 years as crowned head.

Seeing 10 premiers come and go, six men enjoyed two or more terms in office. Viscount Palmerston and the Marquess of Salisbury were two such men, but for more than two decades the dominant politicians were Benjamin Disraeli and William Gladstone. She got on well with the Conservative 'Dizzy', but relations were strained between Victoria and the Liberal Gladstone, who was at the political helm four times in the twenty-four years spanning 1868–92.

When her beloved husband passed away in December 1861, Victoria had already been on the throne for 24 years, yet she was to continue as queen for another 39 years, so making her reign the longest ever enjoyed by a British monarch. In personal and dynastic terms, the reign saw many of the queen's children marry spouses from European royal families, including those of Germany, Russia and Prussia, but she also lived so long that she outlived her daughter, Alice, and sons, Alfred and Leopold.

The Victorian era was also the age of the British Empire. With colonies all over the globe, during the queen's long reign Britain's empire incorporated territories as far apart as Africa, Australia and Canada. India was another cherished colony and in 1876 Victoria was given the title of Empress of India. Twenty years earlier, the first major war of the queen's reign had come to an end. Beginning in 1854, Britain and France had fought against Russia in the Crimean War, a conflict best-known for the Charge of the Light Brigade at Balaclava near Sevastopol and the care and compassion of the nursing heroine Florence Nightingale.

Years later, British soldiers were active in Sudan, but in 1884 General Gordon and his men died in Khartoum at the end of a siege lasting 10 months. However, this was not the end of Britain's military involvements during Victoria's reign as in 1899 the Boer War began in southern Africa. Closer to home Ireland suffered a terrible potato famine in the years 1845–48, while in the last decades of the nineteenth century Irish Home Rule was the subject of parliamentary bills in 1886 and 1893. On the British mainland, the Industrial Revolution witnessed the advent of iron and steel, canals and railways, while the first 'horseless carriages' (cars) powered by internal combustion engines appeared. Primary education became compulsory in 1870 and there were concentrated attempts by reformers to improve sanitation and hygiene. An age of plenty for some, many Victorians lived tough lives in acute poverty and there were workhouses at the heart of the great British Empire.

Changing times, often turbulent ones, in the Victorian era even the woman who gave the period its name was a target for extremists. The subject of seven assassination attempts, the queen survived each and every one to live to the age of 81. Dying in her bed at Osborne House on the Isle of Wight, she was buried beside Prince Albert at Frogmore, Windsor, and was succeeded by her eldest son, Albert, who was crowned Edward VII.

))))➤ *Edward VII, William IV*

WESSEX, HOUSE OF

Thought to have been established about AD 495 by Cerdic, the West-Saxon kingdom soon became a force in southern England. King Ceawlin, who ruled in the second half of the sixth century, was so powerful that the monk, Bede, named him as one of the seven English *bretwaldas* (i.e. king of kings).

Later still Egbert was a dominant ruler. Reigning from AD 802, he extended the Wessex borders defeating Mercia and overrunning Essex, Kent and Sussex. After Egbert's death his son, Ethelwulf, became king. The father of several sons, four went on to wear the Wessex crown. The reigns of Ethelbald, Ethelbert and Ethelred I were all short, but then in AD 871 came the accession of the most famous West-Saxon king of them all: King Alfred.

Establishing and fortifying his kingdom after finally defeating the Danes, the king was also a lawmaker and a writer who promoted literacy. At his death Alfred was succeeded by his son, Edward the Elder. Like his father he fought and defeated the Danes and was

acknowledged by other British kings as overlord from AD 917. Edward's son, Athelstan, was also recognised as a king of kings in Britain, while simultaneously forming wedding alliances with Continental royal houses. At home he continued the legal and administrative reforms of his father and grandfather before him.

After Athelstan, the Wessex line was hit by a series of short reigns with five kings ruling in the period AD 939–978. Athelstan's half-brothers, Edmund I and Edred, Edmund's son, Edwy, and Edward the Martyr came and went in the space of a few years, with only Edward's father, Edgar, enjoying a long and peaceful reign during this period, one that lasted 16 years. Then, in AD 978 Ethelred II the Unready ascended the Wessex throne.

Another son of King Edgar, he ruled over Wessex and much of England for 38 years in all, but his troubled reign was interrupted by the brief rule of the Dane, Svein Forkbeard. Ethelred II was later succeeded by his son, Edmund II Ironside, although he died a short time later. There then followed a period of Danish rule with Svein's son, Cnut, reigning until 1035. His successors were his sons, Harold I Harefoot and Harthacnut, but after the latter's death the House of

Wessex was restored when Edward the Confessor became monarch.

The longest-reigning king since his father, Ethelred II, Edward the Confessor was the founder of Westminster Abbey and was succeeded by the last Anglo-Saxon king, his brother-in-law, Harold II. King Harold ruled for just nine months, however, before he was killed at the Battle of Hastings in 1066. His death, and the subsequent accession of the Norman duke, William the Conqueror, marked the end of the line for the Wessex dynasty.

LEFT: A Saxon church in Northamptonshire
TOP LEFT: A replica Sutton Hoo helmet
ABOVE: King Ozric of Mercia, early Anglo-Saxon royalty from Gloucester Cathedral

EVENTS OF THE ERA OF WESSEX (FROM AD 871)

AD 874	Iceland settled by Vikings
AD 885–86	Paris raided by Vikings
AD 899	Alfred the Great dies
AD 911	Rollo (or Rolf) the Ganger becomes Count of Normandy
AD 919	The Viking kingdom of York is established
AD 937	King Athelstan wins the Battle of Brunanburh
AD 965	Harald III Bluetooth of Denmark converts to Christianity
AD 982	Greenland is settled by Vikings
AD 991	Byrhtnoth of Essex is defeated by Norse raiders at the Battle of Maldon
c. 1000	Leif Ericsson reputedly discovers North America
1002	Many Danes living in England are killed during the St Brice's Day Massacre
1014	The high king of Ireland Brian Boru dies following the Battle of Clontarf
1016	Svein's son, Cnut, succeeds Edmund II Ironside
1042	Edward the Confessor succeeds the last Danish king of England, Harthacnut
1060	Fourteen years after invading southern Italy, the Normans invade Sicily
1066	Harold II is killed at the Battle of Hastings by the Normans, whose leader is later crowned William I of England

THE LATER HOUSE OF WESSEX

AD 871–99	Alfred the Great
AD 899–924	Edward the Elder
AD 924–39	Athelstan
AD 939–46	Edmund I
AD 946–55	Edred
AD 955–59	Edwy
AD 959–75	Edgar
AD 975–78	Edward the Martyr
AD 978–1013, 1014–16	Ethelred II the Unready
1042–66	Edward the Confessor
1066	Harold II

was also home to another member of the ruling Norman family, the future English king, Edward the Confessor.

Successfully negotiating the hazards of his early years, William then had to head off challenges from fellow Normans, and he also fought against neighbouring states. The vast experience of military campaigns that he gained at this time stood him in good stead for his invasion of England in 1066. Yet in the years before the death of Edward the Confessor and the accession of Harold II, Norman sources claim that Edward himself had made William his heir. William of Poitiers wrote that the duke had been promised the English crown when he had sailed to England to meet the Confessor in 1051 or 1052, while the *Bayeux Tapestry* shows Harold II (when he was still Earl Harold of Wessex) journeying to Bayeux in Normandy to swear an oath pledging his support for William's right to succeed King Edward.

However, following the death of Edward the Confessor on 5 January 1066, it was Harold II who was crowned. Duke William did not launch an immediate attack on hearing the news of Harold's coronation, but instead set about recruiting soldiers from Normandy, Boulogne, Brittany and Italy. Then, having assembled an army of 6-7,000 men he sailed for England. Landing at Pevensey Bay on 28 September 1066, William and his troops met no opposition as King Harold's army was doing battle about 300 miles away. So it was that the Normans and their allies had 16 days to prepare for action, while the king's army came to the battle having just defeated Harald Hardrada and Harold's brother, Tostig, at Stamford Bridge in faraway Yorkshire.

However, when the Battle of Hastings commenced on the morning of Saturday, 14 October 1066, the English forces resisted valiantly and so the fighting raged all day. But then, as dusk fell, Harold II was killed. Still the battle continued for a few hours more before the Normans could celebrate victory. An important battle had been won at Hastings, yet the war to win a kingdom had only just begun.

WILLAUME LE CONQUÉRANT

WILLIAM I (c. 1027–87)

King of England (1066–87); first Norman king; known as William the Conqueror; as Duke of Normandy he defeated Harold II at the Battle of Hastings in 1066. Later crowned king, he led the Norman Conquest. In his reign great castles and churches were built, the *Bayeux Tapestry* was completed and the Domesday Book was begun. Related to Edward the Confessor, William I was the father of 10 children including William II Rufus (who succeeded him) and Henry I.

Born at Falaise in Normandy in 1027 or 1028, he was the bastard son of Robert, Duke of Normandy, and his mistress, Herleva. However, William's illegitimacy did not prevent him becoming duke. Barely seven years old at the time of his accession, his childhood years and his adolescence were fraught with danger. All the young duke's chief protectors were killed as challengers sought to overthrow William and his supporters in a duchy, that

RIGHT: A messenger reaching William, from the Bayeux Tapestry
TOP RIGHT: William I with Bishop Odo and Robert de Mortain, from the Bayeux Tapestry

The major ports needed to be seized and William's conquering army descended on Canterbury, London and Winchester before the leading English earls, by then supporting the claims of Edmund Ironside's grandson, Edgar the Atheling, finally capitulated. Acknowledged as king at Berkhamsted Castle in Hertfordshire in December, the Norman duke was crowned William I on Christmas Day 1066 at Westminster Abbey.

Still the new king continued to meet resistance as the first five years of his reign were relentlessly punctuated by rebellions. However, the Normans' response was decisive. Resistance forces led by folk heroes such as Hereward the Wake were defeated and land was seized and secured by implementing a vast programme of castle building, with Norman earls imported to replace native-born landowners. The English clergy, too, was similarly routed, churchmen being evicted from office and replaced by Normans, the newcomers including the king's half-brother, Odo of Bayeux, who as Earl of Kent came to rule over more English land than anyone except William the Conqueror.

After 1071 the king's own attentions turned back towards Normandy, where the dangers posed by France and Anjou were complicated by the defection of his eldest son, Robert, and by other intrigues, attacks and counter-attacks. Ultimately, it was just such a retaliatory raid in 1087 that proved to be William's undoing. Riding into

battle, as an attack was launched on Mantes, his horse bolted. Suffering severe internal injuries, England's first Norman monarch survived some weeks before passing away on 9 September 1087 at a priory near Rouen. Then, in a grotesque postscript, William's swollen corpse burst open as funeral attendants tried to force it into its final resting place at the Abbey of St. Stephen in Caen, Normandy.

Twenty-one years England's king, William I was survived by his wife, Matilda, the mother of his 10 children. Leaving his English crown to his second son, William II became king just as one of the greatest historical surveys was being completed. Commissioned in 1085 by William I, the Domesday Book bears witness to the extent to which English life had been changed radically by the Norman Conquest, a conquest led by William.

))))➤ *Edward the Confessor, William II*

WILLIAM I THE LION (c. 1142–1214)

King of Scotland (1165–1214); grandson of David I. William succeeded Malcolm IV the Maiden following his elder brother's death in 1165. He established the Auld Alliance with France, but was defeated and captured by the king of England: Henry II. Surrendering Scottish independence by signing the Treaty of Falaise in 1174, William bought back his kingdom's sovereignty in 1189. A modernising influence, who beat off attempts to dethrone him, he retained the crown until his death at the age of 71 and was succeeded by his son, Alexander II.

The younger son of Henry, Earl of Northumbria, he was just a child when his father died and his elder brother was crowned Malcolm IV. Then, when Malcolm died young, in 1165 William ascended the Scottish

Richard I King of England and Earl of Anjou Duke of Normandy & Aquitaine surnamed Cœur de Lion

throne. Promptly agreeing a deal with France to forge what would later come to be known as the Auld Alliance, the new king of the Scots did not make his first attack on England until 1174. A disastrous assault led by William himself, at Alnwick in Northumbria the Lion-king was tamed. Taken prisoner by his enemy, he was then led away to meet Henry II in Normandy, where he was made to sign the Treaty of Falaise, a treaty that completed William's humiliation.

Surrendering the independence of the kingdom and its church, further crushing blows were dealt to the Scots by the enforced garrisoning of castles and the concession of Northumbria to English rule. Eventually William I regained control of his realm, but before that occurred he had to put down uprisings led by Scottish rebels. In Galloway, in the south-west of the country, there were insurrections, while a sustained attack on William's crown was led by Donald MacWilliam. A descendant of Malcolm III Canmore and his wife, Ingeborg, his challenge was not extinguished until he was put to death in 1187.

Two years after the death of Donald MacWilliam, the king of the Scots, William I the Lion, entered into a deal with England's new king, Richard I the Lionheart. Needing money to fund a crusade, in an agreement known as the Quitclaim of Canterbury Richard agreed to give Scotland back its independence and its castles in exchange for 10,000 marks. Finally freed from English oppression, William I enjoyed 25 more years as king, his death in 1214 coming just two years after he had defeated and killed Donald MacWilliam's son, Guthred. Married to Ermengarde de Beaumont from 1085, William was succeeded by their son, Alexander II.

))))➤ *Alexander II, David I, Malcolm IV*

WILLIAM II RUFUS (c. 1056/60–1100)

King of England (1087–1100); son of William I. William succeeded his father in 1087. A warrior-king, he had to fight his brothers, Robert Curthose and the future Henry I, to keep his crown. He appointed the astute bishop, Ranulf Flambard, as his main administrator, but fell foul of other churchmen such as the Archbishop of Canterbury, Anselm. Killed while hunting, William II Rufus was succeeded by his younger brother, Henry I.

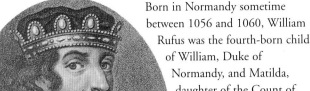

Born in Normandy sometime between 1056 and 1060, William Rufus was the fourth-born child of William, Duke of Normandy, and Matilda, daughter of the Count of Flanders. Little is known of his early life. Just a boy when his father triumphed at the Battle of Hastings, the early death of his elder brother, Richard, in 1075 then lifted young William one step up the royal ladder. Three years later his stock rose higher still when his eldest brother, Robert Curthose, betrayed the family by siding with enemy forces. William, though, stayed loyal to his father and was at the Conqueror's side in his last, dying days.

Succeeding his father on 9 September 1087, William II was crowned at Westminster Abbey 17 days later. The second Norman king of England, he is usually referred to as William Rufus owing to his red hair or because of his ruddy complexion, but during his reign he was also known as William the Younger and William the Red. Like his father he was a capable soldier with a powerful personality, but in other ways William II did not resemble William I at all. The father was a no-nonsense, tough, sometimes brutal ruler, whereas the son was a more devious, pleasure-seeking man.

However, there was little time for relaxation in the early months of his reign. With unrest rife in England in 1087, barons with estates in both Normandy and England sought to dethrone William II Rufus in favour of his elder brother, Robert, himself newly installed as the Duke of Normandy. The barons' revolt of 1088 foundered, though, their cause not helped by Duke Robert's decision not to join the fight. With this threat stubbed out, William's attentions switched from England to Normandy, just as Robert's attention switched to

FAR LEFT: William I the Lion of Scotland
TOP LEFT: Richard I
LEFT AND ABOVE: William II Rufus

waging war in the Holy Land as part of the first crusade. So, in 1089, the elder brother pawned Normandy to the younger brother in exchange for 10,000 marks. Set on recapturing lost Norman territories, eventually William succeeded, while in England in 1095 his forces successfully put down an insurrection led by Robert Mowbray, Earl of Northumberland. Battleground triumphs were one thing, but winning over the English Church was quite another.

The twelfth-century writer, William of Malmesbury, referred to the effeminate men to be found at William's court, while earlier chroniclers were even more damning. Mostly monks and other members of the clergy, they had lamented the long hair, the flamboyant clothes and the sexual antics of William and his inner circle. Yet, if their accounts were not objective, the king's attitude towards the church was often hostile and self-serving, the justiciar (or chief justice) Ranulf Flambard proving to be a skilled, if cunning administrator, who oversaw the heavy taxation programme that transferred Church monies into the

Crown's coffers. William was also slow to appoint abbots and bishops, although an appointment he did make in 1093 he soon regretted.

Choosing Anselm as the new Archbishop of Canterbury, king and cleric were frequently at loggerheads until finally the quarrelling came to an end in 1097 when Anselm left for Rome, two years after provoking the king by declaring that his first loyalty was to the pope. However, with Anselm in exile and his Canterbury estates then in his royal possession, the king headed west in 1098. Marching to Wales, there he crushed a rebellion by Gruffudd ap Cynan of Gwynedd. This success in Wales mirrored his victory over the Scots five years before when Malcolm III had been killed in battle at Alnwick in Northumbria.

By 1100, then, William II Rufus was in full flow, his realms largely secure. Then in his early forties, the unmarried king had reigned in England for almost 13 years when, on 2 August, his life ended. Out hunting that day in the New Forest, like his brother before him he died in an accident there. However, while no controversy had surrounded Richard's death, that of William II Rufus occurred in highly suspicious circumstances.

The official line was that the king was killed by accident when struck by a wayward arrow loosed by Walter Tirel. A member of the royal hunting party, it was claimed that Tirel had fired at a stag as it burst into view, but hit the sovereign instead. Other versions of William's last moments deny that Tirel was in the New Forest that day. One man who definitely was in the vicinity at the time of the monarch's death was his younger brother, Henry, who raced to claim the crown soon after the fatal shooting.

Then, as the new king, Henry I, headed for London and his coronation, so the body of the old king was carted off to Winchester Cathedral, where a hasty burial took place. However, there was further ignominy still to come for William II Rufus as in 1101 the tower above William's burial plot came crashing down, much to the delight of his enemies, who saw the collapse as divine retribution for the former monarch's godless, anti-clerical behaviour.

TOP RIGHT: Insignia of William III
LEFT: William Rufus is slain by an arrow

WILLIAM III (1650–1702)

Grandson of Charles I and nephew of Charles II and James II, better known as William of Orange. He was married to Mary II, the couple reigning jointly from 1689 following the abdication of Mary's father, James II, in 1689. Swept to power by the Glorious Revolution of 1688, after his wife's death in 1694 William III reigned alone and as the war with France ended, James II died and the Act of Settlement was passed. The last Stuart king, William, was succeeded by his sister-in-law, Queen Anne.

Born in The Hague, Holland, on 4 November 1650, he was the only son of William, Prince of Orange, and Mary, who was the sister of Charles II and James II. The young Prince of Orange and Count of Nassau never knew his father, who had died shortly before his son's birth, and so young William was brought up by his mother. A good scholar and talented linguist during his schooldays at Leyden, at 17 he became a member of the council of state of the Dutch Provinces.

Soon drawn to military matters, the serious-minded prince proved himself to be a capable officer, rising to the rank of captain general of the Dutch forces. Then locked in battle with the English in the Third Anglo-Dutch War, which ended in February 1674 with the signing of the Treaty of Westminster, two years earlier, at the age of 21, he had succeeded his father as *Stadhouder* or Chief military commander.

William's star continued to rise as he made a successful marriage to Mary, the eldest daughter of the future James II. Thus, from the moment William of Orange married the future Mary II on his 27th birthday, he was nephew

to the reigning king, Charles II, and nephew and son-in-law to the next sovereign, James II. Nearly twice Mary's age and some 10cm(4inches) shorter than her, William was also stooped and dressed without style. His hooked nose marred his looks, while he was also cursed with ill health, coughing frequently due to asthma. In addition his severe, humourless personality did not present Mary with the most enticing of marital prospects, yet the marriage proved to be a great success.

The couple's wedding ceremony took place in November 1677 at St James's Palace in London. Then, on 11 April 1689, William and Mary returned to the English capital, this time to be crowned jointly as king and queen. Four years earlier Charles II had died without a legitimate son and heir and had been succeeded by Mary's father, James II. However, the reign of the Catholic king was doomed to end with the Glorious Revolution.

Invited to become king in July 1688, following the birth of James's son and heir, the Protestant pretender, William of Orange, arrived in Devon four months later at the head of a 20,000-strong army, which had sailed to England aboard a vast fleet of 250 ships. Marching towards London the force encountered little opposition

and so, when James II hurriedly left the country, the Glorious Revolution had achieved its aim.

Proclaimed king on 13 February 1689, that same day Mary was proclaimed queen. Also crowned together, their joint coronation took place on 11 April 1689 at Westminster Abbey. Earlier it had been decided that William III and Mary II would rule jointly, William declining to be his wife's 'gentleman usher'. Effectively, though, it was the king who played the leading role, the queen deputising in her husband's absence, but otherwise staying in the background until her death.

A king alone from 1694, the first significant event of William's kingship was the peace treaty agreed in 1697. Long at war with France, where the former king James II was still living, the Treaty of Ryswick brought to an end a period in which William III's soldiers had battled with Jacobite and French troops at the Battle of the Boyne in Ireland (in 1690) and in Flanders, too.

Another notable year was 1701. A major alliance was formed that year with Austria and Holland, while at home the Act of Settlement determined a Protestant succession. Passed in the year of James II's death, this legislation guaranteed the accession of the head of the House of Hanover in the likely event of William's successor, Anne, not producing an heir.

The younger sister of the king's late wife, Queen Anne duly succeeded William III the following spring. Dying on 8 March 1702 at Kensington Palace, from injuries he had sustained when the horse he was riding stumbled on a molehill, William of Orange was buried at Westminster Abbey. The last Stuart king, the manner of his death was not forgotten by Jacobites, who would raise an ironic toast to 'the little gentleman in the velvet coat'.

WILLIAM IV (1765–1837)

Son of George III and brother of George IV, he succeeded the latter in 1830. A naval officer as a young man, he was 64 years old when he became the last Hanoverian king. Reigning just seven years, he was succeeded by his niece, Queen Victoria.

The third son of George III and Queen Charlotte, Prince William Henry was born on 21 August 1765 at Buckingham House. The first royal baby to be born at the mansion later remodelled and renamed Buckingham Palace, he grew up in the shadow of his older brothers,

George and Frederick. At that stage in his life there seemed little likelihood of William ever becoming king and so, when he was 14 years of age, he started out on a career in the navy.

Beginning his life at sea as an ordinary seaman, during the next few years he rose steadily through the ranks. Commander of the *Andromeda* by 1787, two years later William was made Duke of Clarence. Then 24 years old, his elevated status allowed him to take his seat in the House of Lords. Soon retiring from the navy, it was then that he fell in love with an actress whose stage-name was Dorothy Jordan. Before long an affair developed that was to last 20 years and produce 10 children.

In time, though, William decided to marry. However, his bride was not Mrs Jordan, but Adelaide of Saxe-Meiningen. Fifty-three years old when he wed Adelaide in July 1818, she was then a 25-year-old princess. Yet despite the difference in age and background, the marriage was a success, although three pregnancies failed to produce a child that lived more than three months.

Just eight months before King William's royal wedding, there occurred the first of three deaths that were to alter the Hanoverian line of succession drastically. The 21-year-old daughter of William's older brother, George, Princess Charlotte died in November 1817. A full decade

TOP LEFT: James II at the Battle of the Boyne
ABOVE: Coronation of William IV
RIGHT: Cartoon illustrating George's naval upbringing

then passed before the death of Frederick, Duke of York. An older brother of William, his death was followed three years later by that of his other brother, George III, the latter's death seeing William become the fifth and last Hanoverian king.

Ascending the throne on 26 June 1830, William, Duke of Clarence, wanted to be crowned Henry IX, but was persuaded to reign as William IV. Crowned at a joint coronation service with Queen Adelaide on 8 September 1831, later the new monarch's adventurous approach proved popular, but he clashed frequently with politicians and parliament alike.

King for less than seven years, William's reign was notable for the high turnover of prime ministers. The grand old Duke of Wellington had completed a brief term of office in 1830, then came Earl Grey. He lasted for four years before Robert Peel took over, while in 1835 he was followed by the king's personal choice of premier: Viscount Melbourne.

Despite the turmoil at the top of the political ladder, there were several important

Acts passed. The Reform Act of 1832 opened out the election process to more voters, while the Factory Act made it illegal for children under the age of nine to be employed and restricted the number of hours that older children could work. Passed in 1833, that year also saw another major change take place in the British Empire when slavery was finally abolished. The 1830s was also a boom time for the economy and for the up-and-coming form of transport: the railways.

The last Hanoverian king, William IV, died on 20 June 1837 at Windsor Castle and was buried at St George's Chapel at Windsor. Survived by his young queen, he was succeeded by an even younger woman, his niece, Queen Victoria.

WINDSOR, HOUSE OF

 The present-day dynasty, it came into being on 17 July 1917. Previously known as the House of Saxe-Coburg-Gotha (or Wettin), during World War I this Germanic title became a source of embarrassment for the reigning monarch, George V. A cousin of the German emperor, Wilhelm II, in 1917 King George opted to change his family's name to Windsor. The Kaiser was not amused, but in Britain the decision to call the royal house after its best-known castle proved popular.

As the first Windsor monarch George V reigned for 26 eventful, often traumatic, years. However, as crowned head of a parliamentary democracy, the king played a back-seat role as prime ministers such as Asquith (Liberal), Baldwin (Conservative) and MacDonald (the first Labour premier) wrestled with the problems presented by World War I, Irish independence, the women's suffrage movement, the General Strike and the Great Depression.

Then, in 1936, came the year of the three kings. In January George V died and was succeedded by his eldest son, Edward VIII. However, he reigned only 11 months, the second Windsor monarch abdicating in December 1936. Faced with the choice of marrying the woman he wished to wed, the twice-married Wallis Simpson, or

remaining a bachelor king, Edward VIII put love before duty. Later marrying Mrs Simpson, as Duke of Windsor the former king then faded into the background as his brother stepped into the foreground.

Like his father, George V, the second son of a king, George VI had not expected to be crowned king himself, but crowned he was, together with his wife, Queen Elizabeth. Then, just as George V had become monarch of a nation fighting a world war, so George VI reigned as Britain became embroiled in World War II.

Staying in England throughout the 1939–45 conflict, the king, queen and their two young daughters, Elizabeth and Margaret, soon came to be seen as symbols of the

THE HOUSE OF WINDSOR

1910–36	George V
1936	Edward VIII
1936–52	George VI
1952–*present*	Elizabeth II

British resolve to win through. An even more potent symbol was the wartime prime minister, Winston Churchill, the man whose leadership and speeches rallied people to the cause during the darkest days before, during and after the evacuation of Dunkirk, the Battle of Britain and the Blitz.

A one-time Liberal MP, who had defected to the Conservatives, Churchill and his party were defeated in the first post-war election in 1945. However, there was still life in the old politician and he returned to power in 1951, the year before George VI passed away. The late king was succeeded by his eldest daughter, Elizabeth II, who was just 25 years old at the time of her accession in February 1952. Later coming to be known simply as 'The Queen', the fourth Windsor sovereign had married Prince Philip, Duke of Edinburgh, in 1947 and came to the throne as the mother of two children, Charles and Anne.

Crowned in 1953, the beginning of the second Elizabethan age also marked the start of a new chapter in the life of the widow of George VI. Taking the title of Queen Elizabeth the Queen Mother, her popularity then increased with each passing decade until in 2000 she reached another personal landmark. Celebrating her

ABOVE: The Duke and Duchess of Windsor
BOTTOM LEFT: Elizabeth II in robes of the thistle

100th birthday that year, the Queen Mother could then look back on a century that began with one long-reigning queen on the throne and ended with another, her daughter Elizabeth II, poised to enter her sixth decade as sovereign.

As monarch for half a century the Queen has reigned at a time when her role, like that of the United Kingdom, has been forced to change. No longer at the hub of an empire, Britain has allied itself with its NATO partners and then with the European Community, while at home government has been devolved in Scotland, Wales and, after three decades of the 'Troubles', in Northern Ireland.

Meanwhile, the House of Windsor has been the subject of many attacks from politicians, media and public alike. Yet, for the most part, the Queen herself has remained an admired figure, retaining a respect not given to many members of the royal family. Celebrating her Golden Jubilee in February 2002, on her many royal tours Elizabeth II has travelled further and to more countries than any previous British monarch. A passionate believer in the Commonwealth and a hard-working, if conservative monarch, she is a grandmother and the mother of four children: Anne, Andrew, Edward and her son and heir, Charles.

Invested with the title Prince of Wales in 1969, like his great-great-grandfather, Edward VII, the future Charles III has spent years as a king-in-waiting. The father of two sons by his ill-fated marriage to Princess Diana, who was killed in a car crash in 1997, Charles's eldest son, William, is second-in-line to the throne.

EVENTS OF THE WINDSOR ERA

1911 Roald Amundsen reaches the South Pole

1912 China becomes a republic

1914 The assassination of the Austrian archduke, Franz Ferdinand, triggers the outbreak of World War I

1918 The signing of the Armistice signals the defeat of Germany and ends the 'war to end all wars': World War I

1919 Alcock and Brown complete the first direct transatlantic flight

1921 The Irish Free State is established; Albert Einstein is awarded the Nobel physics prize

1924 The Russian revolutionary, turned, statesman, Vladimir Ilyich Ulyanov Lenin, dies

1929 The Wall Street Crash takes place on the New York stock exchange

1930 The novelist and poet D.H. Lawrence dies, as does Sir Arthur Conan Doyle, the inventor of the fictional detective, Sherlock Holmes

1933 Adolf Hitler is appointed chancellor in Germany

1936 The Spanish Civil War breaks out

1938 Prime Minister Neville Chamberlain returns from a meeting with Hitler and Benito Mussolini of Italy promising 'peace in our time'

1939 Chamberlain tells the nation that war has been declared on Germany following the invasion of Poland. World War II begins

1940 Battle of Britain rages throughout the summer, the RAF repelling the German Luftwaffe

1945 World War II ends with victory for the Allies; The United Nations Charter is signed in San Francisco; Alexander Fleming is one of three British scientists to share a Nobel prize for his work on the antibiotic properties of penicillin; The minimum age at which British children can leave school is raised to 15; The automobile pioneer, Henry Ford, dies

1953 A British-led team makes history by scaling the world's highest mountain, Mount Everest, for the first time

1954 Roger Bannister becomes the first man to run a mile in under four minutes

1956 Third-class travel is abolished on Britain's railway network

1961 Yuri Gagarin becomes the first spaceman when he flies around the world in 108 minutes

1963 John F. Kennedy becomes the fourth US president to be assassinated

1965 The great wartime prime minister, Sir Winston Churchill, dies

1966 England's footballers win the World Cup for the first and only time

1969 The first man to set foot on the Moon, Neil Armstrong, makes 'one small step for man, one giant leap for mankind'; Concorde successfully completes its maiden flight

1971 Britain introduces decimal currency

1979 The Conservative leader, Margaret Thatcher, becomes Britain's first female prime minister

1982 British troops defeat Argentinian forces in fight for control of the Falkland Islands (Las Malvinas)

1993 The Channel Tunnel linking the British Isles with France is completed; The Nobel Prize-winning author of *Lord of the Flies*, William Golding, dies

1996 The 100th anniversary of the modern Olympic Games sees the sporting festival return to the USA for the third time

1998 The signing of the Good Friday Agreement promises peace in Northern Ireland

2000 Amid arguments about the correct starting date for the third Christian millennium (2000 or 2001?) huge New Year celebrations take place around the world

2001 At the same time as the world's six billionth human being is born, the Human Genome project maps out man's genes

appearance later that year (1483) was the last anyone was to see of the Princes in the Tower, so Edward V was never crowned. Gloucester took the throne as Richard III, but had no more luck than the nephew he had plotted against. The last Yorkist king was killed at the Battle of Bosworth Field in 1485, and a new line, the Tudors, was established.

THE HOUSE OF YORK

1461–70, 1471–83	Edward IV
1483	Edward V
1483–85	Richard III

YORK, HOUSE OF

Like the House of Lancaster, the House of York was a branch of the Plantagenet family tree. The dynasty was founded by Richard, Duke of York. His claim to the throne came from Lionel, Duke of Clarence, from whom he was descended. Clarence was the third son of Edward III. York's challenge for the throne came up against the Lancastrian Henry VI, who was a descendant of the the fourth son of Edward III. York thus claimed seniority of birth. It was this claim that sparked the famous Wars of the Roses between these rival Plantagenet branches. Although the Duke of York did not live to see his house established on the throne (he was killed at the Battle of Wakefield in 1460) his son eventually deposed the now-insane Lancastrian Henry VI and seized the throne for himself and his heirs.

It was not to prove a successful or long-lasting dynasty. Edward's son was the target of the manipulations of his uncle, Edward's brother, Richard of Gloucester. When Edward IV died Edward V was travelling to London for his coronation when he was seized by Gloucester and sent, with his brother, to the Tower of London. A brief

EVENTS OF THE YORKIST ERA

1483 The Princes in the Tower are locked away and are never seen alive again

1485 Richard III is killed at Bosworth Field. The last Plantagenet king, he is also the last English king to die in battle

GENEALOGICAL CHART – SCOTLAND

Constantine III

THE HOUSE OF MAC ALPIN AD 834–1034

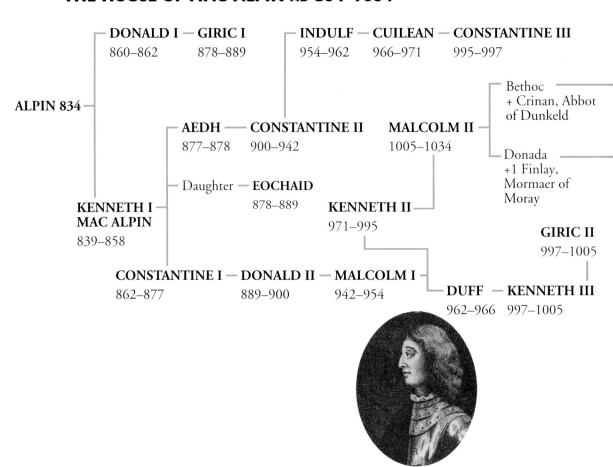

Alpin

Macbeth

THE HOUSE OF DUNKELD 1034–1371

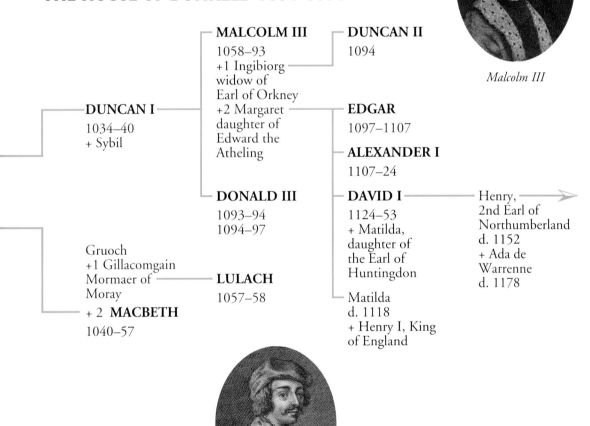

MALCOLM III
1058–93
+1 Ingibiorg
widow of
Earl of Orkney
+2 Margaret
daughter of
Edward the
Atheling

DUNCAN II
1094

Malcolm III

DUNCAN I
1034–40
+ Sybil

EDGAR
1097–1107

ALEXANDER I
1107–24

DONALD III
1093–94
1094–97

DAVID I
1124–53
+ Matilda,
daughter of
the Earl of
Huntingdon

Henry,
2nd Earl of
Northumberland
d. 1152
+ Ada de
Warrenne
d. 1178

Gruoch
+1 Gillacomgain
Mormaer of
Moray
+ 2 **MACBETH**
1040–57

LULACH
1057–58

Matilda
d. 1118
+ Henry I, King
of England

Donald III

THE HOUSE OF DUNKELD 1058–1371 *(continued)*

MALCOLM IV
1153–65

WILLIAM I THE LION —— **ALEXANDER II** —— **ALEXANDER III** ——
1165–1214   1214–49   1249–86
+ Ermengarde de Beaumont   +2 Marie de Coucy   + Margaret,
d. 1234   daughter of
                                                    Henry III, King
                                                    of England

Henry,
2nd Earl
of
Northumberland

David, 3rd Earl of ——   Margaret ——   Dervorguilla ——
Northumberland   d. 1228   d. 1290
d. 1219   + Alan, Lord   + John Balliol
+ Matilda de Keville   of Galloway   d. 1269
d. 1233   d1234

                        Isabella ——   Robert Bruce, ——
                        d. 1251   Lord of Annandale
                        + Robert Bruce,   d. 1295
                        Lord of Annandale
                        d. 1245

Alexander II

Margaret
d. 1283
+ Erik II, King of Norway
d. 1299

MARGARET
1286–90

John Balliol's seal

THE HOUSE OF BALLIOL

JOHN BALLIOL
1292–96
+ Isabella de Warenne

EDWARD BALLIOL
1332–41

Marjorie Bruce
d. 1316
+ Walter, the Steward
d. 1326

THE HOUSE OF BRUCE

Robert Bruce
d. 1304
+ Margaret,
Countess of Carrick

ROBERT I
1306–29
+2 Elizabeth de Burgh
d. 1327

DAVID II
1329–71
+ Joan, daughter of
Edward II, King of England

David II

THE HOUSE OF STEWART 1371-1567

James III

ROBERT II	ROBERT III	JAMES I	JAMES II	JAMES III
Marjorie Bruce	1371–90 + Elizabeth Mure d. 1355	1390–1406 + Annabella Drummond d. 1401	1406–37 + Joan Beaufort d. 1445	1437–60 + Mary of Guelders d. 1463	1460–88 + Margaret of Denmark d. 1486

JAMES IV	JAMES V	MARY	JAMES VI
1488–1513 + Margaret Tudor, daughter of Henry VII, King of England d. 1541	1513–42 + 1 Madeleine, daughter of François I, King of France + 2 Mary of Guise d. 1560	**Queen of Scots** 1542–67 +1 François II, King of France d. 1560 +2 Henry, Lord Darnley d. 1567 +3 James, 4th Earl of Bothwell	1567–1625 (James I of England 1603–25) + Anne of Denmark d. 1619

Continued on page 211

James V

GENEALOGICAL CHART - ENGLAND

THE HOUSE OF NORMANDY 1066–1135

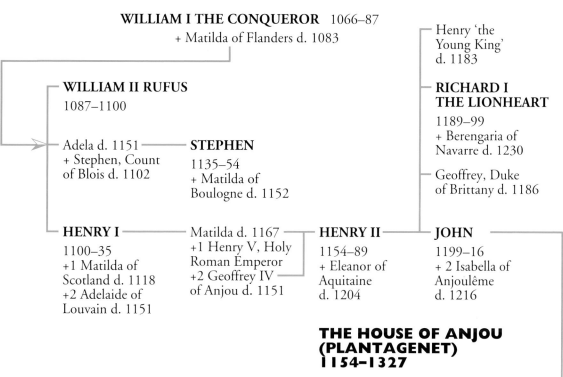

WILLIAM I THE CONQUEROR   1066–87
+ Matilda of Flanders d. 1083

Henry 'the
Young King'
d. 1183

WILLIAM II RUFUS
1087–1100

**RICHARD I
THE LIONHEART**
1189–99
+ Berengaria of
Navarre d. 1230

Adela d. 1151 —— **STEPHEN**
+ Stephen, Count   1135–54
of Blois d. 1102   + Matilda of
Boulogne d. 1152

Geoffrey, Duke
of Brittany d. 1186

HENRY I
1100–35
+1 Matilda of
Scotland d. 1118
+2 Adelaide of
Louvain d. 1151

Matilda d. 1167
+1 Henry V, Holy
Roman Emperor
+2 Geoffrey IV
of Anjou d. 1151

HENRY II
1154–89
+ Eleanor of
Aquitaine
d. 1204

JOHN
1199–16
+ 2 Isabella of
Anjoulême
d. 1216

THE HOUSE OF ANJOU (PLANTAGENET) 1154–1327

HENRY III
1216–72
+ Eleanor of
Provence d. 1291

EDWARD I
1272–1307
+ 1 Eleanor of
Castile d. 1290

EDWARD II
1307–27
+ Isabella of
France d. 1358

EDWARD III
1327–77
+ Philippa of
Hainault d. 1369

Eleanor d. 1275
+2 Simon de
Montfort, Earl
of Leicester d. 1265

EDWARD III

Edward, the Black Prince
d. 1376
+ Joan of Kent d. 1385 ——————— **RICHARD II**
1377–99
+1 Anne of Bohemia d. 1394
+2 Isabella of France d. 1409

Lionel 1st Duke of Clarence d. 1368

THE HOUSE OF LANCASTER 1399–1471

John of Gaunt, 2nd Duke of ——————— **HENRY IV**
Lancaster d. 1399
+1 Blanche of Lancaster d. 1369
1399–1413
+1 Mary of Bohun d. 1394
+2 Joan of Navarre d. 1437

+3 Catherine Swynford ——————— John Beaufort,
d. 1403
Earl of Somerset d. 1410
+ Margaret Holland

THE HOUSE OF YORK 1461–1485

Edmund of Langley,
1st Duke of York d. 1402
+1 Isabella of Castile ——————— Richard, 4th
Earl of Cambridge d. 1415
+ Anne Mortimer, great-granddaughter
of Lionel, 1st Duke of Clarence
d.1411

Henry V

THE HOUSE OF LANCASTER 1399–1471 *(continued)*

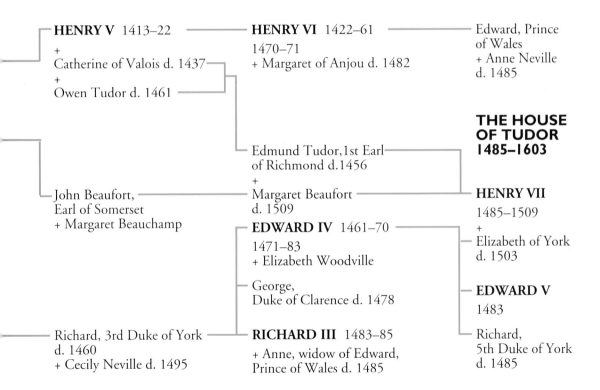

HENRY V 1413–22
+
Catherine of Valois d. 1437
+
Owen Tudor d. 1461

John Beaufort,
Earl of Somerset
+ Margaret Beauchamp

Richard, 3rd Duke of York
d. 1460
+ Cecily Neville d. 1495

HENRY VI 1422–61
1470–71
+ Margaret of Anjou d. 1482

Edmund Tudor, 1st Earl
of Richmond d. 1456
+
Margaret Beaufort
d. 1509

EDWARD IV 1461–70
1471–83
+ Elizabeth Woodville

George,
Duke of Clarence d. 1478

RICHARD III 1483–85
+ Anne, widow of Edward,
Prince of Wales d. 1485

Edward, Prince
of Wales
+ Anne Neville
d. 1485

**THE HOUSE
OF TUDOR
1485–1603**

HENRY VII
1485–1509
+
Elizabeth of York
d. 1503

EDWARD V
1483

Richard,
5th Duke of York
d. 1485

Henry VIII

Elizabeth I

THE HOUSE OF TUDOR 1485-1603 *(continued)*

HENRY VII

Margaret Tudor d. 1541
+ James IV King of Scots d. 1513 ——— James V King of Scots ——— Mary, Queen of
+2 Mary of Guise d. 1560 ——— Scots d. 1587
+2 Henry,
Lord Darnley
d. 1567

HENRY VIII 1509–47
+1 Catherine of Aragon d. 1536 ——— **MARY I** 1553–58
+ Philip II, King of Spain

+2 Anne Boleyn d. 1536 ——— **ELIZABETH I** 1558–1603

+3 Jane Seymour d. 1537 ——— **EDWARD VI** 1547–53

+4 Anne of Cleves d. 1557

+5 Catherine Howard d. 1542

+6 Catherine Parr d. 1548

Mary Tudor d. 1533 ——— Frances d. 1559 ——— **LADY JANE GREY**
+2 Charles Brandon, + Henry Grey, d. 1554
Duke of Suffolk d. 1545 Duke of Suffolk d. 1554

THE HOUSE OF STUART 1603–1714

Elizabeth d. 1662
+ Frederick V,
Elector Palantine of
the Rhine d. 1632

Sophia d. 1714
+ Ernest Augustus,
Elector of Hanover
d. 1698

THE HOUSE OF HANOVER 1714–1901

CHARLES I
1625–49
+ Henrietta
Maria
of France
d. 1666

CHARLES II
1660–85

GEORGE I →
1714–27
+ Sophia Dorothea
of Celle
d. 1726

Mary d. 1660
+ William II,
Prince
of Orange
d. 1650

WILLIAM III
1689–1702
+

MARY II
1689–94

JAMES I
1603-1625
(James VI of
Scotland)
+ Anne of
Denmark
d. 1619

JAMES II
1685–88
+1 Anne Hyde
d. 1671
+2 Mary of
Modena
d. 1718

ANNE
1702–14
+ George of Denmark
d. 1708

James, the Old
Pretender d. 1766

Charles, the
Young
Pretender
d. 1788

Charles I

THE HOUSE OF HANOVER 1714–1901 *(continued)*

Augusta d. 1813
+ Charles, Duke
of Brunswick
d. 1806 —— Caroline of
Brunswick
d. 1821

+

GEORGE II
1727–60
+ Caroline of
Brandenburg-
Ansbach d. 1737 —— Frederick Louis,
Prince of Wales
d. 1751
+ Augusta of
Saxe-Gotha-
Altenberg
d. 1772 —— **GEORGE III**
1760–1820
+ Charlotte
of Mecklenburg-
Strelitz d. 1818 —— **GEORGE IV**
1820–30

WILLIAM IV
1830–37

Edward, Duke of
Kent d. 1820
+ Victoria of
Saxe-Coburg
d. 1861 —— **VICTORIA**
1837–1901
+ Albert of
Saxe-Coburg-
Gotha d. 1861

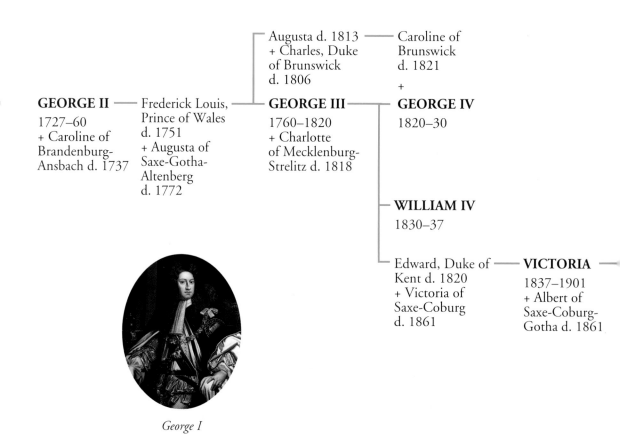

George I

Edward VIII

Victoria,————————— Wilhelm II, Emperor
Princess Royal   of Germany d. 1941
d. 1901
+ Frederick,
Emperor of
Germany d. 1888

THE HOUSE OF WINDSOR 1917–

EDWARD VIII
1936 d. 1972
+ Wallis Simpson
d. 1986

THE HOUSE OF SAXE-COBURG-GOTHA 1901–17

EDWARD VII ———— GEORGE V ———— GEORGE VI ———— ELIZABETH II

1901–10   1910–36   1936–52   1952
+ Alexandra of   + Mary of Teck   + Elizabeth
Denmark d. 1925   d. 1953   Bowes-Lyon   +

Alice d. 1878 ———— Victoria of ——— Alice d. 1969 —— Philip, Duke
+ Louis IV,   Hesse d. 1950   + Andrew of   of Edinburgh
Grand Duke of   + Louis of   Greece d. 1944
Hesse d. 1892   Battenberg d. 1921

                     Alice of Hesse   Louis, Earl
                     d. 1918   Mountbatten
                     + Nicholas II, Tsar   d. 1979
                     of Russia d. 1918

Elizabeth II

GLOSSARY

ABDICATION
The renunciation of the throne, usually voluntarily but sometimes enforced, by the reigning monarch. The most famous abdication occurred in 1936, when Edward VIII gave up the throne so he could marry the twice-divorced Wallis Simpson.

ABSOLUTE MONARCHY
Rule by a monarch in which they wield absolute authority, without reliance on government or parliament for approval of decision-making.

ANGLES
Name given to one of the great Germanic tribal groups (with the Saxons and Jutes) who invaded and settled in the British Isles from the seventh to ninth centuries. The Angles claimed the kingdoms of East Anglia, Mercia and Northumbria.

ANGLO-SAXONS
Name given to the descendants of the Jutes, Angles and Saxons who invaded the British Isles between the fifth and seventh centuries. They were finally overthrown by the Normans in 1066.

BEAKER PEOPLE
Some of the earliest settlers in the British Isles, from about 1900 BC. Beaker folk were essentially warriors and were the first to make regular use of metals in tools.

BRETWALDA
Saxon word meaning 'overlord'. The Bretwalda came into existence in AD 825 after centuries of in-fighting between the Angle, Saxon and Jute settlers in Britain, when the kingdoms fell under the overlordship of Wessex.

BURHS
Network of fortified towns ordered by Alfred the Great to protect his people, goods and livestock against invasion from the Vikings. The suffix 'borough' to a place name indicates an area that was once an Anglo-Saxon burh.

CELTS
Ancient settlers of the British Isles who migrated there from mainland Europe. The Celts were eventually marginalized by the conquering Romans and later invaders.

CLIENT-KING
Ruler of a province or kingdom, normally Welsh or Irish, who acknowledged an overlord elsewhere. Although the client-king was nominally in charge of their region, effective power was asserted by the more dominant monarch.

COMMONWEALTH
Name first applied to the republican parliamentary protectorate under the leadership of Oliver Cromwell in the mid-seventeenth century. The term is now also used to describe the association formed since World War II comprised of now-independent ex-British colonies.

CONSTITUTIONAL MONARCHY
Method of rule by which the powers of the monarchy are subject to parliamentary control. Introduced in 1689, constitutional monarchy limited the monarch's rights to wage war, and curtailed his or her power of veto and choice of when to dissolve parliament.

COUNTER-REFORMATION
Sixteenth-century movement instigated by the Catholic Church as a reaction to the Protestant Reformation. Key amongst its methods was the European Inquisition and the development of the Jesuit Order.

CRUSADES
Series of wars from the eleventh to thirteenth centuries, originally to recover territories lost to Muslim control in the Holy Land, but later gaining imperialist foundations.

DANEGELD

Money raised by taxation and paid by the English in exchange for peace with the Danes during the tenth and eleventh centuries.

DANELAW

Area of north-east England settled by the Danes in the eleventh century in which they were entitled to live by their own laws, customs and language. It was formed as part of an agreement to secure peace and prevent further invasion and infiltration on Anglo-Saxon territory.

DIVINE RIGHT OF KINGS

Belief that the monarch is God's representative on Earth and is therefore not subject to the laws or will of any man, being answerable only to God. Charles I's staunch belief in his Divine Right led to the English Civil War and eventually his execution.

DRUIDS

Celtic priests and one of the most respected positions in the Celtic social hierarchy. Druidism involved belief in spirits of the Earth and centred their rituals around the sacred oak. The practice of Druidism was eventually obliterated by the Romans.

EISTEDDFODS

Welsh tradition in which poets meet and recite verses to one another, established in the twelfth century by Rhys ap Gruffudd.

ELEVEN YEARS' TYRANNY

Name given to the period 1629–40 during which Charles I refused to convene parliament and ruled without their advice.

ENGLISH CIVIL WAR

Series of battles (1642–48) between the royalist supporters of Charles I and republicans under the leadership of Oliver Cromwell, later Lord Protector of England. The Civil War was caused by Charles's refusal to convene parliament and rule with their guidance for a period of 11 years.

GLORIOUS REVOLUTION

Name given to the overthrow of the Catholic James II and the establishment of his Protestant daughter Mary II and her husband William of Orange (William III) on the throne of England in 1689.

HEIR APPARENT

Eldest son of a reigning monarch, with a right to the throne senior to all others. The Heir Apparent is certain to succeed the throne unless they predecease the reigning monarch or are disinherited.

HEIR PRESUMPTIVE

A near relation (daughter, brother, sister, cousin) of the reigning monarch who is presumed to be the heir to the throne until a child is born to the monarch and supersedes them.

JACOBITES

Followers initially of the overthrown James II, and later also applied to supporters of his descendants, who wished to restore the usurped king and the Stuart line to the throne.

JUTES

Name given to one of the great Germanic tribal groups (with the Angles and Saxons) who invaded and settled in the British Isles between the seventh and ninth centuries. The Jutes claimed the kingdoms of Kent and South Hampshire.

MAGNA CARTA

'Great Charter' – agreement sealed at Runnymede on 15 June 1215 between the king, John, and his barons, who objected to the king's foreign policies and what they saw as the tyrannical nature of his reign. Copies of the original document can still be found in Salisbury and Lincoln Cathedrals and the British Library.

NEW MODEL ARMY

Army created by Oliver Cromwell and commanded by Thomas Fairfax during the English Civil War, and maintained throughout the Commonwealth, to help him establish the Puritan 'Society of Saints'. The New Model Army wielded significant power during this period.

ORDER OF THE GARTER

Highest order of English knighthood, established by Edward III in 1344. Its motto is 'shame to be him who thinks evil of it'.

PICTS

Scottish tribes who inhabited Britain prior to the arrival of the Celts. The Picts and the Scottish Celts joined forces in the mid-ninth century. The name means 'painted people'.

PRETENDERS

Name given to those who assume the identity of a royal figure in order the claim the throne, normally under the control of an opposing faction in order to overthrow the reigning monarch.

PRIMOGENITURE

The right to succession of the eldest son of the reigning monarch or the right to inherit all his father's property and titles. In early times, kings were often elected rather than having automatic rights of succession, although they were normally selected from among members of the royal family.

PRINCESS ROYAL

An honorific title conferred on the eldest daughter of the reigning monarch. Princess Anne is the current Princess Royal.

PRESBYTERIANISM

Strict Puritan branch of Protestantism which emerged in the sixteenth century, notably in Scotland, and eliminated many traditional Catholic rituals in church services.

PROTESTANTISM

Christian denomination which emerged in the early sixteenth century as a 'protest' against corruption in the Catholic Church. Henry VIII used this to break with the Church of Rome and establish the Church of England, while in Scotland extreme forms of Protestantism such as Calvinism were adopted.

PUPPET-KING

Derogatory term given to a monarch who reigns but does not rule and who is under the control of a stronger character. Richard Neville, Earl of Warwick controlled the weak Henry VI after he suffered bouts of insanity.

REFORMATION

Sixteenth-century European movement to instigate reforms in the Catholic Church, resulting in Protestantism and its denominations. In England, Henry VIII established the Church of England.

REGENT

Figure elected to rule the country in the absence of a monarch who is at majority age or who is deemed unfit to rule. The most famous regency period in the UK was between 1811–20, when Prince George (later George IV) ruled in place of George III.

RENAISSANCE

Intellectual and artistic movement across Europe, beginning in the fourteenth century and spanning some 300 years. The Renaissance ('rebirth') saw a revival of interest in the arts, science and exploration.

RESTORATION

Name given to the re-establishment of the monarchy in England. Charles II was restored the throne in 1660 after 11 years of government as a republic under Oliver Cromwell.

REPUBLICANISM

Belief in a system in which the head of state is not a monarch. England's only period of republic was after the English Civil War when Oliver Cromwell was the head of state, taking the title 'Lord Protector'.

SAXONS

Inhabitants of the German state of Saxony, applied loosely to one of the great tribal groups (with the Angles and Jutes) who invaded Britain in the fifth and sixth centuries. The kingdoms of the West, South and East Saxons gave rise to the territorial divisions or counties of Wessex, Sussex and Essex.

STONE OF SCONE

Also known as the Coronation Stone and the Stone of Destiny; the stone upon which Scottish kings were crowned at Scone. The stone was seized by Edward I and kept in the coronation chair at Westminster Abbey. It was returned to Scotland in 1996.

TANISTRY

Method of electing the next monarch from within the ranks of the royal family, rather than being nominated by the reigning monarch.

TORIES

Political party, forerunner of the modern Conservative Party, and advocating Conservative values. The Tories were traditionally supported by the upper classes and were the main opponents of the Whigs.

VIKINGS

Warriors, traders and settlers from Scandinavia with fearsome reputations for plundering and pillaging the lands they invaded. The Vikings first made coastal attacks on England in the ninth century and established settlements in the country, most notably at York.

WARS OF THE ROSES

Dynastic civil wars (1455–85) over claims to the throne between two branches of the Plantagenet line, the House of Lancaster and the House of York. The wars were ended when Richard III was killed at the Battle of Bosworth Field by Henry Tudor.

WHIGS

Political party, forerunner of the Liberal Party and main political opponents of the Tories. The Whigs had their heyday in the eighteenth century.

WITAN

Anglo-Saxon council, established in the ninth century and seen as the precursor to modern parliament. The Witan gave advice to the king on matters of state and checked and balanced the power of the monarch. It also proceeded with government business during times when there were no kings.

BIBLIOGRAPHY

Arnold, C.J., *An Archeology of the early Anglo-Saxon Kingdoms*, Routledge, London, 1998

Ashley, Maurice, *Charles I and Oliver Cromwell*, Methuen Publishing Co, 1987

Ashley, Mike, *Mammoth Book of Kings and Queens*, Constable Robinson, 1999

Baumgartner, Frederic, *Henry II*, Kendall/Hunt, 1996

Brooks, Edward Charles, *Life of St. Ethelbert, King and Martyr*, 779AD-749AD, 1995

Brooman, Josh, *Bloody Mary: Cruel Queen or Good Catholic?*, Longman, 1998

Bruce, John (ed.), *Charles I in 1646, Letters of King Charles the first to Queen Henrietta Maria*, 1984

Bruce, Mary Louise, *The Usurper King: Henry of Bollingbroke 1366-99*, The Rubicon Press, 1998

Bryant, Arthur, *King Charles II*, House of Stratus, 2000

Campbell, Marion, *Alexander III, King of Scots*, House of Lochlar, 1999

Carlton, Charles, *State, Sovereigns and Society in Early Modern England: Essays in honour of A.J. Slavin*, St Martins Press, 1998

Cecil Wingfield-Stratford, Esme, *Charles, King of England, 1600-1637*, Greenwood Press

Coward, Barry, *Oliver Cromwell*, Longman Publishing, 1991

Delderfield, Eric, *Kings and Queens of England and Great Britain*, David & Charles, 1998

Douglas, Mary and Humphreys, Graham (Illustrator), *Collins Fact Books: Kings and Queens of Britain*, Collins, 1999

Elton, Sir Geoffrey, *England under the Tudors*, Routledge, 1991

Erickson, Carolly, *Her Little Majesty; the life of Queen Victoria*, Robson Books Ltd, 1999

Eyton, Robert William, *Court, Household and Itinery of King Henry II*, Golms Verlag, 1974

Fraser, Antonia (ed.), *The Lives of the Kings & Queens of England*, Weidenfeld and Nicholson, London, 1993

Fraser, Antonia, *Mary Queen of Scots*, Arrow, 1989

Fraser, Antonia, *King Charles II*, Arrow, 1993

Gardiner, Judith, *The History Today Who's Who in British History*, Collins and Brown, London, 2000

George, Margaret, *Mary Queen of Scotland and the Isles*, Pan, 1993

Goodman, A., *The Wars of the Roses, Military Activity and English Society, 1452-1497*, London, 1981

Grant, Neil, *Collins Gem of Kings and Queens*, HarperCollins, 1999

Gregg, Pauline, *King Charles I*, Phoenix Press, 2000

Griffiths, R.A., *The Reign of King Henry VI*, Sutton Publishing, 1997

Guy, John, *Charles I and Oliver Cromwell*, Ticktock Publishing, 1998

Haigh, Christopher, *English Reformations: Religion, Politics & Society under the Tudors*, Clarendon Press, 1993

Hawkins, Michael, *Politics and administration of Tudor and Stuart England*, Harvester P Microform Publishing, 1980

Hefin, Mathias, *Wales and Britain in the Early Medieval World c.1000-c.1500*, London, 1996

Hennessy, James-Pope, *Queen Mary*, Phoenix Press, 2000

Hibbert, Christopher, *Queen Victoria*, Harper Collins, 2000

Hibbert, Christopher, *Queen Victoria in her Letters and Journals*, Sutton Publishing, 2000

Higham, N.J. & Hill, David (eds.), *Edward the Elder, 899-924*, Routledge, 2001

Holmes, Richard, *The English Civil War*, Peter Young, 2000

HRH Queen Victoria, *Queen Victoria's Highland Journals*, Hamlyn, 1997

Lace, William W, *The Little Princes in the Tower (Mysterious Deaths)*, Lucent Books, 1997

Lasky, Kathryn, *Elizabeth I: Red Rose of the House of Tudor, England, 1544, (The Royal Diaries)*, Scholastic, 1999

Lewis, Jayne Elizabeth (ed.), *The Trial of Mary Queen of Scots,* Palgrave, 1990

Loades, David, *Mary Tudor: a Life*, Blackwell Publishers, 1992

Loades, David, *Power in Tudor England*, Palgrave, 1996

Luke, Mary, *The Nine days Queen*, Buccaneer Books Inc, 1994

Macinnes, Alan, *Clanship, commerce and the House of Stuart, 1603 – 1788*, Tuckwell Press, 1996

MacCulloch, Diarmaid, *The Boy King: Edward VI and the Protestant Reformation,* St Martins Press, 2001

Melchior, Giorgio (ed.), *King Edward VI and the Protestant Reformation*, Cambridge Uni Press

Morillo, S., *Warfare Under the Anglo-Norman Kings, 1066-1135,* Woodbridge, 1994

Morrow, Ann, *Without Equal, The Queen Mother,* House of Stratus, 2000

Munich, Adrienne, *Queen Victoria's Secrets*, Columbia University Press, 1998

Newman, P. A., *A Companion to the English Civil Wars,* Oxford, 1990

Owen, Morfydd, Charles-Edwards, Thomas, and Russell, Paul (eds.), *The Welsh King and his court*, 1990

Partridge, Robert B., *"O Horrible Murder": the Trial, Execution and Burial of King Charles I,* The Rubicon Press, 1998

Pimlott, Ben, *A Biography of Elizabeth II*, 1998

Potts, D.M. and W.T.W., *Queen Victoria's Gene*, Sutton Publishing, 1999

Reanell, Tony, *Last days of Glory: the death of Queen Victoria*, Penguin Books, 2001

Ross, Josephine, *Kings and Queens of Britain*, London, 1982

Smout, T.C., *A History of the Scottish Peoples* , London, 1969

Steele, James, *Queen Mary*, Phaidon Press, 2001

Thurley, Simon, *The Royal Palaces of Tudor England*, Yale University Press, 1993

Warren, W.L. and Green, Judith, A., *Henry II*, Yale University Press, 2000

Wormald, Jenny, *Mary Queen of Scots*

Zeepvat, Charlotte, *Queen Victoria's family*, 2001

PICTURE CREDITS

Art Archive: 8 The Art Archive, 10(cl) The Art Archive/Salisbury and S.Wilts Museum/EileenTweedy, 14 The Art Archive/Devizes Museum/Eileen Tweedy, 18(t) The Art Archive/Stationers' Hall/Eileen Tweedy, 26(t) The Art Archive, 27 The Art Archive/Musee de Versailles/Dagli Orti, 31 The Art Archive/British Library, 33 (tr) The Art Archive/British Museum (b) The Art Archive/Musee du Louvre Paris/Dagli Orti, 34(t) The Art Archive/Christ's Hospital/Eileen Tweedy, 35 The Art Archive/Tower of London/Eileen Tweedy, 38(r) The Art Archive/British History, 42 The Art Archive/British Library, 50 (l) The Art Archive, 54 The Art Archive, 61(t) The Art Archive/British Library, 63 The Art Archive/Garrick Club, 64(tl) The Art Archive/National Gallery London/Album/Joseph Martin, 65(tl) The Art Archive/Eileen Tweedy (c) The Art Archive/Dagli Orti (A), 68(br) The Art Archive, 72 The Art Archive/Victoria and Albert Museum London, 73 The Art Archive, 80 The Art Archive/Musee de Versailles/Dagli Orti (A), 81(tl) The Art Archive/Handel Museum Halle/Dagli Orti (A) (br) The Art Archive/Royal Navy College Greenwich/Eileen Tweedy, 82(bl) The Art Archive/Handel Museum Halle/Dagli Orti (A), 84(tl) The Art Archive/Dagli Orti (A) (c) The Art Archive/Gripsholm Castle Sweden/Dagli Orti (A), 86 The Art Archive/British Museum/Eileen Tweedy, 89 The Art Archive/Imperial War Museum/Eileen Tweedy, 90(br) The Art Archive/Eileen Tweedy, 101(tl) The Art Archive (br) The Art Archive/Musee de la Tapisserie Bayeux/Dagli Orti, 103(bl) The Art Archive/British Library, 104 The Art Archive 105(t) The Art Archive/Musee de Versailles/Dagli Orti, 107(t) The Art Archive/British Museum/Eileen Tweedy, 108(bl) The Art Archive/Museum der Stadt Wien/Dagli Orti (A), (br) The Art Archive/British Museum/Eileen Tweedy, 109(bl) The Art Archive/Bibliotheque Nationale Paris, 111(tl) The Art Archive, (br) The Art Archive/Bibliotheque Nationale Paris, 112(br) The Art Archive/Musee Calvet Avignon/Dagli Orti, 114 The Art Archive/Windsor Castle, 119(b) The Art Archive/Galleria Sabauda Turin/Dagli Orti (A), 123(tl) The Art Archive/Doge's Palace Venice/Dagli Arti, 125 The Art Archive/Musee de Versailles/Dagli Orti, 127(br) The Art Archive/Pitti Palace Florence/Dagli Orti, 130(tl) The Art Archive/British Library/Harper Collins Publishers,(b) The Art Archive/Guildhall Library/Eileen Tweedy, 134 The Art Archive/British Library 138(tl) The Art Archive/Garrick Club, 140(tl), 146 The Art Archive/Museo del Prado Madrid/Dagli Orti, 150 The Art Archive/Musee de Versailles/Dagli Orti, 151(bl) The Art Archive, 157 The Art Archive/Bibliotheque Municipale Castres / Dagli Orti, 162(tr) The Art Archive, 163(t) The Art Archive / British Museum, 164(tl) The Art Archive/British Library, (br) The Art Archive/ British Library, 166 The Art Archive/Garrick Club, 172(tr) The Art Archive/Musee de Versailles Paris/Dagli Orti (A), 177 The Art Archive/Victoria and Albert Museum London, 183 The Art Archive/Victoria and Albert Museum London, 186(bl) The Art Archive/Dagli Orti (A), 188(t) The Art Archive/British Museum/Eileen Tweedy, 190(b) and 191(bl) and (tr) The Art Archive/Musee de la Tapisserie Bayeux/Dagli Orti, 193(bl) The Art Archive, 196(br) The Art Archive/Musee de Versailles/Dagli Orti, 198(br) The Art Archive/Co of Merchants, City of Edinburgh

Bill Doyle: 140(br), 152(t)

Foundry Arts: 154

Impact: 92(b) Michael George/Impact, 198(c) and 200 David Martin/Impact

National Library of Wales: 46(b), 97(tr), 137(tl), 156(bl), 161(all),

National Portrait Gallery of Scotland: 48(tl), 49, 51, 120(br), 133, 145, 176

Mary Evans: 11, 16(all, tl: Mary Evans/Institution of Civil Engineers), 18(b) Mary Evans/Edwin Wallace, 20, 22(all), 28, 29(all, tr: Mary Evans/Edwin Wallace), 32, 39, 40(r), 41, 44, 45(r), 46(tl),48(br), 53, 55, 57(l), 59, 61(br), 62, 69, 70(br), 74(l), 78, 82(r), 83, 87(br), 88(all), 92(t), 93, 96, 97(tl), 98(c), 99(l), 100, 102, 103(t), 108(t), 109(tr), 112(tl), 115(tr), 116(all), 117(Mary Evans/Edwin Wallace), 118, 120(bl), 121(tr), 122, 123(br), 124(all), 126, 131, 132(all), 135(all), 136 (Mary Evans/Edwin Wallace), 138(c), 139, 141, 142(all), 143, 147(all), 148(c), 156(c), 158, 167(tl), 168(tl), 169, 170, 171(all), 173, 174, 175, 178(tl), 178/179, 184, 185, 187, 190(tl), 192(all), 193(t), 194, 195(cl), 196(tl), 197(r), 201(all),

Still Moving Picture Company: 47: Michael Brooke, 144: Scottish Tourist Board

Topham: 9(all), 10(br),12, 13, 15, 17, 19, 21(all), 23, 24, 25, 26(b), 30, 30/31, 34(b), 36, 37(all), 38(tl), 40(l), 43, 45(t), 50/51, 52, 56, 57(t), 58(all), 60, 64(br), 66, 67, 68(tl), 70(bl), 71(r), 74/75, 75(r), 76, 77, 79, 85, 87(tl), 90(t), 91, 94, 95(all), 98(br), 105(c), 106(t), 107(b), 110, 113, 119(tr), 121(bl), 127(t),128, 129, 137(b), 148(bl), 149, 151(tr), 152(b), 153, 159, 160, 162(bl), 163(br), 165, 167(br), 168/169, 172(l),181, 182, 186(tr), 188(b), 189, 195(tr), 197(tl), 199

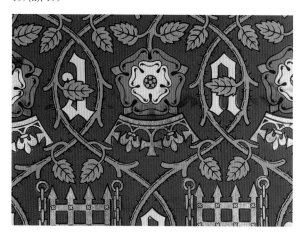

INDEX